PERSUASION IN PRACTICE

Dedicated to
George McCune
a warm, kind stranger who with a bit of a smile told a young
professor, "It just so happens that I do know an editor,"

and

Sara McCune
the editor who took a chance on a "kid,"

to both of them as publishers and most of all as dear friends.

PERSUASION IN PRACTICE

Kathleen Kelley Reardon

SAGE PUBLICATIONS
The International Professional Publishers
Newbury Park   London   New Delhi

For information address:

SAGE Publications, Inc.
2455 Teller Road
Newbury Park, California 91320

SAGE Publications Ltd.
6 Bonhill Street
London EC2A 4PU
United Kingdom

SAGE Publications India Pvt. Ltd.
M-32 Market
Greater Kailash I
New Delhi 110 048 India

Printed in the United States of America

Library of Congress Cataloging-in-Publication Data

Main entry under title:

Reardon, Kathleen Kelley.
     Persuasion in practice / by Kathleen Kelley Reardon.
          p.   cm.
     Includes bibliographical references and index.
     ISBN 0-8039-3316-9. — ISBN 0-8039-3317-7 (pbk.)
     1. Persuasion (Psychology)   Title.
   BF637.P4R33   1991
   303.3′dc20   90-23689
                                                                   CIP

FIRST PRINTING, 1991

Sage Production Editor: Judith L. Hunter

Contents

Preface

Persuasion in Practice was written for the scholar who wishes to understand the theoretical and research origins of current wisdom regarding persuasion, and for the practitioner in all of us who wants to know how this current wisdom translates into practice. This balance is not easy to achieve. There are those who will read this book and long for more theory and research. Let me direct those people to my earlier book, *Persuasion: Theory and Context,* and other academic sources of such information. Others may desire more practical cases. Unfortunately, there are fewer sources to turn to here. Robert Cialdini's excellent book, *Influence,* is one choice. Cialdini too provides an understanding of theory and research but includes a wide variety of examples. I hope there will also be those who find the attempt to combine research and practice useful for their purposes.

It will become clear as you begin to read this book that it was not written for the novice. It is not a book for lower-level undergraduate classes by any stretch of the imagination. It was written for people who have some background in the study of persuasion or at least some background in the study of it in their daily lives. Most of the examples are business oriented, in part because I am a business professor but also because most of us are involved or soon to become involved in some sort of business. Many examples have nothing whatsoever to do with business, but you will probably experience this book as having a leaning toward that discipline.

You may also experience this book as an attempt to cover a lot of bases. It is that. As such, it may cover some issues in less detail than you desire. I hope you will find that it teaches you a fair amount about persuasion and encourages you to reflect on the styles and strategies you use when you attempt to be persuasive and those others use when attempting to persuade you. I also hope you will enjoy reading it as much when it gets deeply into theory as when it provides practical examples or cases. Feel free, however, to skim those sections that just aren't for you. For example, if you don't care to know about the origins of attitude research, skim or skip that chapter. The two purposes of this book are to share with you some old and new perspectives on persuasion and to look at how persuasion operates in a variety of contexts. Whether you study, read, skim, or skip, my hope is that your approach or combination of approaches will improve your understanding of persuasion.

—Kathleen Kelley Reardon

Acknowledgments

My gratitude must go first and foremost to my colleagues and students in various regions who took time to comment on my earlier book, *Persuasion: Theory and Context*. They were my inspiration to write again about persuasion. Among them was Bill McGuire at Yale, who encouraged me to do a sequel. Sara McCune's unceasing, but always gentle, urgings to write this book were an object lesson in the patience and persistence persuasion often requires. Ann West has my appreciation too for her encouragement and consistent interest in this project. Many friends and colleagues whose ideas shaped my work are cited in the book. Other colleagues not only influenced my thinking with their work but supported my efforts with their friendship, including Gail Fairhurst, Sandra Ball-Rokeach, Mark Harris, Shelley Taylor, Mary Anne Fitzpatrick, Margaret McLaughlin, and Linda Putnam.

I am grateful to the Executive MBA students at the University of Southern California whose persuasion and negotiation experiences are a part of this book and to four USC School of Business colleagues—Barry Leskin, Larry Greiner, Steve Kerr, and Warren Bennis—for their integrity, genuine kindness, and respect. My thanks to my colleagues in the Management and Organization and Business Communication departments for their support, especially Ian Mitroff, who reminded me of something that daily hassles have a tendency to blur in memory: The most important thing is to have a passionate interest in what you do.

My gratitude is extended to my family. Lively, lovable, persuasive 3-year-old Devin took occasional naps so mom could stare blearily at the computer. Our 3-day-old bundle of joy, Ryan, contributed to the completion of this book by sleeping and cooing while mom read proofs. My deep affection belongs to Chris, my husband, who thinks I'm brilliant, which makes all contrary opinions pale by comparison.

1 What Persuasion Is, What It Is Not, and How It Is Maintained: Debunking Some Myths

Through frequent associations with ulterior motives for human behavior, "persuasion" has come to be considered by many an activity reserved for the unethical. On the contrary, persuasion is a form of communication in which every person who ventures forth into the company of others must participate. Persuasion is necessitated by the single fact that all of us differ in our goals and the means by which we achieve them. The inevitable result is that our goals are often at cross-purposes with those of others. When one person's goal achievement is blocked by the goal-seeking behaviors of another, persuasion is one means of achieving cooperation.

Encouraging changes in another person's behavior may be for the good of that person, since it is possible for a persuader to have as one of his or her goals the improvement of some aspect of the persuadee's situation. The persuader may also be either totally or primarily focused on his or her own goals without regard for the good of the persuadee. Persuasion, like most other activities, is not inherently good or bad. Its purpose and outcome may or may not be ethical.

Whether persuasion is intended to improve the state of the persuadee or merely to further the goals of the persuader, it does differ from manipulation and coercion. Manipulation involves furthering the goals of the manipulator at the expense of the person being manipulated. It essentially involves "pulling the wool over the eyes" of others. The people being manipulated are not encouraged to reason about the situation, but are entranced by false promises, deceived by insincere verbal or nonverbal behaviors, or "set up" in the sense that the situation is contrived to limit their choices. Manipulation differs from persuasion in that it does not involve up-front reasoning with others. It robs them of choices through deceptive tactics rather than attempting to guide them to make, of their own free will, the persuader's preferred choice.

Coercion is another means of influencing behavior that does not involve up-front reasoning. Coercion involves physical force or some form of threat. Children are often coerced into behaving as their parents wish them to behave. While there are times when reasoning with children is not as important as removing them from harm's way, coercion as a practice in child rearing does not teach children to reason on their own. Since much childhood learning occurs by example, or modeling, parents who do not reason with children are not likely to encourage those children to reason on their own (see Bandura, 1977). With children and adults, coercion may occasionally appear expedient, but, in most cases, the result is compliance for the moment. Once coerced persons are no longer under surveillance, they are likely to revert to behaviors they prefer. Coercion is less likely than persuasion to lead to long-term changes in behavior because the persuadee has not *chosen* to adopt the new behavior and thus is not committed to retaining it.

This does not mean that persuasion at its best is totally spontaneous and uncontrived. There are effective and ineffective ways to present ideas. The skill is in identifying what matters to the people being persuaded, shaping one's arguments to guide the thinking of those persons, presenting oneself in a credible manner, and encouraging people to see one's perspective without setting them up as in manipulation or backing them into a corner as in coercion.

Persuasion involves guiding people toward the adoption of some behavior, belief, or attitude preferred by the persuader through reasoning or emotional appeals. It does not rob people of their ability to choose but presents a case for the adoption of a persuader-preferred mode of action, belief, or attitude. It does not use force or threat and does not limit the options of others by deceit. Persuasion is not always in the best interests of the persuadee. Even the persuader with good intentions may lead persuadees to do what might not be in their best interests. In all cases, however, persuasion does not deprive persuadees of other choices by deceit or force.

PERSUASION DEFINED

Now that we know what persuasion is not, the question remains, what is persuasion? First, persuasion is always a conscious activity. Gerald Miller and Michael Burgoon (1973) advocate this position. While they would not deny that people can unintentionally influence, their perspective implies that it is impossible unintentionally to persuade. Persuasion involves conscious intent.

The second characteristic of persuasion is the persuader's perception of threat to his or her goals. The threat need not be explicit—merely sufficient in the eyes of the persuader to warrant an attempt to change the behavior of other(s).

Third, persuasion often involves threat to the persuadee's self-concept. Self-concept plays a much more central role in interpersonal persuasion than it does in mass communication, since the message is directed to one or a few people. The implicit message is, "There is something wrong with the way you're thinking or acting, so you should change." The suggestion that one should change always implies some level of inadequacy on the part of the persuadee. This distinction makes persuasion a delicate activity. Effective persuaders know how to elicit change without eliciting defensiveness, a skill I will discuss in the chapter on interpersonal persuasion.

With these three criteria in mind, the following definition of persuasion emerges: Persuasion is, in all cases, the activity of attempting to change the behavior of at least one person through symbolic interaction. It is conscious and occurs (a) when a threat to at least one person's goals is observed and (b) when the source and degree of this threat are sufficiently important to warrant the expenditure of effort involved in persuasion. It is a delicate activity, since any attempt to change another person can be seen as a suggestion that the individual's beliefs, attitudes, and/or actions are faulty.

It is important to note that the term *persuasion,* like *communication,* is not used in this text as an implication of success. Persuasion and communication are activities involving at least two persons whose joint actions determine the outcome. Persuasion is not something one person does *to* another but something he or she does *with* another. Even if the persuader does not feel that the goal of changing the behavior of another has been accomplished, persuasion, as an activity, has still occurred. Use of the terms *persuader* and *persuadee* in this text is not intended to imply that persuasion is a unidirectional activity. A person rarely changes another's perspective or behavior without altering some of his or her own perspectives or behaviors in the process.

Moreover, persuasion is, more often than not, an incremental activity. It is rarely a one-shot effort. Most of us prefer to obtain results right away. We carry a model of persuasion in our minds that looks like this:

```
        Persuadee                    Persuadee
        Position                     Position
           A                            C
        ─────────────────────────────────►
                      Change
```

We expect our efforts to result in immediate change. Actually, most persuasion looks more like this:

```
                        Partially            Full Desired
                        Changed              Change in
        Initial         Persuadee            Persuadee
        Persuadee       Position             Position
        Position


        Position                 Position             Position
           A                        B                    C
                1    2    3              1    2    3
                                 Change
```

Not only are there usually other positions (attitudes and behaviors) between where the persuadee is now and where the persuader would like him or her to be, but there are subpositions as well. Persuasion involves considerable patience and a talent for identifying how far an individual can be encouraged to move at any particular point in time.

Even this model distorts persuasion, however, because as we attempt to change others, we are often changed ourselves, especially with interpersonal persuasion, where all persons involved have opportunities to give feedback and argue their positions. So the model above may be useful prior to the actual activity of persuasion as a planning tool (i.e., identifying ideal changes), but it does not represent what typically occurs during persuasion. A more accurate model would leave room for change in the persuader's position as he or she attempts to change someone else.

Another important characteristic of persuasion is its tendency to involve at least some strategizing. While persuasion is not the same as manipulation—which, as discussed earlier, involves "slipping one by" the target in order to achieve one's own ends—it often involves dressing one's intentions in an acceptable fashion. After all, the goal of persuasion is to change someone's attitudes and/or behavior. Since most people are naturally protective of their views and their behaviors, this intention, if not properly presented, can encourage people to close their minds to change.

HOW UP-FRONT IS PERSUASION?

Persuasion has been defined above as involving the persuadee in reasoning and attempting to guide his or her choices. The implication here is that persuasion, while requiring skillful development and presentation of ideas and arguments, is up-front. The fact is that it is more up-front than manipulation and certainly less controlling than coercion, but it is important to point out that all forms of human communication involve, by necessity, some degree of indirectness.

The disguising of intentions is a prevalent communication behavior in our society. It is an accepted and often expected means of avoiding conflict. Even young children learn that saying what one means can sometimes be a very sure way of not getting what one wants. Recognizing the prevalence of indirectness in communication can be disturbing unless we consider what life would be like if all of us were to say exactly what we think. Economizing of truth is a necessity, especially when the truth might hurt. If each of us were always motivated by selfless concerns, then this might not be the case. However, given that selflessness is not the norm, a certain amount of restraint is appropriate when dishing out truth. To assure our cooperation, rules have been developed to assist us in the restraint effort.

For example, indirectness is especially prevalent in our everyday interpersonal communication. Here, too, disguised purpose is the norm. Terms like *hidden agenda* and *ulterior motive* carry negative connotations because they suggest that people may hide their true purposes. Actually, people often collaborate in deceiving each other about their true purposes. Mark Knapp and Mark Comadena (1979) consider deception, like other forms of communication, to be mutually negotiated: "Sometimes we consider ourselves innocent recipients of another's deceit, but even then it is difficult to discount the role our own needs, values, and expectations play in another's message decisions" (p. 272).

In his book *Interaction Ritual,* Erving Goffman (1967) explains how people engage in "facework" to avoid too much truth. They often cooperate in interactions to protect each other's "face" from threat. Whenever people engage in conversation, they place their "faces," which Goffman defines as the positive social value people effectively claim for themselves, in jeopardy. The individual expects that others will not purposely attempt to place his or her worth in question.

People do not always live up to this obligation to save the face of another. However, we often find that no matter how angry we are at someone, a heartfelt apology leads to a face-saving response: "Oh, I hardly noticed. Don't worry about it. I do the same thing sometimes." In like manner, those who try to raise the value of their own faces by bragging usually find others making remarks that bring them back into line: "Well, I guess you're pretty pleased with yourself, huh?"

Sometimes it is necessary to attempt to tell someone the truth about some negative trait. To do so directly is often unacceptable. Goffman (1967) points out that we tend to prefer tactful communication. Tact, in regard to facework, depends on the tacit agreement to communicate via hint: "The *rule* here is that the sender ought not to act as if he had officially conveyed the message he has hinted at, while the recipients have the right and obligation to act as if they have not officially received the message contained in the hint" (p. 30). Goffman further explains that people find communication through hint useful because hintable communication is deniable and can be used to warn others that, should they persist in the annoying behavior, they may lose face. Rather tricky, you say? Surely, but also extremely important to competent communication in a society where people do not expect direct communication of unpleasant intentions.

The following dialogue provides an example of communication via hint:

Fred: How are things, Sue?
Sue: Okay, Fred. How about you?
Fred: I'm fine. I just spent some time reading your report.
Sue: How did you like it?
Fred: It's well organized, carefully researched, and clearly written.
Sue: Did you think the content was accurate?

Fred: Sure. It was accurate. It's sure gutsy too. It ought to get their attention upstairs.
Sue: Maybe it's too direct? They told me to tell them how it really is out there.
Fred: Well, you'd know better than anyone. Good piece of work.

In this example, Fred is letting Sue know that her candidness might get her into trouble with her bosses. Fred does not quite say, "You know, Sue, this could get you into trouble upstairs," but he does hint at that. He gives Sue the information he wants her to have while reserving for himself the option to deny intending to do so. Is this manipulation or persuasion? Fred is not attempting to set Sue up (manipulation) or force her to change her report (coercion). He is guiding her toward reconsideration of her report style. He is persuading her to *choose* to change that style.

Given the fact that telling the "whole truth and nothing but the truth" is reserved for courtrooms and not conversations, it is easy to see why persuasion is such a complex activity. The task of discovering why individuals decide to behave in a certain manner is a formidable one if they engage in efforts to disguise their true purposes. Research provides little reason for optimism in this matter. It appears that members of our culture are not very good at detecting lying strangers (Bauchner, Brandt, & Miller, 1977; Ekman & Friesen, 1974a; Hocking, Bauchner, Kaminski, & Miller, 1979; Shulman, 1973). Moreover, familiarity does not always increase detection ability (Bauchner, 1978).

Even in the best, most well-intended persuasive efforts, there is likely to be some indirectness—attempts to avoid blatant expression of the truth that might offend the persuadee. It is difficult to know when indirectness becomes lying. Is the person who chooses to say "I find your work unique" rather than "I find your work weird" merely selecting words with care or lying? The fact is that words are very weak vehicles of meaning. They are often spoken before less offensive ones are selected. Sometimes we forget to filter out offensive statements. If the purpose is to reason rather than to manipulate or coerce, to allow people choices while presenting the best arguments for the choice(s) preferred by the persuader, then we can safely say that the activity is persuasion.

Aside from engaging in "indirectness," people also engage in another less than candid method of communicating. This is embellishment—making an idea, product, or behavior, for example, more attractive than it is in reality. What's the harm in a little embellishment here or there?

you may ask. Probably nothing. It is not uncommon for people to use makeup, hair coloring, or specially fitted clothes to enhance their more natural look. Is this so bad? It brings no harm to anyone, and it makes people feel better about themselves. Where, then, is the line to be drawn in making ideas, products, or behaviors look good? How much embellishment is too much? There are no easy answers, although most of us would agree that there must be a limit somewhere.

Cialdini (1987a, 1987b) has identified characteristics of influence attempts that render them unethical. These can be helpful in separating embellishment from deceit. Embellishment often involves the employment of what Cialdini calls "triggers of influence." These are appeals or images that encourage the persuadee to respond in a manner preferred by the persuader. According to Cialdini, ethical persuaders locate triggers of influence that naturally exist in the situation. For example, a car salesperson might point out the advantages of small cars with regard to miles per gallon of gas. Persuaders who use triggers of influence in an unethical manner operate like smugglers. They import these triggers into situations where they do not naturally reside. For example, if an organization uses an actor who plays a doctor on television to advocate the health benefits of its product, it is smuggling a trigger of influence (the actor as doctor) into a situation. The actor is not really a doctor. The organization has injected into the selling situation something that does not inhere there. An ethical use of a trigger of influence involves the persuader in honing his or her abilities to "uncover, bring into focus, and engage resident trigger principles" (p. 162)—to locate characteristics of the idea, product, or the situation that are not counterfeit or fabricated.

Three of the most frequently employed trigger principles described by Cialdini (1985, 1987a, 1987b) are reciprocity, scarcity, and authority. *Reciprocity* refers to the obligation to give back to others the kind of behavior they have given to us. The salesperson who gives a potential buyer a free roll of paper towels before beginning her sales pitch about a new detergent is using reciprocity as a trigger of influence. She is hoping that the potential buyer will feel obligated at least to listen to her sales pitch since he has received a gift. *Scarcity* refers to the impression (accurate or inaccurate) that something is limited in supply or for some reason not readily available. The person who invites all potential buyers for his car to view the car at the same time is using scarcity as a trigger principle. He is creating the impression that there is a high demand for the one car. *Authority* involves employing an expert as an advocate of the idea, product, or behavior being promoted. Each of these triggers of influence may be used in ethical or unethical ways. To the extent that the trigger of influence employed naturally resides in the product, idea, or behavior being advocated or is natural to the situation (e.g., a real doctor advocating a pain relief medication), the use of that trigger of influence is ethical. According to Cialdini, to the extent that it is smuggled into the promotion attempt, it is being used in an unethical manner.

In later chapters we will look more closely at trigger principles and their use and misuse. The point here is that the most ethical form of persuasion is one that does not import characteristics, or what Cialdini calls "trigger principles," into the situation. Skillful persuaders are adept at locating trigger principles that belong to the idea, object, or situation surrounding it. Use of these inherent trigger principles embellishes but does not deceive.

HOW PERSUASION IS MAINTAINED

Now that we have debunked the myths that persuasion is a form of manipulation or coercion, that it is something done *to* rather than *with* people, that it is a one-shot effort, and that it must be completely up-front to be ethical, we turn to a final and important myth—that persuasion endures without effort. If this is a myth it is because of the focus of past research. For the many decades that persuasion researchers have been exploring what it takes to change behavior, the emphasis has been on immediate change. As Miller (1980) explains:

> In the heat of a political campaign or fund-raising drive it may be tempting to center efforts on potential converts at the expense of ignoring those whose prevailing response tendencies already coincide with the intent of the political candidate or the fund raiser. Such an approach can yield low vote counts or depleted treasuries. (p. 20)

Taking for granted that once an individual is persuaded he or she is always persuaded is a good way to lose employees or even a spouse. People must be rewarded for change if it is to endure. To lose weight, an obese person must remain convinced that he or she can and should diet. This takes more than one persuasive message and a pat on the back after a milkshake has been rejected. There are three main steps in achieving long-term change: motivation, participation, and reward.

Motivation refers to encouraging people to adopt a mental set conducive to change. For example, persuading a reluctant employee to take on greater responsibility on the job is not something that can be done without first giving him or her some incentive to do so. For some employers, that incentive is fear of losing one's job. The problem with fear is that it often breeds resentment and certainly does not encourage commitment to the change. It may bring about short-term acquiescence, but it is not likely to encourage what persuasion researchers call "private acceptance." The latter involves truly believing in the value of the specific change. For example, a woman who quits smoking because she truly believes that it is good for her to do so is more likely to remain a nonsmoker than the person who quits merely to please others.

Motivation to change is the first step in achieving private acceptance. In and of itself it is not usually sufficient to the achievement of long-term change, but it is the foundation of such change. A number of strategies, several of which are described in subsequent chapters, can be used to encourage people to see the value of a particular change. A boss could let an employee know that she perceives him as a valuable asset to the company and that he is being asked to take on added responsibility because he has the skills to handle it. Of course, these words may fall on deaf ears, so to speak, if the employee is already overburdened and concerned about not being able to meet the responsibilities he already has. The competent persuader operates like a detective to find out if concerns of this type exist. The greatest enemy to persuasion is *assumption*. Assuming that one knows how others think is the crux of many a persuasion failure. To motivate people to change one must know what *does* matter to them, not what *should* matter to them. The boss who discovers through skillful probing that the employee harbors concerns about meeting all his responsibilities might find it feasible to work with the employee to remove some responsibilities until he is secure in the new position.

The point here is that *motivation to change involves finding out what matters to the persuadee and shaping one's initial message(s) to address those concerns and needs.* Marketers do not attempt to sell their products by appealing to what the consumer *should* think. Effective marketing involves knowing what the consumer *does* think. All persuasion, whether between spouses, parent to child, boss to employee, or salesperson to buyer, starts at this point—exploring the mind of the persuadee for clues regarding what might be said or done to encourage him or her to give change a try.

The second step in persuasion maintenance is *participation*. This step is borrowed from a body of persuasion research indicating that the best form of persuasion is self-persuasion. Theories of counterattitudinal advocacy and self-attribution suggest that when people observe themselves engaging in particular behavior, they are inclined to accept that behavior as their own. In other words, it is one thing to motivate people to attempt change, and quite another for them to feel at home with that change. By involving them in activities that they can successfully accomplish, one gives them opportunities to see themselves as capable of carrying out the change they were motivated to make.

Sometimes participation means trying a small part of the planned change rather than attempting a total change overnight. Returning to the dieter example, giving up all high-fat foods may be too much for someone who is used to a high-fat diet. Giving up some subset of high-fat foods may lead to greater success; it may enable the dieter to see himself actually carrying out the change that he previously considered impossible. Later, this dieter might move on to greater change and eventually achieve a low-fat, low-calorie diet. So the persuader who wishes to accomplish long-term change must not only be a detective of motivational appeals but of opportunities for participation in change that are palatable for the persuadee and likely to lead to observable success.

The next step in persuasion maintenance is *reward*. People do not change easily. They do not remain changed easily, either. Most of us are skeptical of the phrase, "He's a changed man." There is something almost as powerful as gravity about the status quo. We cling to what we know even if it is not particularly good for us to do so. Change brings with it uncertainty and fear of failure. Persons who have been motivated to attempt change and have successfully participated in at least some phase of the proposed change may still be quite uncertain of their ability to sustain it. Here is where reward comes in. People need visible signs of their progress. They need pats on the back, words of encouragement, gold stars, M&Ms, trophies, or whatever makes them feel successful. Here is the third type of detective work involved in persuasion maintenance. The persuader must investigate to find out what makes persuadees feel good about their changed behavior and how often they need to receive such rewards. For some people, a simple "Nice work" is all that is needed to keep them on track. For others the demands are greater.

One vice president of a Los Angeles insurance company gives little toys and gadgets to her people whenever they complete a difficult project. Once she took all of them bowling and provided the best and worst bowlers with prizes. This may not be everyone's style, but it works for her. The point is that persuasion is an incremental process requiring at least occasional reminders that the persuadee's efforts are appreciated.

SUMMARY

In this chapter I have differentiated persuasion from manipulation and coercion. Persuasion involves encouraging someone to *choose* to make a change in beliefs, attitudes, and/or behaviors. This does not mean that persuasion is always totally up-front. People expect a certain amount of economizing on truth. There are times, of course, when people are admired for having "the courage of their convictions," for "calling things as they see them," so to speak. Yet communicators who always "speak their minds" run the risk of being seen as insensitive and boorish. Moreover, speaking our minds can commit us to positions to which we may not subscribe a few hours or even a few minutes later. Perhaps the most admiration goes to those who "hold themselves in check" until their ideas are solidified and they know what truth really is for them. Being a good persuader, then, means knowing where and how to present one's version of reality so that others will *choose* to adopt it.

2 How People Interpret Reality: Constructs, Schemata, Rules, and Illusions

With each person thinking somewhat differently from others and social pressure encouraging indirectness in communication, persuasion is a major challenge. How can one ever know what another person is thinking? Fortunately, people do share certain patterns of viewing themselves and the world around them. A host of terms have been used to describe patterns of human thought that guide action. This chapter introduces four perspectives on human thought, focusing on constructs, schemata, rules, and illusions. Each of these contributes to a fuller understanding of the challenges faced by those who engage in persuasion.

PERSONAL CONSTRUCT THEORY

According to George Kelly (1955), people strive to make their worlds predictable. They develop constructs to interpret phenomena. According to Kelly, constructs are analogous to yardsticks. They serve to measure the meanings of objects, actions, and contexts. They operate much like bipolar adjectival scales. Consider, for example, the characteristics one must have to be a friend. Some of them might be a sense of humor, talkativeness, consideration for others, and punctuality. Kelly contends that each adjective one uses to describe a person, object, or event has a polar opposite. The above set of constructs, then, reflects the following set of opposites for a friend: sense of humor/morbid, talkative/quiet, considerate/inconsiderate, punctual/tardy.

Constructs are developed by individuals to assist them in their inter-pretations of their worlds. They differ from person to person because different experiences generate different constructs. Yet in all cases they operate to make events more predictable. The amount of predictability required for comfort is a personal matter. We do know from the works of Berlyne (1960, 1963), De Charmes (1968), and others that some novelty is required by the human mind to keep it alert. Humans are "driven" to explore. Too much novelty, however, is dysfunctional to productive thought and behavior. Since the world we live in provides many opportunities to experience novelty, people expend much of their mental energy searching for and maintaining order and predictability.

Motives or drives alone do not impel persons to action. Kelly (1955) states: "Suppose we began by assuming that the fundamental thing about life is that it goes on; the going on is the thing itself. It isn't that motives make a man come alert and do things; his alertness is an aspect of his very being." In essence, Kelly implies that people do not react to the past, but seek to address accurately the problems of the future. They seek to develop cognitive schemata that will facilitate their ability to anticipate the future. The following fundamental postulate and corol-laries constitute the central tenets of Kelly's personal construct theory:

- *Fundamental postulate:* A person's processes are psychologically chan-neled by the way he or she anticipates events.

This fundamental postulate indicates that a person's main purpose in life is to make sense of the world and to test conclusions on the basis of their predictive capacities. Like scientists, all people construct hypotheses on the basis of past experiences and then proceed to test those hypotheses by applying them to the world. This fundamental postulate is elaborated in the following 11 corollaries:

- *Construction corollary:* A person anticipates events by construing their replications.

People do not live in a world of consistently different happenings. On the contrary, much of what is done one day (getting out of bed, getting dressed for work, eating breakfast, and so forth) will be repeated the next. Bannister and Fransella (1977) interpret Kelly's construction corollary as meaning that "basic to our making sense of our world and of our lives is our continual detection of repeated themes, our categorizing of these themes and our segmenting of the world in terms of them" (p. 20). There would be no attempt to predict accurately if we could not detect replications of events. Unlike most animals, we are creatures of the future, a time period given meaning by our interpretations of it in light of our past.

- *Individuality corollary:* People differ from each other in their construction of events.

No two persons ever see a single event in exactly the same way. Their past experiences, even for two identical twins residing in the same womb, are not equivalent. Since it is our past that gives meaning to the present and future, our interpretations and anticipations are never identical to those of others, a fact that exacerbates the problems of communication.

- *Organization corollary:* Each person characteristically evolves, for convenience in anticipating events, a construction system embracing ordinal relationships between constructs.

This corollary implies that a person's constructs are interrelated. Larger, more abstract constructs subsume more concrete constructs. For some people "persuasion" is a construct that may be subsumed by the construct "communication." The subordination of some constructs by others formulates within the human mind a logic system used primarily to anticipate the future.

- *Dichotomy corollary:* A person's construction system is composed of a finite number of dichotomous constructs.

Kelly considers it useful to see constructs as having two poles, affirmative and negative. For every positive descriptive term in a person's repertoire, a negative counterpart exists. As Kelly explains, even when we are unable to provide a label for contrast, we do not affirm without implicitly negating. In other words, to state that a person is attractive is to imply that he or she is not unattractive.

- *Choice corollary:* People choose for themselves that alternative in a dichotomized construct through which they anticipate the greater possibility for the elaboration of their own system.

People do not become permanently imprisoned by a construct system. On the contrary, these systems are elaborated upon and occasionally disconfirmed over the course of many years. Books such as *The Women's Room,* by Marilyn French, *The Seasons of a Man's Life,* by Daniel Levinson, and *Passages,* by Gail Sheehy, suggest the occurrence of evolution and revolutionary changes of evaluative schemata throughout the life cycle. In contrast to the Freudians, who view people as the victims of their infancies, Kelly argues that people are not the victims of their pasts, though they may enslave themselves by adhering to unalterable visions of what the past means, thereby fixating the present (see Bannister & Fransella, 1977, p. 19). The change of a construct system, then, is a matter of choice, an action rather than a reaction.

- *Range corollary:* A construct is convenient for the anticipation of a finite range of events only.

The "range of convenience" of any construct is all those things to which one might eventually find that construct applicable. The construct *girl,* for example, is used by many persons to refer to all females. The individual who has been sensitized to the inequities inherent in our language might use *girl* as the child female equivalent of *boy* and *woman* as the adult female equivalent of *man,* thereby limiting the range of convenience of each construct.

- *Experience corollary:* A person's construction system varies as he or she successively construes the replication of events.

This corollary is related to the choice corollary in that it implies change. It steps beyond that corollary, however, by positing that such change is a result of successful and unsuccessful validation of constructs. Constructs are predictive, not merely ways of labeling objects and events in our world. If predictions prove accurate, then it is likely that a construct will be retained. However, if a construct leads consistently to inaccurate predictions, we may feel compelled to dispense with it or modify the overall construct subsystem in which it resides (see Bannister, 1966, p. 366).

- *Modulation corollary:* The variation in a person's construct system is limited by the permeability of the constructs within whose range of convenience the variants lie.

In this corollary Kelly implies that each person has a more or less rigid construct system. Rigidity of constructions leads to more frequent invalidation of predictions, thus requiring more frequent change. The person whose construct system includes permeable constructs may comfortably assimilate the slightly unexpected as a variation upon rather than an invalidation of a construct. The construct *permeable/impermeable* refers to the degree to which a construct can assimilate new experiences into its range of convenience, thereby generating new implications.

- *Fragmentation corollary:* A person may successively employ a variety of construction subsystems that are inferentially incompatible with each other.

This corollary merely indicates that the construing of events is a personal matter. Successful usage of one construct or construct system to explain an event and generate behavior does not guarantee that the same construction of that type of event will occur in the future. The degree of consistency demonstrated by an individual is a matter of personal choice.

- *Commonality corollary:* To the extent that one person employs a construction of experience similar to that employed by another, his or her processes are psychologically similar to those of the other person.

This corollary specifies that people are similar to the extent that they construe events in similar ways. Communication is facilitated by similarity and inhibited by differences in construal processes. The next and final corollary indicates, however, that we need not possess the same construct systems to understand each other.

- *Sociality corollary:* To the extent that one person construes the construction processes of another, he or she may play a role in a social process involving the other person.

Our interpretation of others' construct systems provides the foundation for our influence on others. People recognize that they are not the same as others. They attempt, with more or less success, to understand just where the other individual is "coming from." The success or failure of attempts to persuade another is, to a large degree, a function of the accuracy with which one can construe the construct system of another. To be able to do so successfully provides persuaders with an understanding of what persuadees expect of them. This social perspective-taking is an invaluable communication skill.

Personal construct theory is important to persuasion because it demonstrates why two people with every good intention of communicating effectively with each other are sometimes unable to do so. People "talk past each other" when they do not share similar constructions of their environments. It simply is not possible to persuade someone whose construction of the world is so foreign to our own that we cannot comprehend it. This is why one of the greatest challenges to becoming skillful at persuasion is comprehending how the persuadee thinks, how he or she views your product, idea, behavior, or even you as a person.

As Kelly explains, people are not necessarily stuck with their constructs for life. Constructs often change as life events teach their owners that they are inaccurate or not useful. It is even possible for an individual to be persuaded to change constructs regarding a particular person, event, or type thereof. For example, a woman who is tired of working late hours each day only to receive a small raise may be ready to hear a friend say, "You know, there are some people who live to work and those who work to live. You might consider trying the latter." These words might finally persuade her to take a vacation or take a few minutes each day to remember what counts in life.

SOCIAL SCHEMATA

Another term describing the types of mental patterns people use to guide their interpretations of experience is *schema*. A schema is "a cognitive structure that represents organized knowledge about a given concept or type of stimulus" (Fiske & Taylor, 1984, p. 140). Researchers who study schemata examine the ways that people use their prior theories and concepts to shape how they view events. For example, suppose you move into a new neighborhood and discover that your neighbor has five dogs and four cats in his small, two-bedroom house. How you receive this information depends on your own experiences with dogs and cats as well as possible experiences with people who tend to have large numbers of animals in their homes. If you later discover that each of the animals had been abandoned and that your neighbor took them in to save their lives, would that influence your perspective? It probably would.

Each of our past experiences contributes to how we view current events. This means that we rarely experience reality firsthand, but instead construct our own versions of reality on a daily basis. If your job involves managing people, each day you are managing a host of individualized versions of reality. Certainly the people who work for you share some conceptions of their jobs and of you, but, by and large, they differ. Some think that you don't like their work if you don't say something positive about it nearly every day. Others may not need frequent reinforcement because their personal schemata are sturdy and thus they need only occasional reminders of their worth as employees. Their previous bosses may have been people who did not provide frequent praise, so their "boss schema" does not include frequent praise.

The same employee who does not expect frequent praise might, however, expect other things from the boss, such as being asked to play a key role in departmental decisions rather than being told of decisions after the fact. Or the employee might think that a good boss should allow occasional long lunches or extra vacation days if an employee works on a weekend to finish an important project. Being a manager of people means being a manager of multiple versions of reality. Persuading employees to see things your way often means seeing things their way first. Then you can formulate your arguments effectively. If you use only your own schemata to determine how you might, for example, persuade an employee to work late without expecting extra vacation time, you are less likely to do so effectively.

Of course, you could merely tell yourself, "I'm the boss, so we'll do things my way." Many bosses do just that. And most bosses do feel that way occasionally. As mentioned in Chapter 1, however, a person who is coerced into doing as you wish is not likely to continue to do so after you leave. The value of persuasion is that people *choose* to cooperate and are thus more committed to continuing to cooperate. So managing people for the long term means getting to know how their schemata regarding work expectations differ from yours. Add to this the fact that telecommunications and ease of travel have increased the chances of doing business cross-culturally and the challenge of understanding the schemata of those with whom one does business becomes quite imposing.

TYPES OF SCHEMATA

Social schema research has identified essentially four groups: person schemata, self-schemata, role schemata, and event schemata (Fiske & Taylor, 1984). The first of these, *person schemata,* refers to people's understanding of the psychology of typical or specific individuals. Many stereotypes are based on person schemata. If a person is tall, we might tend to consider him or her a promising basketball player. In actuality, that person may be completely uncoordinated in basketball or may simply hate the sport. A person who dresses conservatively may be considered by coworkers as someone who would not appreciate off-color jokes. Someone who is always early for work may be considered a workaholic, when in actuality she may be someone who likes to get to work early to avoid rush-hour traffic.

Self-schemata focus on one's own appearance, personality, and behavior. You might consider yourself quite good looking and a pleasure to be around. Others may not agree, but the absence of large amounts of disconfirmation may allow you to maintain your positive self-schemata. If some of your friends decide to tell you that you are actually a bit mousy in appearance and a considerable bore at parties, then you might begin to question the self-schemata you have held dear. Individuals also harbor negative self-schemata about which they may or may not be open with others, such as knowing that one is the "jealous type."

Role schemata constitute the third type of social schemata. These include information about broad social categories such as age, race, sex, or occupation. A man who finds himself depressed for two weeks after his fortieth birthday may have a schemata that places 40 in the "over the hill" range. Another person might consider 40 the time when life really begins. People who think they would rather be at a party with five Hollywood producers than with five investment bankers might think the former more interesting or fun to be with. Of course, if you are an investment banker, you might consider Hollywood producers less interesting and less fun than your peers. The nature of one's schemata depends a great deal upon one's own experience. As Tom Wolfe says in *The Bonfire of the Vanities,* "A liberal is a conservative who's been arrested."

Event schemata include information about what typically happens on certain occasions. You know how to act in a restaurant because you have schemata that tell you what is and is not expected. You know how to depart from a friend's home without offense and just how long to stay when visiting. As the old saying goes, "Fish and visitors tend to stink after three days." Each of us has some understanding, even if inaccurate, of how to behave at a cocktail party versus a beach party. We are brought up with a variety of event schemata and, if we're lucky, our friends, acquaintances, and relatives share similar ones.

An understanding of schemata is important to persuasion because it helps explain how it is that people come to have different views of the same person or event. Schemata are what make persuasion easier at one time and more difficult at another. When persuadees share your schemata, it is easier to know what to say to them, since you likely have some idea of what would be persuasive for you. When persuadees do not share your schemata, it is imperative that you find a way to comprehend theirs before attempting to persuade them. Persuasion requires some bridging of schemata, or what might be referred to as a "common ground" of experience. Otherwise, persuasive appeals have little effect—they essentially "fall on deaf ears."

BEHAVIORAL RULES

Whether construct theory or schema theory works best for you as a description of how people interpret and organize their experiences, the next step is knowing how people convert these mental maps into action. Some researchers have argued that people are guided in their actions by rules or prescriptions of how people should or ought to behave given the situation and their goals. Rules help people choose among a variety of behavioral options by identifying certain options as more appropriate, consistent, or effective than others (Reardon, 1981).

Figure 2.1 depicts how behavioral options are selected. In the figure, *antecedent conditions* refers to how the individual construes the situation, the relevant schemata, and *desired consequent(s)* refers to what the individual wants to achieve. Given these two sources of input, certain behavioral options emerge based on the individual's past experiences. For example, if a 2-year-old child sees her dad's car pull into the driveway, a number of options become available to her. If dad always greets her joyfully upon his return from work, she is likely to run to the door to meet him. Her goal in this case would be to experience her father's happiness at seeing her. If, however, she is busy watching a movie, her desire to see what happens to Mickey Mouse might lower

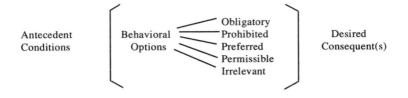

Figure 2.1. Regulative Rule Model
SOURCE: Reardon (1979).
NOTE: See T. J. Smith (1976) for an explanation of preference as a normative force.

the likelihood of her choosing to greet dad at the door, despite positive prior experiences (antecedent conditions).

Behavioral options may be considered in terms of how appropriate (socially acceptable), consistent (personally acceptable), and effective (likely to result in obtaining the desired goals) they are. The phrase "may be considered" is used here since people are not always terribly thoughtful about their actions. If provoked to reason by the importance of the issue, amount of social pressure, or some other extenuating circumstance, people tend to judge their potential actions on the basis of appropriateness, consistency, and/or effectiveness. These three criteria for reasoning about actions or potential actions are derived from decades of research on persuasion, to be reviewed in Chapter 4, and are explained further in Chapter 5 as the ACE model of reasoned behavior. Each behavioral option also carries some degree of necessity or obligation. In other words, in order to act appropriately in a given situation, it may be obligatory to do A but merely permissible to do P. For instance, at a wedding it may be obligatory to be quiet during the ceremony but permissible to laugh aloud or say "Ohhh" or "Ouuu" when the bride and groom kiss.

Imagine for a moment a driver being advised by a police officer that he was speeding. Given that a police officer's job (desired consequent) is to protect the public from speeders, in order to behave in a manner appropriate to a police officer he may consider it obligatory for him to stop the speeder. Suppose, however, that the driver informs the officer that he is driving his pregnant wife to the hospital to have their first child. At this point the officer may rearrange his behavioral options. One of his jobs (another desired consequent) is to serve the public. He may consider a woman in labor sufficient reason to be speeding and may decide that an appropriate, although not necessarily obligatory, action is to let the man go. Essentially, the redefinition of the antecedent conditions, calling up of different schemata, renders delaying the speeder further an inappropriate act in the mind of this policeman.

Should the policeman follow the speeder to the hospital and then serve him with a ticket, we may assume that while the officer felt it was appropriate to be helpful or to behave in a manner consistent with the type of person he likes to think he is, he also considered giving a ticket obligatory. Even the antecedent condition of a wife in labor was insufficient to discourage this policeman from seeing his greatest obligation as one of sending a clear message that speeding is wrong.

This example demonstrates that persuasion involves knowing not only how an individual interprets an event but what he or she thinks ought to occur given that interpretation and the individual's goals. The speeder being handed a ticket as his wife is wheeled into the delivery room might request that the officer reconsider. He might argue that he has never speeded in his life and that he wished only to ensure his wife's safety. If clever, he might agree that the officer has every right to give him a ticket but also encourage the officer to put himself in the same position. It may be stretching reality a bit to assume that any prospective parent might be able to reason in this way while his child is being born, but bear with me for a moment. The policeman has his rules. He knows that it is his duty to give a ticket to a speeder. If he is rigid in the application of his rules regarding crime, the prospective father is up a creek. If, however, he begins to see the antecedent conditions that made speeding this one time a justifiable act (e.g., wife in labor, first child, never speeded before), then he may decide that ticketing in this case is permissible for a policeman but not obligatory. The policeman may consider himself a nice guy, in which case it would be inconsistent for him to give a ticket to this desperate man. The nondefensive manner of the speeder might further encourage the policeman to focus more on his self-image as "nice guy" than to feel compelled to be strident about sending a message that speeding is wrong under any circumstance.

Rules tell people what to do once they have interpreted the situation at hand. Rules are generalizations, so they are never perfect. In fact, each situation elicits a variety of rules that may or may not be followed. A skillful persuader helps the persuadee revise his or her views of the antecedent conditions, desired consequences, or the importance of doing the appropriate, consistent, or effective thing. To be skillful at persuasion, it is important (a) to recognize what rule the persuadee is following, and (b) to determine which conditions of the actual event he or she used to render the rule sensible. This gives the persuader a chance to demonstrate that there are other antecedent conditions that were overlooked by the persuadee that make another action more appropriate, consistent, or effective or that there are certain goals the persuadee might consider that would also make a change of action the logical thing to do. When the persuader is unable to convince the persuadee that there is another way to view the situation, desired consequents, and/or types of pressure associated with a given action, she might just say, "Okay, you're right. We should do X. But just this once it wouldn't hurt to try Q." If the persuadee likes to view herself as a risk-taker, she may abandon her rule "just this once."

Rules, then, are prescriptions for action. They are "shoulds" and "oughts" that people carry around in their minds and apply to situations. They are not etched in stone, so they are subject to revision. Although people do vary in the extent to which they are rigid with regard to their schemata and rules (a condition that may be referred to as "hardening of the categories"), most people are not irretrievably stuck with them. In any event, it is not sufficient for a persuader to know how an individual interprets a person or event; he or she must also know what type of action such interpretations encourage for that individual. Two people may share the same impression of an event but differ in how they think they should respond. For example, seeing an abandoned dog in the street, two friends may feel sorry for the dog. One, however, may feel obliged to take the lonely dog home. The other may see that as a permissible thing to do but certainly not an obligatory action.

ILLUSIONS

As if it were not challenging enough to identify the persuadee's schemata and rules, another set of perceptions exists that researchers call "illusions." Throughout psychological history the dominant view of mental health has maintained that the psychologically healthy person maintains close contact with reality. Taylor and Brown (1988) bring this view into question by suggesting that certain illusions (false mental images) are actually adaptive for mental health and well-being. In other words, there are times when deceiving oneself is conducive to health.

On the basis of prior research, Taylor and Brown (1988) propose that at least three common illusions exist: unrealistically positive views of the self, exaggerated perceptions of personal control, and unrealistic optimism. Unrealistically positive views of the self appear to result from the tendency to dismiss as inconsequential negative aspects of the self and to consider one's favored abilities as rare and distinctive (Campbell, 1986; Marks, 1984). For example, someone who is always late might consider that a minor fault, given that he is always the life of the party once he does arrive. People also tend to perceive that they have improved on abilities that are important to them even if their performance has remained the same (Conway & Ross, 1984).

The second type of illusion includes less than realistic beliefs about personal control over the environment. Of course, people who are mildly or severely depressed are less vulnerable to the illusion of control. Taylor and Brown (1988) argue, however, that most people tend to overestimate the degree to which they are instrumental in bringing about positive outcomes. We tend to pat ourselves on the back when things turn out well.

The third type of illusion is an unrealistic optimism about the future. One might reasonably argue that it is not always unrealistic to assume that positive outcomes will obtain in one's life, but evidence exists that, aside from those people who are experiencing depression, there is a general tendency to see one's personal world through rose-colored glasses.

What does this have to do with persuasion? It means that persuasion strategies cannot always be based on facts. It is important to recognize that people see the world through their own schemata and even harbor illusions that appear to them as reality. The competent persuader is one who seeks a considerable amount of information about the persuadee and his or her views of the world before formulating a strategy. Such a persuader looks not only at what the persuadee should think if he or she is in touch with reality, but what that person does think. It is the latter that forms the base upon which persuasive arguments are constructed.

CONCLUSION

While I cannot do justice in a single chapter to constructivism, schema theory, or rules perspectives, this overview is important as a means of demonstrating the difficult task involved in persuasion. Persuasion is facilitated by a meeting of the minds on some common ground that is often not easily identified. When people do not share the same ways of construing the world around them, it is difficult for them to communicate effectively. To do so requires finding some bridge between their differences—some similar perspectives. These similar perspectives constitute a common ground from which dissimilar people may begin to build a common understanding. *It is not necessary to agree with others in order to persuade them. It is necessary to understand how they think and why such perspectives matter to them.* This is the foundation for persuasion. To reach it the persuader must truly be a detective of the human mind—a Sherlock Holmes of schemata (or constructs), rules, and illusions.

3 Attitudes and Values

Attitudes and values are hypothetical constructs. This means that while we firmly believe that they exist, they cannot be directly measured. Can you touch or see an attitude? If so, you are one up on the rest of us. The only thing we can do is look for something that reflects attitude. During the 1950s and 1960s researchers assumed that they could infer changes of attitudes and values from changes in behaviors. We have since learned that these relationship are far from perfect. It is quite possible for people to change their behaviors while retaining the same attitudes and values. For example, a company might hire more minorities in response to affirmative action demands without feeling good about it.

WHAT IS AN ATTITUDE?

No one really knows what an attitude is. Multiple definitions have emerged (see Reardon, 1981). Some have defined it as a predisposition to respond in a certain manner. For example, someone who has a positive attitude toward her job may be predisposed to respond favorably when her boss asks her to work late.

In 1934, LaPiere brought into question the assumed relationship between attitudes and behaviors. LaPiere reported that, despite strong anti-Chinese sentiment characteristic of that decade, he and a Chinese couple were received at 66 hotels, auto camps, and tourist homes, and were turned away at only one. They were served in 184 restaurants and cafes scattered throughout the country and treated with "more than ordinary consideration" at 72 of them. After six months had elapsed since the overt acceptance of the Chinese couple, LaPiere "questionnaired" the establishments. The results indicated a wide discrepancy between nonsymbolic and symbolic behavior. Of the 128 establishments that responded—81 restaurants and 47 hotels, auto camps, and tourist homes—92% of the respondents from the former and 91% from the latter stated that they would not accept members of the Chinese race as guests of their establishments.

The absence of a direct relationship between attitude and behavior has led to much confusion surrounding the definition of attitude. Leonard W. Doob responded by providing a behavioral definition of attitude. According to Doob (1947), attitude is "an implicit, drive-producing response considered socially significant in the individual's society" (p. 43). He elaborated on this definition for discussion purposes. The result was a definition of attitude as

(1) an implicit response
(2) which is both (a) anticipatory and (b) mediating in reference to patterns of overt responses,
(3) which is evoked (a) by a variety of stimulus patterns (b) as a result of previous learning of gradients of generalization and discrimination,
(4) which is itself cue- and drive-producing,
(5) and which is considered socially significant in the individual's society. (p. 42)

This is one of the most inclusive definitions to come out of early attitude theory. It is inclusive in the sense that it accounts for the origins, functions, and consequences of attitudes.

(1) "Attitude is an implicit response." An implicit response is one that occurs within the individual. It is an intrapersonal response not observable by others. This perspective on attitude has led many to consider its major role one of predisposing the individual to act in a certain manner: an immediate response to a stimulus pattern that sets the tone, so to speak, for further responses.

(2a) "An attitude is an implicit response which is . . . anticipatory . . . in reference to patterns of overt responses." Doob was essentially arguing that all responses have antecedents, even if they cannot be consciously recalled. Through the process of socialization, for example, a child could learn to share. In later years he may not know why he tends to share his wealth with others, but his early training in sharing likely played a significant role.

(2b) "An attitude is an implicit response which is . . . mediating in reference to patterns of overt responses." This aspect of Doob's definition reflects the latent process view of attitude. Attitude is treated as a hidden or hypothetical variable, shaping, acting upon, or mediating observable behavior (see Wicker, 1969). This perspective has been even more popular than probability conceptions of attitude. The attitude is not considered to consist of the behavioral responses themselves or their probability, but is instead an intervening variable, occurring between the stimulus and the response, that can be inferred only from overt behavior.

Unlike the probability conception of attitude, which by definition indicates that for any issue the absence of empirical evidence for a predictable relationship between attitude and behavior is sufficient to assume that an attitude on that issue is nonexistent, the latent process view implies that the attitude is there, but that our measurement techniques are not sufficiently adequate to locate it. Larson and Sanders (1975) have objected to the latter view because, in the absence of empirical evidence, latent process advocates must rely on faith to support their belief in the existence of attitudes.

Doob combined the probability and latent process views in his definition of attitude. Its anticipatory nature is a reflection of the former view, and its mediating nature originates from the latter. As such, it is difficult to conceive of an empirical test that would support or reject Doob's definition. Thus, while Doob's definition may be one of the most inclusive to come out of attitude theory, it may have added to the demise of attitude research by setting up incompatible research demands.

(3a) "An attitude is an implicit response . . . which is evoked by a variety of stimulus patterns." Just as it is possible for an attitude to evoke a repertoire of alternative behaviors, one attitude can be evoked by a variety of stimulus patterns, as depicted in Figure 3.1.

(3b) "An attitude is an implicit response . . . which is evoked . . . as a result of previous learning or of gradients of generalization and discrimination." Doob preferred to explain the complex nature of responding to contextual exigencies (stimuli) in terms of gradients of generalization and discrimination. If, for example, the stimulus *poodle* fails to elicit an anticipatory response of dislike mediating a goal response of running away, whereas *bulldog* elicits a running response, we can assume that the individual discriminates among types of dogs. If the individual runs from all dogs, then we can consider stimulus generalization accountable for that behavior.

(4) "An attitude is an implicit response . . . which is itself cue- and drive-producing." According to Doob, attitudes, like all other responses, have stimulus value. They arouse other responses. Overt behavior is one type of response aroused by an attitude. Doob (1947)

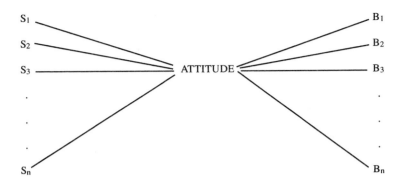

Figure 3.1.

refers to the bond between attitude and behavior as "efferent-habit strength." He views this bond as influenced by the cue and drive strength of a given attitude. As he explains, "An attitude has cue value in the sense that it acts as a stimulus to produce another response, but it also is a drive in the sense that tension is reduced through subsequent behavior leading to a reward" (p. 47).

Although afferent- and efferent-habit strength are theoretically intriguing concepts, the latter especially fails to account adequately for the linkage between an attitude and a given response in those instances where many responses are possible and equally rewarding. Chein (1967) proposes that "conditions (inner and outer) surrounding the bond are different from time to time. It follows that the relative frequency of evocation is a function of the surrounding conditions rather than of 'the strength of the bond' and that, in this respect at least, all bonds are equally strong" (p. 55).

It does not seem useful to take sides with either Chein or Doob on this issue. Both acknowledge the existence of an attachment between attitude and behavior. Chein places primary emphasis on external forces influencing the strength of the bond, whereas Doob favors an internal orientation. It seems feasible to consider both frequency and conditions of occurrence as factors influencing the connection between attitude and behavior. In terms of constructs and rules, we can consider the former to be more resistant to external constraints than the latter. For example, while it is possible to construe women as inferior, changing social norms have influenced male behavior in public places to conform

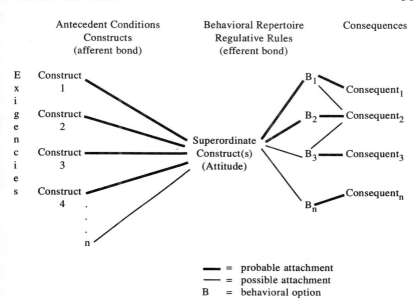

Figure 3.2. Construct-Rule Linkage Model

to demands for equality. It seems reasonable to assume that many people retain the afferent-habit strength between the stimulus *woman* and negative constructs, but adjust the rules to conform to societal pressures, thereby weakening the consistency between afferent (stimulus-attitude) and efferent (attitude-behavior) bonds. It may be very useful to view afferent bonds as consisting of linkages between attitudes and one or more superordinate attitudes, and efferent bonds as linkages between superordinate attitudes and regulative rules. The new model that emerges from this perspective appears in Figure 3.2.

This model suggests that persuasive communication can be used to change constructs (or attitudes), behaviors, or both. If one seeks to change both, the result is more likely to be private acceptance of the persuasive message rather than mere acquiescence (behavior change alone). For example, assume that a particular man normally construes all suggestions offered by female colleagues as worthless and so ignores them. If a persuasive message merely altered his image of female competence but did not provide any face-saving ways whereby he could also change his behavior, the result could be inconsistency between the superordinate attitude toward female colleagues and the behavior toward female colleagues. If, on the other hand, pressure through affirmative action programs, superiors, or peers influenced this man to change his overt behavior toward female colleagues but did not influence his attitude regarding their competence, acquiescence alone would result. Finally, should he be influenced to reconstrue the value of female competence and, on his own or through a persuasive message, find face-saving ways of revising his behavior accordingly, then private acceptance is more likely to be secured. We shall return to this conceptualization of the persuasion process. For now, let us turn to Doob's final description of attitude.

(5) "An attitude is an implicit response . . . which is significant in the individual's society." This aspect of Doob's definition is consistent with the concept of normative constraints. In Chapter 2 the rule model behavioral repertoire is accompanied by normative forces. Although many behaviors might be feasible in a given situation, some are obligatory, others are prohibited, preferable, permissible, or irrelevant to the enactment of a particular episode. It is possible to construe what Doob refers to as "drive strength" as a partially external normative force operating as a constraint on the behavior of the individual. The word *partially* is used here because individuals can exert pressure on themselves as well.

THE ATTITUDE-BEHAVIOR DILEMMA

In a 1975 article, "Faith, Mystery, and Data: An Analysis of 'Scientific' Studies of Persuasion," Charles Larson and Robert Sanders question three assumptions derived from several decades of scientific investigations of persuasion:

(1) Persuasion brings about changes in people's attitudes.
(2) Attitudes are constraints on behavior, or predispositions to respond.
(3) Persuasion brings about changes in what people will (or will not) do, because it affects attitudes which in turn affect behavior. (p. 178)

Larson and Sanders argue that commitment to these propositions is inappropriate, since there has been little direct effort to prove them. They claim that these propositions, the foundation of persuasion research, have been treated like axioms rather than as the "empirical claims they really are."

There has been little support for the relationship between attitude and behavior. We also do not know whether attitude change must precede behavior change. There are occasions when people acquiesce to persuasive arguments and behave in ways inconsistent with their past behaviors. If they are rewarded for the new behavior, they may later convince themselves to change their attitude about that behavior as well. For example, if a person who has hated eating beets for most of his life acquiesces to his wife's request to "just try one" and finds that they taste good, he might change his attitude about beets. He might even develop a more positive attitude toward trying foods that he thinks he will dislike. Of course, he might just tell his wife, "I've tried them, okay? Now lay off!" It appears that changes in attitude can influence behavior but that changes of behavior can also influence attitude.

VALUES

Another hypothetical construct relevant to the study of persuasion is *values*. Values are standards. We acquire them from our families, friends, teachers, television, and other sources of influence. Throughout life they are reinforced or challenged by the people with whom we communicate. Thus values are capable of being arranged and rearranged with regard to their priority. At one point in an individual's life, he may place freedom high in his value hierarchy and equality low in that same hierarchy. With time he may learn that freedom for others is what guarantees it for himself. He may begin to believe that others should have access to the same privileges he wishes to enjoy. In time, he may begin to move equality to a higher level in his prioritization of values.

According to Rokeach (1980), values are interrelated with beliefs and attitudes. It is this combination of beliefs, attitudes, and values that provides us with a cognitive framework for engaging in mental activities that lead to action or the absence of action. Rokeach summarizes this perspective as follows:

A *belief* is any expectancy concerning existence, evaluation prescription-proscription, or cause. An *attitude* is a relatively enduring organization of existential, evaluative, prescriptive-proscriptive, and causal beliefs organized around an object or situation, predisposing one to respond (a) preferentially to the object or situation, (b) discriminatingly to all persons perceived to vary in their attitude to object or situation, and (c) differentially to social controls or pressures intended to coerce expression to specified positions toward object and situation. All such preferential, discriminatory, or differential responses are instrumental to the realization of societally originating "values"—shared prescriptive or proscriptive beliefs about ideal modes of behavior and end-states of existence that are activated by, yet transcend object and situation. (p. 262)

From this perspective, personality is actually an organization of beliefs, attitudes, and values around the self, rather than a set of traits such as honest, sensitive, confident, and warm (see Ball-Rokeach, Rokeach, & Grube, 1984). It is important to point out that emphasis on "cognition" as the guiding component of behavior should not be taken to mean that people do not also have an affective or emotional side. All beliefs have an affective component. If you believe that smoking is dangerous, then you most likely have a negative emotional reaction to being seated next to a smoker while you are traveling or eating dinner in a restaurant. It is virtually impossible to strip emotion from human thinking. The two are inextricably linked. So a cognitive system containing beliefs, attitudes, and values is a system immersed in emotional content as well. This content may be visual memories that creep into one's thoughts or merely physical reactions to words. To a person opposed to abortion, for example, the word *abortion* itself may elicit strong, negative emotional reactions. The person who sees the prohibition of abortion as an affront to women's rights may have a stronger negative emotional reaction to the thought of denying a woman who has been raped, for example, the right to choose not to have the baby than she has to the thought of abortion. This person may not be favorably predisposed to abortion but may find the absence of that option abhorrent.

BRINGING ABOUT CHANGE IN
VALUES, ATTITUDES, AND BELIEFS

Assuming, then, that each of us has a cognitive system composed of beliefs, attitudes, and values, is there a way to bring about change in that system? According to Ball-Rokeach et al. (1984), people are quite unaware of the ways in which their cognitive systems regulate action. The complexity of their cognitive systems, intellectual limitations, and ego defenses conspires to prevent most people from knowing what makes them operate as they do. It seems reasonable, then, to assume that at least some people would predispose to change if they were to be informed of the beliefs, attitudes, and values that constitute their systems and if they were also to learn that among these beliefs, attitudes, and values are ones they would not find particularly satisfying. It is also important to point out that the values that make up their value systems differ in degree of stability. Terminal values are quite enduring. They are ultimate end goals of existence, such as wisdom, equality, peace, and family security. Instrumental values are less enduring than terminal values and thus more easily changed. They are the behavioral means for obtaining the end goals of terminal values. For example, they embody the importance of honesty, ambition, forgiveness, and rationality as means to desired ends.

When people receive information causing them to question the accuracy of terminal and instrumental values, research indicates that such information can encourage change. Ball-Rokeach et al. (1984) argue that "self-dissatisfaction is a noxious affective state that people will attempt to alleviate or terminate and thus provides the impetus for changing whatever is perceived to be causing the state." People are inclined to behave in ways that are self-satisfying, ways that elicit feelings of competence and morality (in the sense of doing what one should do under the circumstances).

Self-dissatisfaction alone is not, however, sufficient to elicit change. Each day people experience vague feelings of self-satisfaction and self-dissatisfaction. There are even days when one or the other dominates. When one is generally dissatisfied with oneself without really knowing why, the typical result is cognitive indecision and behavioral vacillation. A person in this state might seek assistance from others in her attempt to understand why she feels dissatisfied. She may be fortunate and learn the actual reason for her dissatisfaction, and actually feel that she can do something about it. She may discover the reason but have little recourse with regard to bringing about change, or she may merely float about seeking an answer or go to sleep and hope tomorrow will bring greater self-satisfaction.

Ball-Rokeach et al. (1984) propose that "self-knowledge" can be induced in ways that encourage both stability of the cognitive system and change in it. When people receive comparative information indicating that their important beliefs or actions are compatible with their self-conceptions and self-presentations, they should experience feelings of self-satisfaction. These feelings should reinforce and stabilize the beliefs and actions and also make them more available or more easily activated in the future.

When people receive comparative information suggesting that one or more of their beliefs or actions is incompatible with their self-conceptions and self-presentations, they should experience feelings of self-dissatisfaction. These feelings undermine or hinder further expression of such beliefs or actions and make them more susceptible to change. Ball-Rokeach et al. (1984) describe this as an "unfreezing" of the beliefs or actions in question. They become less stabilized and less sturdy resisters of change. To reduce feelings of self-dissatisfaction, people tend to change or reorganize beliefs and actions perceived to be the source of such feelings.

From this it is easy to see how persuaders might use value self-confrontation to bring about changes in beliefs and behaviors. Showing people how their actions, for example, are in conflict with their preferred self-conceptions should, according to Ball-Rokeach and her colleagues, encourage change in those actions toward ones that are more compatible with the self-perceptions. It is, of course, possible for people to live with certain amounts of incompatibility between their preferred self-conceptions and some of their beliefs and/or actions. It behooves the persuader to know how to present the comparative information in a way that encourages change rather than a response of "Sure, I know that. So who's perfect?" Ball-Rokeach et al. list seven criteria for information likely to induce self-knowledge in a manner conducive to change:

(1) If the information appeals to the curiosity that people have to understand themselves better.

(2) If the information is potentially useful, that is, holds out a promise of increasing one's knowledge about something that is truly important to oneself. We assume that the most important information that persons can obtain about themselves is that which directly involves their competence or morality. We further assume that information about one's values, because they are central and because they serve as standards for evaluating self and other, will be more important than information about one's attitudes or behaviors.

(3) If the information is unambiguous and does not require too much specialized training or effort to understand.

(4) If the information appears credible and intuitively correct.

(5) If the information arouses a feeling of self-satisfaction because it reinforces or confirms one's self-conceptions or self-presentations of competence or morality or, alternatively, if it arouses a feeling of self-dissatisfaction because it raises doubts about one's present level of competence or morality and thus becomes an impetus for change.

(6) If it is within the repertoire of the person to act upon the information, either to alleviate or eliminate the focused feeling of self-dissatisfaction or to extend and enhance the focused feeling of self-satisfaction.

(7) If the information is presented under conditions that minimize ego defense. (pp. 35-36)

Obviously, value self-confrontation is not merely the mention of comparative information that conflicts with the self-perceptions or self-presentations of the recipient. The composition and presentation of such information should be guided by a number of criteria inclusive of the ones listed above. It is simply not enough to walk up to someone and tell them, "Do you know that your behavior is completely inconsistent with your self-image?" This persuader might just as well have said, "Do you know that you're a phony?" The seventh criterion listed above indicates that the comparative information must be presented in a way that does not elicit ego defensiveness. Once again we are reminded of the Chapter 1 discussion of the importance of knowing not only what to say but how to say it when wishing to engage in effective persuasion.

APPLICATION OF VALUES
TO MASS PERSUASION

It is one thing to present comparative information to someone face-to-face and quite another to do so via mass media. It is also one thing to know the values of an individual and quite another to be familiar with the values of a society or segment of society. Yet that is exactly what marketers do. Plummer, executive research director at Young & Rubicam, argues that marketers must understand emerging new values in order to encourage consumers effectively to buy their products. According to Plummer (1988), people are now in the midst of profound and enduring changes in basic values: "The long-held beliefs about the function of work in one's own life, relations between sexes, expectations for the future, indeed about many aspects of daily living and important relationships among people are undergoing a re-examination and reappraisal." Plummer argues that the value shifts we are seeing place greater emphasis on ethics of employers, marketers, and political figures. Thus marketers who demonstrate a sense of fair play and even a true sense of altruism are likely to gain respect from the "new-value consumer."

Advertisements depicting a company devoting some of its resources to worthy causes may indeed give people a good feeling about purchasing that company's products, especially in a time when people are becoming increasingly aware of the need for ethical standards and are beginning to demand these standards of those with whom they do business and those they select to be leaders. The recent controversy over the environmental threat posed by disposable diapers has some companies, such as Procter & Gamble, engaging in pilot studies to determine whether the plastic outer lining of diapers might be recycled and used to make such items as plastic flower pots. Such efforts will likely have significant public relations effects on a society that is becoming increasingly conscious of the long-term damage today's environmental nonchalance will have on the future of the entire world.

CONCLUSION

Years of research suggest that while changes in attitude may bring about changes in behavior, it is difficult to identify people's true attitudes. It is also difficult to determine which attitudes are directly linked with which behaviors. People with similar attitudes toward work and play often work and play differently. A person who is always late for work might be persuaded to change his attitude toward lateness. He might begin to think that lateness is wrong. He may still, however, continue to be late if he owns a car that always breaks down or if he finds it nearly impossible to get out of bed early in the morning. Many factors influence whether our attitudes match our actions. The person who has a positive attitude toward being supportive of friends may not come to the aid of a friend if doing so will get her into more trouble than she thinks she can handle.

Bringing about changes in values that will lead to changes in behavior is also a challenge. The prospect of changing people's values has always seemed a rather monumental task to those who study persuasion. After all, as discussed in this chapter, values are more enduring than attitudes and beliefs and are not easily articulated. Yet recent research indicates that values are significantly related to variations in socioeconomic status, age, gender, race, religion, and life-style, and have also been shown to be significant predictors of many social attitudes and behaviors, including consumer behavior (see Rokeach & Ball-Rokeach, 1988).

It is important to note that the study of values offers promise as a means of comprehending the cultures of organizations, norms of groups and societies, and changes of such cultures and norms as the result of crises, education, and other environmental phenomena. As a route for changing particular behaviors, they also offer some promise. As people come to value participation in their own health care, for example, they are more easily persuaded to eat well and to exercise regularly. When people place high value on preserving the earth for future generations, they are receptive to persuasive messages that encourage them to recycle. The only problem with using values to change behaviors is that it often takes a long time to change people's values. Often public opinion campaigns are required, and/or the persistence of organized groups, such as those devoted to civil rights, gun control, or victims' rights. The good news is that when values are finally changed, they tend to endure until extensive efforts are directed at changing them again.

4 Theoretical Orientations of Persuasion Research

A theory tells us how events in the world ought to be related. It is one human being's construal of some aspect of the world. As such, it is subject to human error. No theory can explain everything. All theories have scope conditions or parameters beyond which they cannot provide reliable explanations (see Reynolds, 1975). One of the most common problems associated with attitude theory is the absence of specified scope conditions. The attitude theorists' disregard for contextual considerations set them up for failure: They were looking for one theory to explain all types of persuasion. They did not see the necessity for limiting the scope of their theories to, for example, interpersonal, dyadic, group, or mass persuasion, or for explaining how these theories applied differentially to each context.

A good theory, then, specifies the scope conditions. It provides us some way of explaining some portion of reality. Furthermore, theories are vital to understanding any complex phenomenon because they can

(1) generate predictions about complex functional relationships among variables;

(2) integrate many empirical observations that, on the surface, may appear to be dissimilar;

(3) separate relevant from irrelevant variables, and provide schemes for organizing the relevant ones;

(4) allow for the derivation of nonobvious predictions (that is, statements about reality that one would not make on the basis of intuition); and

(5) explain why variables function as they do, often by postulating hypothetical processes (Zimbardo, Ebbesen, & Maslach, 1977, p. 55).

Unfortunately, many social scientists, in their zeal to prove themselves true scientists, have often opted to emphasize measurement over theory. Quantitative and qualitative measures are to theory as a horse is to a carriage. A theory can provide very little if it remains untested, but variable testing with little regard for theory can only serve to confuse us. While it may be true that some people are more adept at conceptualization than measurement or vice versa, the student of communication must learn both or risk the possibility of inhibiting progress (see Mc-Croskey, 1979). Theories are inextricably associated with measurement. As such, they are "intellectual tools for organizing data in such a way that one can make inferences or logical transitions from one set of data to another; they serve as guidelines to investigation, explanation, organization, and discovery of observable facts" (Deutsch & Krauss, 1965, p. 4). The next section traces the history of persuasion theory and the inferences that guided research.

LEARNING THEORY

The most basic and long-lasting paradigm influencing persuasion theory and research was *classical conditioning*. According to this perspective, when a particular response follows a given stimulus, the repeated pairing of this (conditioned) stimulus with a neutral (unconditioned) stimulus will eventually result in the elicitation of the response from the sole presence of the neutral stimulus. Every student of general psychology encounters the classic example of this paradigm. Pavlov conducted an experiment in which he rang a bell shortly before blowing meat powder into a dog's mouth. The dog initially salivated in response to the meat powder but later came to salivate in response to the bell alone.

Staats (1967, 1968) tells us that all attitudes are acquired through classical conditioning. Watson and Johnson (1972) explain that a word, such as *dangerous,* that generally elicits a negative response, when paired with another word, such as *noxious,* can lead to the same negative response to the second word. They refer to this transference of response tendencies from one word to another as "higher-order conditioning."

The process of persuasion often involves influencing a person to respond to one object or word in the same negative or positive way in which he or she typically responds to another object or word. However, sometimes there is a need to change previous associations. This is achieved through *counterconditioning*. Counterconditioning involves pairing a stimulus that evokes a negative response with one that evokes a positive response. As long as the positive stimulus-response linkage is stronger than the negative stimulus-response linkage, counterconditioning is possible. For example, if the word *child* elicits a slightly negative response from someone, the pairing of that stimulus with *cute* or *refreshing* or *warm* will increase the likelihood of *child* eliciting a positive response in the future. The new stimulus must be strong enough to discredit the person's previously negative connotation of the original stimulus.

Classical conditioning has come to be viewed as too simplistic an explanation for all types of learning. However, one of the most common persuasive techniques is to associate the object of change with some other positive or negative stimulus. Source credibility essentially works on this principle of association. High source credibility, when associated with a message, increases the likelihood of message acceptance. For example, advertisers believe that the association of attractive models with cosmetics increases the likelihood of a person or people responding positively to the advertised product. Similarly, subliminal messages conveyed in grocery store music or embedded in advertisements can quietly and surreptitiously influence cognitive associations.

While few deny the effectiveness of forming associations as a means of persuasion, the same types of learning appear to involve much more than mere association. Teaching a dog to salivate at the sound of a bell is certainly not in the same league as teaching a person to chew with his or her mouth closed. Also, even if associations constitute the basis of all learning and hence all persuasion, humans can identify and choose to accept or reject associations. In short, humans can change their own associations through a higher-level cogitation than Pavlov's dog ever devoted to the experiment.

Operant conditioning is a second form of learning, stemming from an emphasis on response reinforcement. The main principle here is that responses become stronger and more resistant to change the more they are associated with rewards. In contrast to classical conditioning, operants are behaviors emitted by the organism, not elicited by a known stimulus. The important link is between the response and the reinforcement. The stimulus is often irrelevant and sometimes unknown.

Here is an example of operant conditioning. A husband who is used to the traditional division of domestic labor decides to cook his first meal. If he is reinforced for such behavior by praise, the chances of his repeating that behavior are increased. The stimulus for such behavior is not considered important from this perspective. However, it seems reasonable to conclude that recognizing the conditions that lead to a desired response provides an edge for the person who wishes to increase the likelihood of response repetition. In other words, if the wife can determine what she may have said or done to encourage this new behavior, she may be able to repeat that behavior and encourage the same response. However, researchers who concern themselves with operant conditioning realize that the husband's behavior might be the result of several unidentifiable experiences, such as hearing that his boss is a great cook. Therefore, instead of attempting to identify the stimuli, we focus on the response-reinforcement connection.

The influence of learning theory on persuasion research was prevalent during the mid-twentieth century and is still obvious in today's research. During World War II, Carl Hovland, a psychology professor at Yale University, and his associates were concerned with influencing the morale of soldiers and with changing civilian attitudes toward the war effort. After the war, Hovland and several students developed an approach to attitude change that has come to be known as the Yale Communication and Attitude Change Program. Much of their work centered on learning theory. To them, attitude is an implicit approach or avoidance response to some object. As such, it is an emotional reaction. The Yale group focused on belief as the change agent of attitude. Beliefs were defined as the cognitive or knowledge component of attitude. Zimbardo et al. (1977) explain this association:

> Thus we should be able to change people's attitudes toward abortion by changing their beliefs about the age at which a fetus becomes a living human being or by altering their beliefs concerning the right of a pregnant woman to decide what to do with her own body. It is further assumed that the learning of new information in a persuasive communication will change beliefs. An effective communication will raise questions about abortion ("Is a three-month-old fetus human?") and provide whatever answers support the appropriate belief. (p. 57)

In 1953, Hovland, Janis, and Kelley reported many of the Yale program results in their book, *Communication and Persuasion*. They explained that attitude change depends on the "rehearsing" or "practicing" of mental and verbal responses. Furthermore, incentives and motivation are needed to encourage the acceptance of new responses over old ones. In terms of the abortion example, it is not sufficient to rehearse in one's mind the new perspective on abortion as a woman's means of deciding what is right for her. The individual must perceive this change of belief and attitude as potentially rewarding (incentives) and must find the change environment (opinions of others, appeals used, source characteristics, and so on) favorable (motivation).

Fishbein (1963) focused upon the relationship of belief and attitude as part of his theory, thereby extending the conditioning paradigm into the 1960s and 1970s. Unlike Doob (1947) and other theorists who left the exact nature of attitude unspecified, Fishbein utilized the concept of belief as a foundation for attitude. He viewed beliefs about some object, concept, or goal in terms of their relationship to some attribute (i.e., to some other object, concept, or goal). Attitude was viewed as the evaluation associated with the belief. As Fishbein and Ajzen (1975) explain, "Some of the implicit evaluation associated with a response constitutes an attitude which may have been formed as the result of prior conditioning" (p. 29).

To Fishbein, then, attitudes are a function of beliefs and associated evaluative responses. Fishbein's model will be explained at greater length later in the chapter. It is one of the classic persuasion models originating from a learning theory perspective. As early as 1932, however, Tolman was emphasizing the importance of considering human needs as the foundation of attitude and belief. He argued that people learn expectations and perform behaviors that they believe will lead to valued results. Despite the apparent emphasis on learning, this perspective suggests the existence of choice among alternatives rather than rigid stimulus-response associations. Inherent in this emphasis on valued consequences is the implication that there is not necessarily a direct association between attitudes and behaviors. While it is likely that a person associates several attitudes with a given object or event, not all of these attitudes are equally likely to be conducive to obtaining a valued consequent. Before elaborating on this variation of the influence of desired consequences, let us look at some related perspectives.

FUNCTIONAL PARADIGM

According to McGuire (1973), the functional paradigm represents a less "intellectual" stance than learning theory. It stresses that people have many needs that attitudes must gratify. Fishbein and Ajzen (1975) refer to this line of thought as "expectancy-value theories." They point to the work of Tolman (1932), Rotter (1954), and Atkinson (1957) as representing a theoretical perspective that proposes that people hold certain attitudes because those attitudes facilitate the attainment of valued consequences.

One of the most well-known functional theories was developed by Katz (1960). According to Katz, we develop favorable attitudes toward those things in our environment that bring satisfaction, and unfavorable attitudes toward dissatisfaction-producing aspects of our world. This satisfaction-seeking behavior has been referred to as the instrumental, adjustment, or utilitarian function of attitudes.

A second function of attitude introduced by Katz (1960) is ego-defense. We refuse to harbor attitudes that force us to admit to discrediting information about ourselves. Ego-defensive attitudes are defense mechanisms. Prejudiced attitudes are ego-defensive. They secure our superiority over others. For example, by refusing to admit to the equality of all people in business, some of us protect ourselves from the competition that such an admission might create. By suppressing minority groups, some individuals reinforce their own sense of superiority. While such attitudes are dysfunctional to cooperative social relations, they protect what such individuals value most: their own self-esteem.

The value-expressive function of attitude allows us to appear competent, sensitive, assertive, discriminating, and so on. These attitudes are developed to foster preferred impressions. For example, the father who exclaims, "We only watch one program in this house—*Masterpiece Theatre!*" is not merely reporting fact but is suggesting he and his family have higher standards for entertainment than most individuals. The boss who says to the new employee, "Don't say you hope you'll do well, son, just do well," is implying that he values competence and assertiveness.

The fourth attitude function is knowledge. Katz contends that we value consistency over inconsistency and certainty over uncertainty. We therefore need to establish certain frames of reference. The age-old metaphors "There are plenty of fish in the sea" and "Never wait for a lover or a train, there will always be another one along soon" are examples of attitudes that give meaning to uncertain situations.

Knowing why a person holds a particular attitude puts the persuader in a better position to encourage change. This can be accomplished by convincing the individual that (a) his or her present attitude no longer leads to the satisfaction sought, (b) another attitude will meet the individual's needs more effectively, or (c) the individual should reconsider the attitude's value in light of new information.

This perspective suggests that the ego-defensive attitude that seems to make women more defensive with each other than with males (see Frost & Wilmot, 1978) might be altered if women were made aware of this tendency and were encouraged to view each other as "in the same boat" rather than as competitors. Several women's networks have been established to encourage female camaraderie. If successful, these groups will redefine female collegial relationships as sources of support rather than challenges to self-esteem, thus removing the threat that makes ego-defensiveness necessary. Similarly, if the person who will not wait for a train or a lover is encouraged to consider that "all good things are worth waiting for," the proven functional worth of this attitude across situations may lead her to reconsider.

McGuire tells us that the functional approach offers insights ignored by other theories, but the theory has been generally neglected and therefore its success has been limited. Perhaps its simple logic does not sufficiently challenge us, although sometimes it is wise to see value in simplicity. Nevertheless, it is one theory that can be converted into action. Unlike several other theories that speculate about the nature of attitudes with little reference to techniques for changing them, Katz's approach provides both theory and technique. As such, it is worthy of more attention than it has received from those who wish to practice persuasion as well as study it.

COGNITIVE CONSISTENCY APPROACHES

Basic to cognitive consistency theories is the perspective that new information disrupts the cognitive organization developed by an individual. Such disruption is intolerable and therefore tension results. This tension drives the individual toward consistency. A way to assimilate or accommodate the new information into the existing cognitive structure must be located. McGuire (1973) refers to these approaches as representative of a conflict-resolving paradigm. The communication recipient is viewed as a

> harassed honest broker, trying to find resolution among many conflicting demands. He feels his attitude toward the object must take into account his own information, his self-interest, the demands of other people, and this new communication. In the end, he adjusts his attitude to keep from getting too far out of line with any one of these demands. (pp. 227-228)

The work of Fritz Heider (1946, 1958) on balanced configurations reflects the consistency principle. Heider was concerned with a person's perceptions of the relationships among him- or herself (p), another person (o), and an object or event (x). A balanced state is assumed to exist when the relationships among p, x, and o depicted in Figure 4.1 obtain. Imbalanced states exist when the relationships among p, x, and o depicted in Figure 4.2 obtain. Heider (1946) summarizes these relationships by stating, "In the case of two entities, a balanced state exists if the relation between them is positive (or negative) in all respects. . . . In the case of three entities, a balanced state exists if all three relations are positive in all respects or if two are negative and one positive" (pp. 110-111).

Balanced states are not conducive to change. That is to say, unless tension exists in a relationship, change is not considered necessary. Successful persuasion, from this perspective, requires as a prerequisite some degree of imbalance. One limitation of Heider's conceptualization, however, is that his relationships are more akin to preferences than to intense forces such as hatred and love (see Zajonc, 1968). Furthermore, balance theory is limited to the relationships among a maximum of three entities.

Although Heider mentions the possibility of multiple relations between two entities, he does not deal with the strength of bonds and degree of balance. Should the degree of balance be offset by some unexpected behavior on the part of person o, an alteration in the beliefs and/or attitude about o and x is conceivable. Person p, for example, may dislike person o's mother, x, and may therefore dislike person o also. Should person p find person o arguing with his mother x one day, person p may find himself appreciating person o much more. He may realize that person o is obligated to like his own mother and so an indication that given no obligation to mother x, o might then agree with p, may be sufficient reason for p to revaluate his feelings about o. Person p may

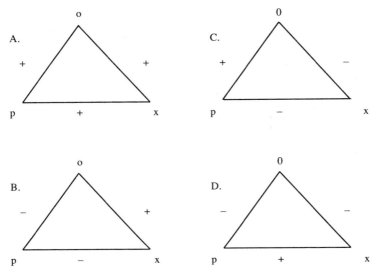

Figure 4.1. Balanced States

perceive o as trapped in an obligatory relationship. In other words, p is expected to like his mother x. The triangle in this case would have originally been as shown in Figure 4.1B, where p dislikes person o and mother x. After person p observes person o violating the obligatory rule, "Be nice to your mother," he may decide to like person o but still dislike his mother. The result is the triangle shown in Figure 4.2A, which, according to Heider, is an imbalanced configuration but one that is justified by reference to the rules impinging on o as x's son.

When this much qualification must accompany a theory, it should lead to some skepticism about the value of its usage. The above example indicates that rules may exist that relieve o from full responsibility for his behavior. Simple triangular configurations that do not specify degrees of balance are limiting. Subsequent theories of cognitive organization attempted to deal with the limitations of Heider's perspective (Abelsen & Rosenberg, 1958; Cartwright & Harary, 1956; T. M. Newcomb, 1953). In any case, Heider's interest in consistency did set persuasion research on a path that still exists today. That path places emphasis on what might be labeled harmony and disharmony in the human cognitive system.

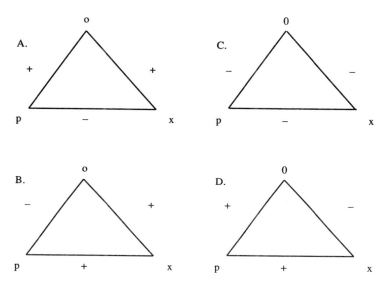

Figure 4.2. Imbalanced States

CONGRUITY PRINCIPLE

Osgood and Tannenbaum's (1955) congruity principle, like Heider's balance model, is based on the associative or disassociative nature of assertions. However, Osgood and Tannenbaum are also interested in the degree of polarization between concepts that are related through assertions. They consider extreme concept polarization as a manifestation of unsophisticated or emotional thinking: "The most simple-minded evaluative frame of reference is therefore one in which a tight cluster of highly polarized and undifferentiated good concepts is diametrically opposed in meaning to an equally tight and polarized cluster of undifferentiated bad concepts" (p. 43). General semanticists refer to this type of thinking as "two-valued." Osgood and Tannenbaum consider it characteristic of lay thinking in any period of conflict and emotional stress.

According to Osgood and Tannenbaum (1955), the principle of congruity can be stated succinctly: "Changes in evaluation are always in the direction of increased congruity with the existing frame of reference" (p. 43). It is only when two or more concepts are associated by an assertion that congruity becomes an issue. In other words, we may entertain two logically incompatible attitudes toward objects, persons, or events in our society (e.g., a person may be charitable but prejudiced) but experience little if any stress until they are brought into association (e.g., charitable people are not prejudiced).

For example, the statement "Mary is a Mormon" may result in negative feelings about Mormonism (neutral concept) if Mary is disliked (negative concept), but positive evaluations of Mormonism if Mary is well liked. The general principle is that when a state of incongruity exists, the evaluations of the two objects will tend to change in the direction of congruity. This is best viewed as a compromise response (see Fishbein & Ajzen, 1975). If an individual with whom you share a friendship (+2 on a scale of −3 to +3) is in favor of abortion, whereas you are opposed to it (−1), incongruity exists. According to the principle of congruity, both the friend and abortion will come to have congruent evaluations (both will be +1).

As the global economy takes hold and political barriers continue to break down around the world, the corporate world will experience more and more incongruity in negotiations. For example, an American company wishing to form a joint venture with a Japanese company might run into differences of opinion with regard to the role of women in business. If the most qualified person for a leadership position from the American side of a joint venture is a woman, the American and Japanese companies may experience discomfort. In Japan, women typically do not play significant leadership roles in business. Placing a woman in the leadership role on the American side of a joint venture could initially make some Japanese businesspeople uncomfortable. The real or potential discomfort of the Japanese on this issue might elicit incongruity for the American businesspeople. On the one hand, they wish to develop a strong relationship that will result in substantial profits to the company. On the other, the woman manager is the most qualified candidate and the company is ethically obliged to place her in the leadership role. According to the principle of congruity, these American businesspeople might begin to find fault with the female candidate and/or they might begin to find fault with the joint venture project. In this way, they allow themselves to establish congruity.

When American troops were sent to Saudi Arabia in 1990 to protect that country from invasion by Saddam Hussein, female soldiers were included. The American press devoted time to the story of how Saudi male soldiers were adjusting to female American soldiers. In Saudi Arabia, women do not serve in the military. They do not vote, and they cover their faces with veils when they appear in public. Having American female soldiers side by side with Saudi male soldiers was viewed by some as problematic. As one general explained, however, before the women arrived, Saudi military leaders were briefed on the need for American female soldiers and informed of the American perspective on this matter. All reports indicated that the women's presence, while a bit of an adjustment for the Saudi men, was accepted.

Congruity theory has been criticized for its simplicity. In the Japanese-American joint venture case, it is possible for the parties involved to find some mutually satisfactory solution. It might be quite comfortable for the Japanese to accept an American female in a leadership role in the joint venture, just as the Saudis accepted American female military personnel. The fact is that people are capable of reasoning through the incongruities in their lives. They do not always do so, of course. Often they allow themselves to be pushed and pulled by incongruity. The American businesspeople could attempt to negotiate the female executive's position. They could do some research to find out how likely it is that the Japanese will respond negatively to female leadership. They could also learn enough about the Japanese culture to facilitate the woman's transition into the job. They could consider involving the Japanese in her selection, so that they feel a part of the process. On the other hand, the Americans might become victims of perceived incongruity and allow themselves to be torn between what they believe the reactions of their Japanese counterparts will be to a female leader and their desires for an effective joint venture. As this example suggests, incongruity can be resolved in more than one way.

COGNITIVE DISSONANCE THEORY

The theory of cognitive dissonance, developed by Leon Festinger (1957), is another variation on the consistency perspective of attitude change. Like Rokeach and Rothman's (1965) belief congruence theory, Festinger's approach focuses on the relationships in "knowledge" about objects, persons, events, and so on. However, Festinger narrows his focus to include only two types of relevant relations, dissonant and consonant. According to Festinger (1957), "Two elements are in a dissonant relation if, considering these two alone, the obverse of one element would follow from the other" (p. 13). For example, if a person in debt bought a car, a dissonant relation between the two cognitive elements "buying a car" and "being in debt" would result (see Insko, 1967, p. 199). A consonant relation, on the other hand, implies an appropriate match of two cognitive elements, or that one "follows from" the other. For example, not buying a car follows from being in debt.

Obviously, not all dissonant cognitive relations elicit the same degree of felt dissonance. The importance of the cognitive elements is one factor influencing dissonance magnitude. The person who recognizes that he or she must save money to survive the winter should experience more dissonance upon the purchase of a new car than the individual who just likes to be thrifty. The magnitude of dissonance also increases with an increase in the proportion of dissonant to consonant cognitions. The more reasons one has for not spending money, the greater the dissonance created by behaving as a spendthrift. Finally, the "cognitive overlap" or similarity among the dissonant elements influences the magnitude of dissonance. Greater dissonance should result from the selection of a boat over a car (low similarity) than results from the selection of one type of car over another.

According to Festinger, people seek to reduce dissonance in one of four ways: revoking the decision, increasing the attractiveness of the chosen alternative, decreasing the attractiveness of the unchosen alternative, or creating cognitive overlap (finding similarities) between the items in question. The magnitude of that dissonance is a function of the extent of reward or punishment used to induce the behavior. The rule is that the greater the reward or punishment used to induce the behavior, the less the felt dissonance. If, for example, an individual is offered $25.00 to state that she likes vanilla ice cream when in actuality she abhors it, we can expect less dissonance than if she is offered 10¢ to induce the same behavior. Obviously, the importance of the issue must be considered as well. For example, a hostage being offered $25.00 to insult his country should experience more dissonance than the woman who for $25.00 claims to like vanilla ice cream.

According to Festinger, forced-compliance situations can be equally as dissonance producing as "free-choice" situations (see Brehm & Cohen, 1962). In forced-compliance situations, however, typical dissonance-reduction behaviors are reducing the importance of the induced behavior, changing one's private opinion to be consistent with the behavior (e.g., "I really do like vanilla ice cream"), and magnifying the reward or punishment used to induce the behavior (e.g., "How could I avoid doing it when I was offered so much?").

It is interesting to note that Festinger does not view intention as crucial to the production of dissonance. On the contrary, he posits that even involuntary exposure to information that is somehow inconsistent with established cognitions results in dissonance. Even the individual who overhears dissonant information must engage in dissonance-reducing activities. Festinger would add that should a large number of persons agree with the overheard information, dissonance will be exacerbated.

The effects of volition (Brehm & Cohen, 1962), self-involvement (Deutsch, Krauss, & Rosenau, 1962), cognitive overlap (Brock, 1963), regret (Festinger & Walster, 1964; Walster, 1964), the greater importance of postdecisional processes over predecisional processes in producing alternative revaluation (Davidson & Kiesler, 1964; Jecker, 1964), and several other variables are exhaustive and well documented in other texts (see Fishbein, 1963; Fishbein & Ajzen, 1975; Insko, 1967). The amount of literature on dissonance theory indicates that its effects have been far-reaching in the field of attitude change. Rather than balance theory and other consistency theories, Festinger focuses on choice from among alternatives. Instead of imprisoning the individual in a triangle of likes and dislikes or entrapping him or her with assertions linking otherwise unrelated cognitive elements, he presents the individual as a choice maker in the environment. However, once the individual has made a choice he or she is seen as obligated to defend it, a condition that may not obtain in the real world (see Aronson, 1968; Bem, 1965; Chapanis & Chapanis, 1964; Eagly & Himmelfarb, 1978; Elms, 1967; Fishbein & Ajzen, 1975).

COUNTERATTITUDINAL ADVOCACY

A derivation of dissonance theory is found in counterattitudinal behavior research. Miller and Burgoon (1973) define the counterattitudinal persuasion technique as the preparation and presentation by the persuadee of a belief-discrepant message for some real or ostensible audience. The example they give involves a father asking his son to prepare a message containing "all the arguments he can muster" against smoking marijuana. The father is hoping that the son will convince himself to stop smoking marijuana.

This same theory can be applied to persuading someone to look forward to a job transfer. An employer who thinks one of her employees might balk at being transferred to another state might ask that employee to visit the proposed transfer site. She might make sure that the employee gets to see the positive aspects of that site. When the employee returns to the original site, the boss might ask him to write a short report describing the positive aspects of his visit. Of course, doing this without telling the employee that he may be transferred could be considered manipulation. Telling the employee before the visit that there is a chance (or a good chance, depending on the likelihood) that he might one day be asked to transfer to the other site keeps things honest.

According to dissonance theory, if the reward for engaging in counterattitudinal advocacy is low, individuals are more likely to construe their behavior as indicative of their own attitudes than when they are paid handsomely to say things in contrast to their prior beliefs. In other words, if the father does not threaten the son with punishment or offer him excessive reward for preparing the belief-discrepant message, the likelihood of self-persuasion is enhanced. This perspective stands in direct contrast to incentive theory, which posits greater self-persuasion when rewards are offered (see Miller & Burgoon, 1973).

INOCULATION THEORY

Another cousin to the straight dissonance approach to persuasion is McGuire's inoculation theory. Relying on the metaphor of immunization against the possibility of future disease, McGuire posits that persuadees can be inoculated against the possibility of encountering counterarguments in the future. McGuire (1961) and Tannenbaum and Norris (1966) have demonstrated that the most effective form of inoculation is combining supportive and refutational messages rather than merely loading the persuadee with supportive arguments. It appears that it is better to arm the persuadee with arguments with which to fight counterpersuasion attempts. For example, if the father who sends his son off to college with much evidence against marijuana smoking also tells his son (a) to expect that others will disagree and (b) how to deal with such arguments, the likelihood of the son retaining his initial antimarijuana position is enhanced. Essentially, the young man has been armed to resist the dissonance-producing capacity of counterarguments.

Inoculation theory can apply to a variety of relationship types. Political candidates can effectively forewarn voters of tactics their opponents might employ to damage their credibility. Corporations planning huge layoffs, rate hikes, relocation, or other major changes can offset some of the shock and anger of employees and customers if the need for such changes is introduced prior to the action. For example, a major chemical company was planning extensive downsizing. Senior management decided to circumvent the possibility of losing valued employees who might move on if they were to learn of the planned downsizing by keeping the plans to themselves. They underestimated, however, the power of the rumor mill. Soon all employees suspected downsizing and none had been assured that their jobs would not be affected. A good many talented employees left before the downsizing was announced. Had this company engaged in effective inoculation, they might have prevented such losses. They could have let people know of the need to downsize, provided counseling and job referral services, and assured a good many employees that their jobs were not at risk. This would have allowed those at risk for termination adequate time to prepare and would have encouraged those not at risk to remain confident that the company would keep them.

The decline of cognitive dissonance theory was probably due to its simplicity. Each research study evolving from a cognitive dissonance perspective added new variables that qualified the claims of Festinger's work. Too many qualifications soon render a theory obsolete. Social situations involve numerous variables in consistent interaction. Any attempt to reduce such complexity to a simple, all-encompassing law of information processing is open to challenge.

Cognitive dissonance theory has resisted researchers' attacks for many years, and it is still alive today. The reason may lie in Kuhn's (1975) description of the resilience of paradigmatic scientific theory as likely to be declared invalid "only if an alternate candidate is available to take its place" (p. 77). Kuhn adds that even the obvious mismatch between theory and the real world is not sufficient reason to discard a theory: "The decision to reject one paradigm is always simultaneously the decision to accept another, and the judgment leading to that decision involves the comparison of both paradigms with nature and with each other." Rather than discard a theory, its scientist defenders will devise numerous ad hoc alterations and qualifications to reduce the conflict. Hence cognitive dissonance theory has not been rejected. Such rejection requires a new paradigm, not merely a new theory. To date no perspective has been offered that has generated the enthusiasm and intersubjective agreement among scientists necessary for a paradigm shift. It may be only a matter of time before one will meet the test. Perhaps then some of the theories described in this chapter will be relinquished to a revered position in history.

The next section looks at a theory that applies indirectly to the process of persuasion. More than any of the perspectives previously presented in this chapter, the next perspective focuses on the formation of cognitions about persons as well as their potential for change in terms of contextual contingencies. We will return finally to a focus on intention, which has generally been ignored by consistency theorists.

ATTRIBUTION THEORY

According to Heider (1946, 1958), the human mind seeks sufficient reasons or explanations for the behavior of others. These take the form of causal attributions. People do this to "make possible a more or less stable, predictable, and controllable world" (1958, p. 80).

The concept of *intention* becomes important to Heider's theory when he distinguishes between personal and impersonal causality. Personal attributions are formulated only when the individual observed appears to have performed a purposive action. Impersonal causality refers to forces outside the actor's control. Jones and Davis (1965) elaborate this perspective by suggesting that there are two prerequisites of intentionality: the knowledge that the effects of an action will result, and the ability to produce the effects. For example, a 3-year-old who announces that your favorite painting is ugly may elicit laughter rather than the assignment of negative attributions (e.g., "little brat"), since the child may not realize the importance of the painting to you and her age suggests that she may not know how hurt you may feel when someone insults your taste in paintings. The assumed absence of both malicious intent and an awareness that hurt feelings might result from her actions excuses the child from responsibility. In this case, then, the normal assignment of negative dispositions is curtailed. Should the child make a series of similar remarks at ages 10 and 16, negative attributions will probably be assigned (e.g., "thoughtless, insensitive twerp").

Jones and Davis (1965) take an interest in the degree of certainty associated with an assigned disposition. They propose that certainty depends upon the desirability of the effect resulting from an action and the extent to which these effects are common to other behavioral alternatives available to the actor. For example, if Mike decides to date

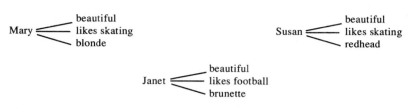

Figure 4.3.

a particular woman named Mary on Saturday rather than two others who are also available, it is likely that Mary has at least one unique characteristic. A closer look at Mary compared with the other two women appears in Figure 4.3.

All three women are beautiful. We can conclude that Mike's selection of Mary indicates that either he prefers blondes or he prefers skating over football. If Janet also liked skating instead of football, we could be more certain that Mike prefers blondes, since the only difference among the three women would then be their hair color. If Mary turns out to be a boring date but he asks her out again, we can then assume with greater certainty that blonde hair is really very important to him.

In each case what the observer is formulating is a correspondent inference (Jones & Davis, 1965). To the extent that several plausible explanations of the observed behavior exist, certainty of attributions decreases. This perspective is consistent with Kelly's (1955) discounting principle, whereby he describes the condition of multiple causality of messages. Kelly emphasizes the importance of behavioral consistency across situations to attribution. If an individual always insists upon having the last word in a discussion, observers might conclude that person is "into power." To the extent that others in the group do not behave in the same manner (distinctiveness), the likelihood of the attribution is increased. In other words, if everyone tries to have the last word, the individual in question will not stand out as being more "into power" than any other individual.

The work of Heider (1946, 1958), Jones and Davis (1965), Jones and Nisbett (1971), and others also points to the characteristics of the observer as influencing attributions. For example, some people are inclined to blame the environment for their own actions, whereas others always blame themselves. The rhyme "A woman thinks about her faults until they seem like double, a man he just forgives himself and saves the Lord the trouble" (Brooks, 1971, p. 214) points to this difference.

A bit sexist perhaps, but it does point out the difference between defining the world in terms of external events and defining it in terms of internal events.

Most theories of message acceptance focus on internal pressures in the form of beliefs and attitudes. Attribution theory is one of the few perspectives on persuasion that also focuses on the impact of contextual cues on message acceptance. Attribution theorists suggest that perceivers are concerned with establishing the validity of the information they receive (see Eagly & Himmelfarb, 1978). Often the accomplishment of this task requires a close look at contextual rather than personal source attributes.

SELF-ATTRIBUTION AND
COUNTERATTITUDINAL ADVOCACY

Attribution theory suggests that people seek reasons or justifications for the actions of others and their own actions in order to understand certain consequences. Berlyne (1960) suggests that this behavior is most pronounced under conditions of uncertainty. Furthermore, response selection appears to be dependent on inferential processes (assignment of attributes) when ambiguity is high (see Bem, 1972; Festinger, 1954; Schachter, 1959). It is through the analysis of causal relations, then, that the individual comes to know which behaviors are appropriate.

Bem (1965; Bem & McConnell, 1970) suggests an attribution explanation for dissonance. He explains that when internal cues are unclear, people infer their own attitudes and internal states from observing their own behavior. For example, a sense of irritability might be construed by the individual as his own jealousy over seeing a close female friend with another guy. Labeling the emotion explains it. To the extent that this man feels that jealousy is an appropriate response to the situation, dissonance will be minimal at best. To the extent that he perceives his jealous behavior as situationally inappropriate or in conflict with his self-image, dissonance is likely. In this way attribution, specifically self-attribution, operates as either a precursor of cognitive dissonance or a means of reducing it (e.g., the labeling of the situationally appropriate emotion may justify the irritable nature of an individual who perceives him- or herself as generally pleasant). It is the nonspecificity of arousal (see Schachter, 1959, 1967) that requires a search for causal attributes. People appear to react physiologically to events before they assign meaning to them.

Self-attribution theory has been used to explain counterattitudinal advocacy. If, as Bem (1965, 1968) contends, people often make inferences about their attitudes by observing their own behavior, advocating a position discrepant with one's initial position on an issue could conceivably lead one to qualify that initial stance. Bem and McConnell (1970) consider the condition of low compensation more conducive to attitude change than that of high compensation.

In the next section, dissonance, attribution, and teleological (choice) explanations of human behavior are integrated into what some may consider optimistic eclecticism. However, as Eagly and Himmelfarb (1978) suggest, "each of these theories embodies some aspect of the truth as we now know it to be, and fitting them together may prove to be as stimulating and insightful as having placed them in opposition in earlier times" (p. 544). This justification for a combined perspective must elicit "diffuse arousal" in the bodies of some social scientists who view eclecticism as a weakness characteristic of those who refuse to make commitments and enemies. Certainly we would get nowhere in social science if all people compromised their perspectives. Yet we need only remember the history of the motion picture camera or the light bulb to realize the value of theoretical integration.

CONSISTENCY:
A SECOND LOOK

The concepts of balance, congruity, and dissonance have in common "the notion that thoughts, beliefs, attitudes, and behavior tend to organize themselves in meaningful and sensible ways" (Zajonc, 1960, p. 280). This perspective presumes human rationality. Inconsistency is viewed as an uncomfortable state that imposes pressure on the individual to reduce it. While it may be true that humans prefer consistency over inconsistency, Zajonc (1960) tells us that the ways humans achieve the former manifest a striking lack of rationality. He points to Allport's (1954) example of human irrationality in inconsistency reduction:

Mr. X: The trouble with Jews is that they only take care of their own group.

Mr. Y: But the record of the community chest shows that they give more generously than non-Jews.

Mr. X: That shows that they are always trying to buy favor and intrude in Christian affairs. They think of nothing but money; that is why there are so many Jewish bankers.

Mr. Y: But a recent study shows that the percentage of Jews in banking is proportionately much smaller than the percentage of non-Jews.

Mr. X: That's just it. They don't go in for respectable business. They would rather run nightclubs.

Zajonc points out that while the concept of consistency may acknowledge human rationality, actual observations of behavior aimed at achieving it reveal irrationality. Zajonc's observation suggests the reason consistency, balance, and congruity theories have not proven useful in predicting behavior. While it may indeed be true that people seek to avoid inconsistency among beliefs, what they define as inconsistent and the means by which they reduce inconsistency are often influenced by idiosyncratic considerations. For example, according to balance theory, individuals do not want their good friends to be liked by their enemies. However, as Zajonc points out, an individual concerned for a friend's welfare may not want his or her enemies to dislike the friend. This concern for a friend creates a situation that is inconsistent with balance theory. The question is, Are these inconsistencies the exception or the rule? In other words, does the human need for consistency exist across situations while the means by which it is achieved are highly situation dependent? If so, it should come as no surprise to find that behavior is not always consistent with attitude.

While it is true that none of the theories discussed in this chapter is presumed to account for all human behavior, the theories do suggest that when other things are held constant, the principles of consistency should provide adequate explanations. As Zajonc suggests, the question to be raised here is, Just what factors operating in the context of human interaction must be held constant?

Let's look again at an individual who does not appear to mind having her friends liked by her enemies. We could conclude that this example merely represents a long line of consistency theory projection failures. After all, the behavior of accepting enemy and friend attraction does not correspond to the tenets of consistency theory. Instead, let's continue for a moment to accept the viability of consistency theory and focus on just what constitutes inconsistency for this individual. It is possible that individuals differ in their tolerance for inconsistency or in their definitions of what constitutes inconsistency. Perhaps the woman in our example did not perceive an inconsistency, or she may have seen a greater inconsistency problem existing in ignoring a friend's welfare by denying her the comfort of other friends (even though, to the woman in our example, these friends are enemies). The problem with inconsistency theory may not be faulty logic but the inappropriate designation of primary inconsistency. It has been demonstrated over and over that inconsistency is a troublesome condition for people, but inconsistency as defined by whom and compared to what other possibilities of inconsistency?

In our friend-enemy attraction situation, a higher-order inconsistency in the woman's rule system for behavior toward friends made it difficult for her to stand in the way of her friend's relationship with enemies. To be a "good friend" one must be generally concerned for the other's feelings and welfare. Requiring that a friend be disliked by an enemy when it may be to the friend's benefit to be liked by the enemy creates an uncomfortable sense of inconsistency. This is an example of the workings of what has been called "conscience" in the psychological literature. The threat of a higher-order inconsistency may require accepting a lower-order inconsistency.

WHO IS DECEIVING WHOM?

Let's return for a moment to the discussion of deception in Chapter 1. Certainly, lying is inconsistent with those societal and personal rules that encourage honesty. However, it appears that most of us accept certain amounts of deception because it is consistent with higher-order rules ensuring relational and even societal maintenance. We reason our perceived inconsistency away by suggesting that particular aspects of the context account for the deception. We deceive ourselves into seeing consistency where it does not exist or into excusing its absence.

In terms of the correspondence between actual conditions and behavior, inconsistency can also be only "in the eyes of the beholder." The person whose behavior appears inconsistent may actually be unaware of those aspects of a context that would render his or her behavior inappropriate. For example, if a man is intimate with a woman who perceives intimacy as an antecedent condition for applying a rule that precludes dating other persons, does his decision to be intimate with other women make him a deceitful character? What if he does not see intimacy as an antecedent condition for exclusivity in relationships? In

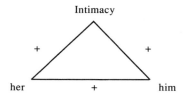

Figure 4.4.

this case the man is not likely to experience inconsistency unless the woman can convince him that his behavior is inconsistent with how he should view intimacy.

The important question here is, What is the superordinate attitude that renders the rule for exclusivity appropriate or inappropriate? For the woman, the relationship superordinate construct could be "lovers," whereas the man's superordinate construct might be "friends." Intimacy may not be an indication of love for him, whereas intimacy may imply more than friendship for her.

The question appears to be, What type of relationship does intimacy imply? Both persons recognize that they are intimate, but they interpret it differently in the designation of appropriate behavior. It is difficult at best to capture this conflict of logics by referring to traditional consistency theories. These two persons both have positive feelings toward each other and toward intimacy. The result is a balanced configuration on this issue alone (see Figure 4.4). But despite this balance, the relationship is in trouble. It is possible that she sees intimacy as a condition that renders exclusivity sensible (Figure 4.5). If he agrees that

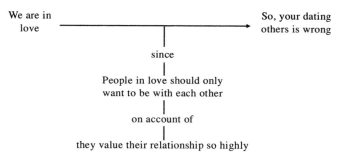

Figure 4.5.

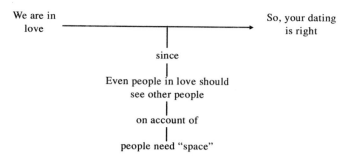

Figure 4.6.

they are in love, his logic might be that shown in Figure 4.6. Balance theory configurations would not provide this overall picture of logic supporting the claims. It would merely supply the configurations shown in Figure 4.7.

It is also possible that both individuals agree on the association of love and exclusivity but differ in their definition of the relationship. This condition is not easily explained by balance theory, because perceptions of each other and exclusivity under conditions of love and friendship are balanced (Figure 4.8).

Apparent balance, then, is not a sufficient basis on which to conclude that all is well. In this situation, the lovers agree on the rules for exclusivity under the conditions of love and friendship but do not agree that intimacy is a sufficient condition to label the relationship one of love rather than friendship. Essentially their rules differ for loving relationships. In the previous example, they were in agreement concern-

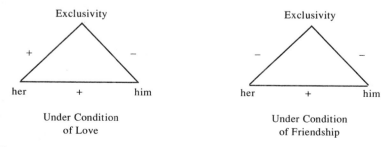

Figure 4.7.

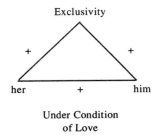

Figure 4.8.

ing what constitutes love, but they disagreed on what behavior love calls for.

The example suggests that while inconsistency is an uncomfortable state for most of us, we differ in our tolerance for it and also in our recognition of its existence. What appears to be inconsistent behavior to one individual might be very consistent to another. The persuader must uncover the underlying logics of the involved parties to determine the origin of the perceived inconsistency.

CONCLUSION

This chapter has described theories of persuasion that downplay the role of reasoning in human behavior. They might be described as push-and-pull theories, since so many of them describe people as torn between inconsistent cognitions, pushed by stimuli or pulled by rewards.

The next chapter will introduce theories of persuasion that do not ignore the potential for people to reason about their behaviors and the behaviors of others. As we all know, people do not always reason. They may not do so most of the time. It is important, however, for persuasion theories to take into account the ability of people to consider their actions and to reason through messages encouraging them to change. This is the case even if people are pushed and pulled through life more than they push and pull on their own. The next chapter reviews theories that describe what happens when people do reason about the persuasive messages they receive from others.

5 Contemporary Theories and Models of Persuasion

In recent years a number of perspectives on persuasion have emerged that focus on the reasoning ability of people during the course of persuasion. As described earlier in this text, persuasion is something people do *with* each other, not *to* each other. Moreover, persuasion involves a spiral of changing feelings and beliefs on the part of each participant (Smith, 1982). This view does not dispute the fact that there are benefits to be derived from learning theories that espouse an S-R (stimulus-response) view of persuasion. Certainly a good deal of what we learn to do and are persuaded to do is the result of associations between behaviors and subsequent rewards and punishments. However, decades of research have taught us that people often reason about their actions. We have learned that attitudes do not reliably predict behavior. There is simply no way to keep people from thinking. Models of persuasion that disregard the fact that people reason can describe only a subset of the activity. Therefore, a number of models and theories of persuasion giving people credit for their ability to reason have emerged. This chapter will review some of them.

SOCIAL LEARNING THEORY

Many theories of human behavior have proposed that motivational forces such as needs, drives, and impulses, frequently operating below the level of consciousness, are the major determinants of behavior. When such theories were brought into question because of the recognition that behavior can be influenced by environmental factors, many theories emerged that focused exclusively on the environmental "causes" of behavior. This perspective was referred to as *behaviorism*.

To make a very long story short, by the mid-1970s members of both sides of the controversy adopted the view that persons and situations influence behavior.

Despite the recognition that both inner thought and situational factors influence human behavior, the question remained as to how these two sources of influence interact. Albert Bandura (1977) proposed a "social learning view" of this interaction. According to this view, "people are neither driven by inner forces nor buffeted by environmental stimuli. Rather, psychological functioning is explained in terms of continuous reciprocal interaction of personal and environmental determinants" (pp. 11-12).

Central to Bandura's theory is learning via modeling. This involves learning by observing the behavior of others rather than through first-hand experience. By observing the behavior of others and associated consequences, people learn vicariously rather than by relying solely on tedious trial-and-error learning. Bandura points out that such observational learning facilitates development and survival. Without it, mistakes are quite costly. In fact, life would likely be quite short if all learning had to occur by trial and error—if we were constantly suffering the consequences of our own curiosity.

Since modeling often does not afford immediate opportunities for the observer to try the observed behavior, the role of reinforcement appears to be a small one in social learning theory. Bandura explains, however, that reinforcement does play a role in observational learning, but mainly as an antecedent rather than a consequent influence. Anticipation of reinforcement is one of several factors that influences what is attended to and retained and what passes unnoticed. If a model's behavior does lead to valued consequences, the observer can be persuaded to adopt the behavior if the persuader finds ways to increase the observer's attention to the model and motivates him or her to perform and rehearse the behavior.

Modeling has the potential of diffusing information to large numbers of people. Television, films, and other visual media play an important role in shaping behavior and attitudes. People also derive the benefits of abstract modeling. This occurs when observers apply the principles underlying specific performances to new or unfamiliar situations. For example, a child who observes Cookie Monster sharing his only cookie with Grover might later share her toy with another child. People learn, among other things, judgmental orientations, linguistic styles, conceptual schemata, information strategies, cognitive operations, and standards of conduct through modeling.

Modeling can also have a profound influence on the diffusion of innovation. It can instruct people in new styles of behavior by allowing them to see the consequences of adopting those styles. People do not, of course, adopt everything they see. They must be persuaded to adopt certain behaviors over others. Stimulus inducements serve as one set of activators. Advertising appeals, for example, are used to stimulate consumers to purchase new products. The more pervasive the stimulus inducements, the greater the likelihood that the new behavior will be adopted.

Of course, pervasiveness of inducements alone does not ensure adoption of a behavior. Innovations spread at different rates because they have different requirements for adoption. Moreover, observers must be encouraged by effective appeals to try the new behavior. Anticipation of reinforcement is one means of encouraging new behavior. Advertisers often display their products as bringing about a host of desired consequences. Negative appeals portray the adverse consequences of failure to purchase the product.

A second means of encouraging adoption of a new behavior involves demonstrating that the potential adoptee would gain attention or status by doing so. Fads are evidence of the power of anticipated social rewards. As the popularity of the new behavior grows, it loses this power and eventually becomes commonplace.

A third way of encouraging adoption of a behavior is by appealing to people's social or moral convictions. Marketers might present their products in ways compatible with prevailing values. Products may be portrayed, for example, as saving the environment (cloth diapers rather than nonbiodegradable disposable ones), supporting the country's economy (savings bonds), or protecting loved ones (security systems).

Other factors such as perceived risk of adoption, economic barriers, and social constraints also influence the likelihood that an innovation will be adopted. As Bandura (1977) notes, it is difficult to predict who will be most receptive to new behaviors. Social and economic factors "set limits on the power of persuasion" (p. 54). Despite these limits, marketers have been quite successful in persuading the public by working with those behavioral determinants over which they do have some control. So, while knowing how people learn and what factors influence their adoption of new ideas and behaviors does not afford perfect prediction, such knowledge does bring us closer to understanding how messages might be formulated to facilitate preferred outcomes.

THE ELABORATION LIKELIHOOD MODEL

The elaboration likelihood model (ELM) specifies a finite number of ways in which source, message, and other persuasion variables have an impact on attitude change (Petty & Cacioppo, 1981). This model is based on the notion that people want to form correct attitudes (i.e., ones that will prove useful in functioning in one's environment) as a result of exposure to persuasion. There are, however, a variety of ways in which a reasonable position may be adopted (Petty, Kasmer, Haugtvedt & Cacioppo, 1987).

Among the several ways of evaluating any persuasive communication is one that involves drawing upon prior experience and knowledge to scrutinize and elaborate the issue-relevant arguments contained in the message. For example, a young person encouraged by a fellow employee to lie to his boss might evaluate that option in light of prior experiences with lying and/or his own set of personal values. According to the ELM, this "central route" method to changing or forming attitudes results in attitudes that are relatively persistent, predictive of behavior, and resistant to change.

Another method for the formation or change of attitudes involves less cognitive effort than the "central route." Since people are often unwilling to exert extensive mental effort, they often act as "lazy organisms" (McGuire, 1969) or "cognitive misers" (Taylor, 1981). Under such conditions, formation of attitudes or changes in them are achieved by relatively simple association (as in classical conditioning), inferences or heuristics. An adolescent may accept a cigarette from a peer simply because she admires that person, not because she has thought through the pros and cons of smoking and decided that it is a safe thing to do. Attitudes formed or changed via this "peripheral route" are less persistent, predictive of behavior, and resistant to change than those formed via the central route.

The ELM predicts the likelihood that the persuadee will attend to the persuasive appeal, attempt to access relevant associations and experiences from memory, scrutinize and evaluate the information in light of the associations drawn from memory, draw inferences about the merit of the arguments, and derive an attitude toward the recommendation

(Petty, Cacioppo, Kasmer, & Haugtvedt, 1987). When elaboration is likely, the probability of a person using the central route to persuasion is increased. When elaboration likelihood is low, the peripheral route becomes more probable.

There are a number of variables that might affect the likelihood of elaboration. One such variable is the personal relevance of the issue-relevant arguments. When personal relevance is high, people are more motivated to scrutinize issue-relevant arguments, leaving attitude change dependent upon the quality of the arguments. In the case of the employee considering whether or not to lie to his boss, he is more likely to scrutinize the issue if he has attended recent lectures on ethics in business and considers ethical conduct important. Individual differences in people's motivation to think about persuasive messages also affect the likelihood of elaboration. If the employee does not typically scrutinize arguments, even recent ethics lectures may not encourage him to do so now. External variables such as distraction, number of argument repetitions, and number of different arguments can also influence the likelihood of elaboration.

It is important to point out that a variable can play different roles in different persuasion situations. The number of arguments contained in a persuasive message can lead to persuasion via the central route or can lead to simple inferences. For example, when the personal relevance of a message is low, increasing the number of messages can enhance persuasion, whether the arguments are strong or weak. This happens if persuadees judge more reasons as better than fewer reasons. When the personal relevance of a message is high, however, increasing the number of arguments is likely to enhance persuasion only when the arguments are strong (Petty & Cacioppo, 1984). For example, newspaper headlines can serve to draw the attention of readers. When a headline points out those aspects of a story that are of personal relevance to a reader, the reader is more likely to read it and more likely to process the information via a central route.

The ELM suggests that in some situations (e.g., low personal relevance) peripheral cues are the primary determinants of attitude change, whereas in other situations (e.g., high personal relevance) it is the processing of arguments that determines attitude change. On occasion, people are either unmotivated to evaluate or incapable of evaluating the true merits of the arguments presented and thus base their judgments on simple cues. In other situations, where motivation and ability are present, judgments are based on the quality of the arguments presented.

Critics of the ELM argue that the model does not adequately account for the effects of parallel processing of central and peripheral information on attitude change (Stiff, 1986; Stiff & Boster, 1987). They argue that if the ELM does depict human beings as parallel information processors, then conditions under which different types of information processing occur must be clearly specified. If these conditions are not specified and a particular piece of information may at any time be classified as either peripheral or central, then the model becomes impossible to falsify and is of little value in making a priori (before the fact) predictions of how information will be used. Stiff and Boster (1987) add:

Furthermore, within any persuasive situation (for example, a shampoo commercial), the same stimulus (a female model's hair) may provide a central cue for some people while providing a peripheral cue for others. This ambiguity allows the ELM to explain all possible outcomes of an experimental study. (p. 251)

These kinds of controversies over the value of theories and models are troublesome to most students of communication and persuasion. The fact is, however, that such controversies are usually healthy. There is nothing more likely to encourage a theorist to improve his or her theory than the presence of detractors. So as the battle over the utility of the ELM continues, it is important to bear in mind that the originators of this model have brought us closer to understanding the different routes persuasive messages may take in the minds of recipients.

THE ACE MODEL

While the ELM focuses on how persuasive messages are received, another model focuses on the types of messages likely to be persuasive. The ACE model (Reardon, 1981, 1987) proposes that when people are motivated to reason and are capable of doing so, they tend to use three criteria as the foundation of that reasoning. In other words, people do not always reason about the information they receive. When they do, they use three criteria to help them determine whether they should respond favorably to the persuader's arguments.

This requirement of motivation and ability to reason is also used by Petty, Kasmer, Haugtvedt, and Cacioppo (1987) as a major factor in the determination of how messages are received. They argue, "Importantly, it is neither adaptive nor possible for people to exert considerable mental effort in processing all of the persuasive communication to which they are exposed" (p. 234). When motivation and ability to scrutinize information are low, it is still possible for people to form a new attitude or change an old one, but they do so through simple associations, inferences, or heuristics rather than by exerting the mental effort involved in reasoning about alternatives.

The ACE model deals with those situations in which people are motivated to reason and capable of reasoning about the alternatives presented in a persuasive message. It proposes that people judge an idea or behavior on the basis of the following criteria: appropriateness, consistency, and/or effectiveness. *Appropriateness* refers to the extent to which the idea or action is approved of by important others or whether it is the right thing to think or do in the situation at hand (based on rules, laws, or the transference of such to a situation similar to the one in which the rules or laws normally apply). An appeal to appropriateness might be, "Everyone in the group is going tonight, so you should join us." *Consistency* refers to the extent to which the idea or proposed action is what the individual perceives to be something a person like him or her would think or do, or something similar to ways he or she has thought or behaved in the past. An appeal to consistency might be, "It isn't like you to miss a great theater performance, so let's go tonight." *Effectiveness* refers to the extent to which an idea or action leads to desired ends. An appeal to effectiveness might be, "If you take a break and go with us to the theater, you'll come back refreshed and ready to do some more writing."

The ACE model also specifies some conditions under which one or the other type of appeal is likely to be more successful. For example, when people are being observed by others important to them, they do not have the "self-autonomy" or freedom to do as they please. In such cases they are more likely to be persuaded by appeals to appropriateness or effectiveness for the group than by appeals to consistency or personal effectiveness. Moreover, there are individual differences that predispose people to be more or less concerned about the opinions of others. People who "follow their own lights" are not as easily swayed by the opinions of others as those whose greatest fear in life is social disapproval. Of course, even people who are prone to do as they see fit rather than as the crowd sees fit may give in to the crowd if the situation is sufficiently formal—if the lines of authority are clear and individualism is discouraged by the type of event or nature of the environment (e.g., in a highly formal organization where lines of authority are clearly demarcated).

The ACE model is derived from decades of persuasion research demonstrating that people are influenced by the opinions of others (appropriateness considerations), troubled by inconsistency between and among thoughts and behaviors (consistency considerations), and motivated to achieve short- and long-term goals (effectiveness considerations) (see Reardon, 1987, pp. 140-145). In fact, people are often torn among these three considerations when determining their positions on particular issues.

A recent dispute in a Los Angeles County city over whether to block certain roads to through traffic demonstrates how people can be torn among appropriateness, consistency, and effectiveness issues. A member of the community visited her neighbors to determine how they intended to vote. One neighbor, Elaine, who had recently moved to the area, had not yet decided how to vote on the issue of closing off streets. Her husband was convinced that doing so would cut down traffic and thereby make the neighborhood safer for children. He argued that the proposed street closings would cut down traffic and pollution and thus benefit the neighborhood as a whole. Elaine was inclined to agree with her husband until a neighbor arrived at her door. The neighbor complained that the closing off of streets was another attempt by a small group of vocal people to cut off the rest of society and create an elite neighborhood. She considered it against her liberal principles to keep people from driving down public streets and considered it a burden to have to weave one's way through one's own neighborhood. She pointed out that none of the people proposing the street modifications had clearly indicated the benefits to the neighborhood as a whole of closing off streets. Moreover, most of the neighbors on Elaine's street were opposed to the modifications. Elaine found herself torn among concerns for the safety of her children (appropriateness concerns for a mother and an effectiveness consideration as well), her own perception of herself as a liberal and a person who gets all the facts before committing to a position (consistency considerations), her desire to be a good neighbor (appropriateness concern) and a supportive wife (appropriateness consideration), and her desire to do what would be best for the neighborhood (effectiveness consideration) while still maintaining the sense that she is the type of person who makes up her own mind (consistency consideration).

Obviously, Elaine is not someone who leaps to decisions. As a person who considers alternatives, she found herself enmeshed in a conflict among appropriateness, consistency, and effectiveness considerations. Such dilemmas are not uncommon. When a boss reprimands an employee in front of others, the employee may find himself torn between two considerations. The formal rules of the office might encourage him to keep his complaints to himself (appropriateness consideration), whereas his own personal disdain for such treatment of employees might encourage him to complain (consistency consideration).

Since people do use the three criteria of appropriateness, consistency, and effectiveness in their decisions about issues and incidents, it is easy to see how these criteria can also be used by persuaders to encourage one form of behavior over another. Effective persuaders are detectives of sorts, trying to locate the criteria that carry the most weight with persuadees. They then formulate strategies to show how the persuader-recommended behavior favorably responds to those considerations. They might also locate the conflict among the three criteria and suggest how the persuader-recommended behavior actually satisfies two or all three criteria.

Now, if Stiff and Boster were here they might rightly ask, as they did of the ELM, Can the ACE model predict a priori whether a particular appeal is likely to be effective in a given situation with a given type of person? The answer would have to be that the jury is still out. Recent research with adolescents does, however, indicate that the ACE model proves useful in categorizing reasoned refusals of offers to smoke. Two studies indicate that reasoned noncompliance responses and attempts to gain compliance fall into categories similar to those proposed in the ACE model (social approval, personal rules, and goals) (Friedman, Lichtenstein, & Biglan, 1985; Newman, 1984). These studies provide some consensual validation for the findings of Reardon and her colleagues. Reardon, Sussman, and Flay (1989) asked junior high school students to respond to eight different scenarios in which the students were being invited to smoke. The scenarios differed in the number of people present (dyad or group), amount of pressure (first versus second offer), and nature of the relationship (friend versus acquaintance). The researchers were interested in how noncompliance responses might differ across these situations. In support of the ACE model, they found that the reasoned responses fell into the three categories of appropriateness, consistency, and effectiveness. They found that adolescents were more likely to provide reasoned compliance-resisting strategies in dyadic situations with a friend and when pressured once rather than two times. They also found that, across situations, the adolescents preferred to use reasoned appeals that focused on consistency (their own personal rules) rather than appropriateness (whether it is wrong to smoke or not something people should do) or effectiveness (the extent to which it might bring about undesirable ends such as death or cancer). Effectiveness strategies were their second choice. Reardon et al. propose that while this preference for consistency may appear counterintuitive, given that teenagers are supposedly concerned about what others think, teenagers may think it inappropriate to say that they are dependent on others for their own opinions. Saying "I don't smoke because it is wrong" or "I don't smoke because my friends don't smoke" may be uncomfortable for them, since it implies that they cannot make up their own minds.

Reardon, Sussman, and Flay (1989) did find a preference for statements of typical behavior and attitudinal statements in dyadic versus group situations and in first pressure versus second pressure situations. In other words, the adolescents preferred to say things like, "I never smoke" (typical behavior) or "Smoking is bad for your health" when they were talking to one other person and being pressured for only the first time. The adolescents in this study were not inclined to use statements about their personal views (consistency statements) when pressured a second time to accept a cigarette and when confronted by strangers. Statements of personal behavior may not seem persuasive to them when they hardly know someone and/or when they are faced with considerable pressure.

This research indicates that the ACE model can be used to categorize reasoned strategies and that preferences for appropriateness, consistency, and effectiveness strategies do differ with variations in situational factors such as relationship, number of people present, and amount of pressure.

The ELM and the ACE model are actually somewhat complementary perspectives on persuasion. The ELM focuses on the routes taken by various messages within the cognitive system of the recipient. The ACE model focuses on strategies likely to be effective with those people participating in persuasion when they *reason* about the messages being received. Since persuasion is done *with* others, not *to* others, each of the people involved in persuasion receives messages containing strategies and creates such messages in return. Each may use his or her knowledge of the situation to select appropriateness, consistency, or effectiveness appeals to elicit the desired response from the other(s). If the recipient of these appeals (the persuadee) is motivated and capable of reasoning rather than merely inclined to react without reason to the message, then these appeals to reason may prove influential. This type of reasoning is more likely to occur when the messages being received are processed via the central route described in the ELM.

COMMUNICATION/PERSUASION MODEL

Another model of persuasion describes the components out of which messages to change attitudes and actions may be drawn (columns in Figure 5.1) and the successive behavioral processing substeps (rows in Figure 5.1) that the messages must evoke in the persuadee if persuasive impact is to occur (McGuire, 1989). The input factors in Figure 5.1 are independent variables and persuasive message options that can be manipulated in the construction of a persuasive communication.

Source factors are characteristics of the persuader, such as age, socioeconomic status, gender, and ethnicity. In Chapter 6, the effects of these source factors on the persuader's impact will be discussed. There are times when being young is more persuasive than being old and when being female is more persuasive than being male. The recent increases in female car salespeople reported in the *Wall Street Journal* (September 21, 1989) are a case in point. The article states, "Car selling isn't the man's world it once was." The number of women enrolled in the National Automobile Dealers Association's ownership training school has more than doubled in the last few years. Frank McCarthy, the group's vice president, has been quoted as saying, "Car dealers are no longer the good ol' boys who sit around and drink coffee, read the paper, and smoke cigarettes." A few years back, women apparently began complaining about condescending salesmen who assumed that women cared only about a car's color. Since approximately 45% of new car purchases are made directly by women and another 30% are influenced by them, car dealers have begun to realize that the credible salesperson for the female buyer might well be a female.

Message factors include such things as organization of the materials presented, types of appeals, delivery style, and length and relevance of message. As will be discussed in Chapter 6, there is much to be considered in the construction of a persuasive message. How much to say about the topic and at which point in the conversation or presentation

OUTPUT: Dependent Variables (Response Steps Mediating Persuasion) / INPUT: Independent (Communication) Variables	SOURCE	MESSAGE	CHANNEL	RECEIVER	DESTI-NATION
	number unanimity demographics attractiveness credibility · ·	type appeal type information inclusion/omission organization repetitiveness · ·	modality directness context · ·	demographics ability personality life style · ·	immediacy/delay prevention/cessation direct/immunization · ·
1. Exposure to the communication					
2. Attending to it					
3. Liking, becoming interested in it					
4. Comprehending it (learning what)					
5. Skill acquisition (learning how)					
6. Yielding to it (attitude change)					
7. Memory storage of content and/or agreement					
8. Information search and retrieval					
9. Decoding on basis of decision					
10. Behaving in accord with decision					
11. Reinforcement of desired acts					
12. Post-behavioral consolidating					

Figure 5.1. The Communication/Persuasion Model as an Input/Output Matrix
SOURCE: McGuire (1989, p. 45).

to say that amount is only a small part of the many issues to be considered when formulating a persuasive message. As Figure 5.1 indicates, message formulation is a major component in evoking in the persuadee those information-processing behaviors that lead to effective persuasive outcomes.

Channel refers to the modalities through which the persuasive message is conveyed to the target (persuadee). Written, audio, visual, nonverbal, and verbal are only a few of the possibilities. There are those who cogently argue that the growing dependence on FAX machines and other less personal means of communicating can lead to breakdowns in trust between, for example, customers and suppliers. How much dependence on technology is too much? These and other questions regarding the benefits of face-to-face persuasion versus telephone or other machine-mediated types of persuasion remain unanswered at this time. McGuire's model reminds us that they are important considerations in the formulation of persuasion strategies. McGuire (1989) argues, "Too often public persuaders choose the channel solely on the basis of the number of people it reaches, as when television ads are placed according to Nielsen ratings without consideration of differences in perceived credibility, likability, and comprehensibility" (p. 47). Channels are also chosen solely on the basis of how quickly they convey a message. Speed, however, is only one criterion to consider when attempting to communicate effectively. The company that becomes overly dependent on quick but nonpersonal forms of communication with customers is likely to lose those customers to companies willing to provide personal attention.

A recent airline television ad shows how choosing the wrong channel can lead to negative outcomes. The ad shows a boss sadly telling his employees about the loss of a customer who has done business with them for years. The boss explains that new technology has allowed them to lose that personal touch with customers. He hands all the employees airline tickets, so they can visit important customers in person. When one employee asks where the boss will be going, the boss replies that he will be visiting the long-time customer they've just lost. The message implicit in this ad is that new technology may be fast and convenient, but there is nothing like face-to-face interaction when you are attempting to make a customer feel that you care.

Receiver factors refer to such persuadee characteristics as age, intelligence, education, interest in the topic, gender, ethnicity, personality, and life-style. The more one knows about the person to be persuaded, the better prepared one is to construct an effective message. Talking above people's heads, in a condescending manner, or in some other manner not acceptable to them is a surefire way to undermine the persuasive impact of a message. Remember, it was those irate female customers who were tired of being treated like ignoramuses who brought about the recent increase in female car salespeople. Sometimes tone alone can alienate. The more willing a persuader is to go beyond obvious characteristics such as gender to discover how intelligent, informed, and interested a persuadee is, the better his or her chances of constructing and delivering a persuasive message.

Destination factors include the types of persuadee behaviors at which the message is aimed, such as short- or long-term change, change on a specific issue or across a whole ideological system, and change in existing belief versus change plus preparation for future attempts by others to change that belief back to the way it was. It is important for persuaders to consider how much to ask for at each juncture. Persuasion is often incremental. There is a tendency to want the whole pie in the first bite, so to speak, when one is attempting to persuade. Clever persuaders have a good idea of what they can expect each time they approach a persuadee. This is one reason it is often useful in off-site business negotiations for a persuader not to buy a round-trip airline ticket. Knowing that one must leave by a certain time or date forces one to rush the persuasion process. In such cases, especially in cross-cultural negotiations, where the concept of time used by one's counterpart may be different from one's own, the savings in airline fare may impose far greater costs on the effectiveness of negotiation.

The *output factors* in Figure 5.1 provide a useful checklist for constructing and evaluating a communication campaign or even dyadic communication. Of course, it is rare for any of us to sit down with such a checklist before attempting to persuade someone. Yet the output factors in Figure 5.1 are important whether the goal is to persuade 500,000 people or one person. To use the model effectively, it is important to consider at each of the 12 substeps how each input factor can be constructed or modified to increase the likelihood of that substep's being evoked. For substep 1, exposure to the communication, this means determining the best way to get your audience to notice the new idea or product you are advocating. Specifically, you must determine how to handle source, message, channel, receiver, and destination factors in a manner conducive to eliciting persuadee notice of your idea or product.

While the 12 steps may seem demanding, they are also important to successful persuasion. Too often, advertisers spend billions of dollars on exposure, as if getting people to notice their products were tantamount to getting them to buy those products. McGuire (1969, 1985) has found that audiences often take shortcuts that shorten or even reverse the 12 steps. Petty and Cacioppo's elaboration likelihood model may be used to determine the relative importance of each step. For example, if it is clear that the persuadee is attending more to what Petty and Cacioppo describe as the central route of persuasion, the persuader may decide to give less attention to peripheral considerations such as source credibility and more attention to message factors such as evidence and argument.

There are perspectives on persuasion that contradict McGuire's 12-step approach. A number of researchers advocate that attitude change follows behavior change. If you can get a man to engage in a kind act toward someone he dislikes, for example, he may come to like that person more. This view is totally contradictory to the view espoused by McGuire. In McGuire's model, behavioral change is step 10 in the 12-step process involved in persuasion. McGuire (1989) argues that attitude change does follow behavior change more often in the laboratory setting than in naturalistic settings. He argues, however, that the two views are not mutually exclusive, but complementary. There may be times when behavior change does precede attitude change. There is no reason to discount that possibility, especially since much basic research stemming from dissonance theory supports the view that behavior change can precede attitude change.

CONCLUSION

The theories and models described in this chapter tend to give human beings more credit for their reasoning abilities than did earlier theories of persuasion. Each focuses on a slightly different aspect of persuasion. Bandura's social learning theory explains how patterns of behavior are acquired and how these patterns are influenced by both the self and external sources of influence. It demonstrates how people learn from direct and vicarious experience. Petty and Cacioppo's elaboration likelihood model explains why certain aspects of a persuasive message are sometimes more powerful than others in bringing about behavioral change. The impact of persuasive elements depends on the information-processing route used by the persuadee. McGuire's communication/persuasion matrix model demonstrates how factors such as source, message, receiver, channel, and destination variables can be manipulated to evoke the 12 steps needed to bring about persuasion. The ELM can be seen as a complement to McGuire's model, because it informs the persuader as to the priority he or she might want to attribute to factors affecting the central route versus the peripheral route. The ACE model applies when the persuader is hoping to encourage the persuadee to reason about his or her behavior. It is consistent with Bandura's view that certain stimulus inducements can operate to encourage the adoption of a new behavior (e.g., fads, concerns about status, personal convictions) and suggests three categories of inducements. The ACE model can provide insight into how messages might be developed that encourage central route processing of information described in the ELM. For example, if a person is provoked by consistency appeals to reason about how her weight threatens her health (e.g., "It's hard to believe that someone as health conscious as yourself would continue to overeat"), she might begin to attend to media messages about weight loss. The ACE model can also provide some assistance in message formulation directed at evoking liking or interest, comprehension, skill acquisition, and yielding (steps 3 through 6 in McGuire's model).

Each of the contemporary theories and models introduced in this chapter can be seen as a complement to the others. None describes all of the ways that persuasion occurs, and much research remains to be done in support of each. However, these models do provide us with sturdy alternatives to earlier views of human beings as nonreasoning organisms pushed and pulled by stimuli in their environments.

6 Persuasion Variables

This chapter reviews research regarding those variables that influence persuasion outcomes. If you are not a researcher by trade, you may find that this chapter provides far more than you ever wanted to know about any persuasion variable. Let me suggest, however, that you at least skim the material. You may be surprised to find hidden in historical accounts of persuasion variable research some relevance to your own life. The discussion starts with a variable that has received considerable attention from persuasion researchers: source credibility.

SOURCE CREDIBILITY

Studies of source credibility by communication researchers have clearly demonstrated that this construct is multidimensional. Recent work also suggests that the components of credibility may not be the same across situations but instead depend on the role a communicator is expected to perform in a given context. For example, at very formal schools and colleges professors are expected to convey knowledge to students but may not be expected also to provide entertaining examples.

Anderson and Clevenger's (1972) summary of experimental research on source credibility (or ethos) indicates that studies of source characteristics differ widely in theoretical and methodological features. Most studies prior to the mid-1960s treated source credibility as a fixed characteristic. It was assumed that sources possessed characteristics that made them credible. However, later studies recognized the influence of situational factors as well as the possibility of changes occurring in the receiver's impressions during the communication act.

Credibility studies also differ in the extent of attention paid to source and audience characteristics. However, even today, credibility research reflects a tendency to ignore the interaction of source and subject

characteristics. The few studies that have focused on audience characteristics have clearly demonstrated that communicator-audience reciprocal influence is not something researchers can afford to ignore.

More flexible perspectives on credibility than those afforded by a
"fixed-ethos model" led to temporal considerations. Put succinctly, the
question of credibility effects over time became an area of research
focus in the 1950s. These studies introduced the sleeper-effect phenomenon. Hovland and Weiss (1951) found that, over a period of one month,
the favorable effect of high-source-credibility attitude change diminished, and low-source-credibility negative attitude reactions became
more positive. They postulated that, in the absence of further stimuli,
agreement with high-credibility sources decays while agreement with
low-credibility sources grows. It is good to know that while you may
not leave your audience in awe, a few weeks or months later they may
begin to see you in a more favorable light.

It was Hovland's belief that the source is forgotten over time. However, in a later study Kelman and Hovland (1953) provided support for
a disassociation of message and source explanation. They found that
reintroduction of the speaker three weeks subsequent to the initial
meeting removed the sleeper effect. Also, they found that in the absence
of reintroduction, those persons who best remembered the source
showed the greatest sleeper effect. They assumed, therefore, that the
logical explanation of sleeper effects is disassociation of message and
source rather than mere forgetting of the source.

Gillig and Greenwald (1974) and Cook and Flay (1978) have questioned the existence of sleeper effects. They point out that limited
empirical support exists. As early as 1955, researchers questioned
Hovland's experimental procedures, which failed to control for the
possible experiment-related discussions of subjects during the time lag
between experiments. Nevertheless, the sleeper effect has not been laid
to rest; it lives on in most persuasion texts, if not in reality.

Greenberg and Miller (1966) sought to determine whether a negative
image of a source adversely affects receiver attitudes toward a persuasive message. Their results did indicate that the positive appeal of
the message was vitiated by the negative image of the source. However, Greenberg and Miller discovered that, on 7-point scales, their
experimental group subjects had actually found the source generally
trustworthy (4.4) and competent (4.7), despite exposure to a seemingly
negative introduction message. The introduction read as follows:

> For your information: The piece you are about to read was included in a sales brochure written and distributed in several American communities by a small group of men recently indicted for unethical business practices. The men traveled across the country trying to persuade school systems to build schools which could be used as fallout shelters. The salesmen would then offer to be "advisers" to the school board about this possibility. They charged a sizable fee for their services, and made up some kind of report without doing any work. (Greenberg & Miller, 1966, p. 129)

Greenberg and Miller explained the unexpected, rather positive source impressions as resulting from a normative standard that predisposes audience members to respond somewhat positively in the absence of personal experience with the source. They added that audiences may give unfamiliar sources the "benefit of a doubt." Perhaps these authors had not taught an MBA class or were not thinking of business groups who want to be sure the speaker lives up to his or her honorarium.

Rosenthal (1972) developed an alternative explanation. He held that the high source ratings given by the control group (5.1 on trustworthiness and 5.4 on competence) indicated that the content and style of the message provided sufficient information for the control subjects to glean a positive impression of the source. The experimental group received the same high-quality message and, according to Rosenthal, probably experienced some dissonance over experiencing a positive message response to a criminal source. He explained that this dissonance could account for the lower source ratings by experimental group subjects. However, the quality of the message appeared to have offset any negative feelings toward the source, since the ratings on both trustworthiness and competence on a 7-point scale were still above 4 points.

Rosenthal criticized Greenberg and Miller for their attempt to explain the absence of low source ratings by referring to the existence of a "benefit of the doubt" normative standard. Such a claim was unwarranted in Rosenthal's view, since Greenberg and Miller (1966) themselves concluded, on the basis of control subject ratings, that "the quality of the message was apparently sufficient to induce subjects to create a somewhat favorable perception of the source. It would appear that these subjects reasoned that such a good message could only have come from a good source" (p. 130). Since this same high-quality message was administered to the experimental group, Rosenthal reasoned that they too experienced the favorable perceptions of the source.

Furthermore, Rosenthal disagreed with Greenberg and Miller's contention that the subjects' lack of personal experience with the source could account for their willingness to give him the benefit of a doubt. Rosenthal suggested that in the "cogitation of a persuasive message," the subjects received a direct message about facets of the source's personality. While Rosenthal acknowledged that a persuasive message cannot provide an abundance of information, it does supply some information, and subjects will use this to form impressions.

On the basis of his rejection of the Greenberg and Miller "normative standard" and "absence of personal experience with the source" explanations, Rosenthal (1972) concluded that "the failure to induce a negative image of the source was the result of internal paramessage dissonance. Put succinctly, there were more source data operant in this communication than the experimenters apparently were aware of" (p. 24). Rosenthal's perspective emanates from his belief that people recognize some information as firsthand and therefore of a higher "evidentiary order" than "hearsay evidence," such as that provided by the Greenberg and Miller source introduction. Being confronted with information of different evidentiary orders created dissonance for the experimental group subjects, but they opted to give greater credence to their own sense experiences of the source. In terms of the elaboration likelihood model, discussed in Chapter 5, the subjects attended to peripheral and central route information about the source but derived conclusions by giving greater weight to the latter.

If we assume, as Thibaut and Kelly (1978) contend, that people use what information they can to reduce the uncertainty in their environment by forming impressions of others, Rosenthal's explanation has a certain appeal. Yet it is not totally inconceivable that there exists a normative standard that leads subjects to give credit to individuals they do not know personally. In any case, both the Greenberg and Miller and the Rosenthal perspectives point to one very important source of error in our research practices: We would prefer to rely on our own justifications for subject behavior rather than to ask subjects for theirs. Whether Greenberg and Miller's explanation is inaccurate or accurate, their recognition of subject input gave Rosenthal (and me) support for the realization that "because a factual assertion is true or untrue does not mean it will be perceived as such by the receiver" (Rosenthal, 1972, p. 30). It questions the faith we have placed in experimenter interpretations of subject responses and, I hope, sets us on a new track of self-skepticism when determining how much we can assume to be true about audiences and subjects.

Besides encouraging some healthy skepticism about experimenter judgments of receiver reactions to source information, the Greenberg and Miller study indicates that subjects' message-based interpretations of source characteristics cannot be made with absolute confidence. Bowers and Osborn (1966) found that different types of metaphors resulted in differences in the ratings of the message source. Wheeless (1974), using scales developed by McCraken et al. (1972), found that receivers selectively expose themselves to messages based on their attitudes toward the sources and message concepts. These researchers' results indicate that source competence is the best predictor of selective exposure, with homophily and attitude involvement "meaningfully" improving the predictive model. Even such often overlooked message aspects as speed of speaking (Miller, Maruyama, Beaber, & Valone, 1976), vocabulary and style (Carbone, 1975), and nonverbal expression (London, 1973) have been found to influence credibility and persuasion effects.

It is obvious, then, that the study of source credibility is not without its complications. Research indicates that numerous factors (including ones not anticipated by researchers) influence credibility. McGarry and Hendrick (1974) have shown that the assumed direct linkage between credibility ratings and message influence is mitigated by the subject's perception of message importance and direction. What is needed is a theory of persuasion that integrates the findings on source, message, and receiver influences.

Norman Anderson (1971) proposes a model of persuasive impact that treats source impressions as a weighting factor for the persuasive impact of a message. His model represents a general theory of information integration that credits the message recipient with a history impinging on his or her present judgments:

> In even the simplest investigations of attitudes and opinions, the stimuli typically carry information at a cognitive level not often reached in other areas of research. Information stimuli . . . impinge on the person, in life or in the laboratory, and he must integrate them with one another as well as with his prior opinions and attitudes. (p. 171)

Anderson's formula for information integration is as follows:

$$R = \frac{ws + (l - 2)I}{s + (I - w)}$$

where R is the response, s is the scale value for an item of information, I is the initial impression, w is the weight associated with the item of information, and $(l - w)$ is the normalized weight associated with the initial impression. In attitude change research, Anderson suggests, the weight (w) and information (s) concepts should be considered analogous to the source and message. Thus, while including separate values for both the source and the message, Anderson also hypothesizes a relationship between them. Eagly and Himmelfarb (1978), in their review of mathematical models of credibility effects on message acceptance, state that, in general, research supports Anderson's assumption that source credibility can be considered a weight that amplifies or multiplies the value of message information.

Donald Lumsden (1977) applied the Anderson model in a personality impression task. While his research supports the linearity of the source-message relationship (the impact of a message is a function of the strength of the message multiplied by the strength of the source), he notes three limitations of the applicability of his results. First, his study structured all the variables (source, message, and target ratings) along a likability dimension. This provided a high degree of control for the variables, but it is unreasonable to assume that likability is the only important dimension in attitude formation. Second, the context of the design—rating targets to select a method of selecting college room-mates—implies some question concerning "unsuspected limitations" of likability as a criterion in this situation. Finally, a number of important variables, of which source and message are only two, were not included in the study.

Hence, while Anderson appears to have been on the right track, the application of his model to attitude change is limited to source and message characteristics. Furthermore, how applicable would his model be to situations in which the source impression is more important than the message effects? For example, political campaign messages are developed with the source impressions as the central variable and message as the weight. Whether or not Anderson's model is useful in such situations is open to question.

One reason that even integration approaches like the Anderson model fall short is the absence of a theoretical base explaining the functional relationships among persuasion variables. Perhaps it was necessary to generate enough conflicting evidence to call for a comprehensive theory. Whether variable testing should precede theory or vice versa is not the question to be addressed any longer. We have at our disposal research that at least indicates which variables appear to play major roles in the persuasive process. The quest now should be to determine the functional relationships among them and how they are used to create conditions conducive to persuasion.

The elaboration likelihood model, described in Chapter 5, suggests that the importance of source credibility and how it interacts with other aspects of persuasive events depends on the extent to which persuadees process persuasive messages via central or peripheral information-processing routes. When persuadees are involved in the topic being discussed, they are more likely to attend the arguments presented and to evaluate the merits of those arguments. Under such conditions, the role of source credibility may be less important than in situations where the persuadees are not motivated to evaluate arguments and are influenced by simple cues such as their impression of the persuader.

Of course, there may be times when source credibility is a central cue. For a young person enamored of a movie star, anything the star says may seem accurate merely because the youngster is so impressed with the star that he is not inclined to evaluate the merits of her arguments. This effect has not escaped the notice of advertisers, who often employ highly regarded actors to persuade audience members to buy products.

Obviously, we still have much to learn about source credibility. Perhaps the safest route for the communicator to take is to assure that persuadees are aware of his or her expertise and as impressed as possible with his or her dynamism, attractiveness, and trustworthiness. The communicator may achieve the former by making sure to be introduced by someone who is not reluctant to describe the communicator's better traits. The latter is in the hands of the communicator him- or herself.

PERSUASIBILITY AND SEX

Rokeach's (1960) theoretical propositions about dogmatic personalities imply that people are predisposed to openness or closed-mindedness as a function of enduring personality characteristics. McCroskey and Burgoon (1974) found support for Rokeach's perspective. Their research indicates that "people have relatively invariant widths or latitudes of acceptance and rejection across topics and sources" (p. 425). They did, however, find reason to question Rokeach's emphasis on dogmatism. They could find no evidence demonstrating that it affects latitudes of acceptance or rejection. McCroskey and Burgoon suggested that his finding may reflect a construct validity weakness in the dogmatism scale.

Research such as that discussed above has given credence to the study of personality traits as predictors of attitude change. Janis and Field (1956) set a strong precedent for looking at personality as the characteristic of being susceptible to persuasion regardless of the source or message topic. Much research in this vein attests to higher persuasibility among women than among men. Some researchers, however, have found that women do not seem more persuasible when the speaker is a woman. Also, researchers have suggested that differences in persuasibility between the sexes may be more culturally than biologically determined. However, Cronkhite (1976) claims that the more dominant tendencies of males, which are culturally and perhaps hormonally induced, make men less persuasible.

The controversy over who is more persuasible continues today. In the meantime, another controversy over whom people choose for opinion leaders, males or females, has drawn attention. Research has generally suggested a male bias in our society. Richmond and McCroskey (1975), however, shed some new light on this subject. In contrast to Goldberg's (1968) finding that women are prejudiced against women, they found that, while the generalization holds true for politics, other topics, such as fashion, show a definite female preference for female opinion leaders. Richmond and McCroskey qualify their results by suggesting that their subjects were better educated than the general adult population in our society, but at least a trend toward more faith in women as opinion leaders seems evident.

Recent research on language use differences between males and females offers some insights into why women continue to be perceived as more persuasible and often less credible than their male counterparts. A number of social scientists have argued that women tend to use verbal behavior that is perceived as weak or powerless when compared to the linguistic behavior of men. Lakoff (1975) argues that women are more likely than men to use language forms suggesting uncertainty and emotionality. Moreover, women are more likely than men to use formal, grammatically correct language and to add qualifiers to their assertions (see Zahn, 1989, for an overview of this research). These and other sex-linked forms of expression are yet another reason women are perceived as more persuasible than men.

Mulac and his colleagues have provided evidence that people do respond differently to the speech of men and women (see, e.g., Mulac, Incontro, & James, 1985; Mulac & Lundell, 1980, 1982, 1986). Male speakers are typically rated as more dynamic, whereas female speakers are given higher ratings for aesthetic quality. Mulac and his colleagues argue that speech differences between men and women may be the reason women are treated as outsiders or perceived as less powerful than their male counterparts. Males and females can be seen as constituting two different sociolinguistic communities. For example, men use more interruptions ("Let's go on to the next topic . . . ") and more directives ("Why don't you write down your answers?") and maintain the floor by using more conjuctions/fillers at the beginnings of sentences ("And another thing . . . "). Women make greater use of questions ("What's next?") and justifiers ("The reason I say that is . . . "). They use more intensive adverbs ("I really like her") and show an interest in people as opposed to objects through the use of personal pronouns. They also use a more indirect, qualified style than men ("Surprisingly, it was an easy assignment" rather than "It was an easy assignment") (Mulac, Wiemann, Widenmann, & Gibson, 1988).

There is a body of research attesting to the existence of convergence effects between interactants. This means that as people communicate they tend to speak in ways typical of the recipients of their communication. According to Street and Giles (1982), this occurs (a) when the communicator desires the recipient's social approval and the perceived costs of converging his or her speech do not outweigh the rewards, (b) when the communicator desires a high level of communication efficiency, and (c) when social norms are not seen as dictating alternative speech patterns. When these conditions do not exist, convergence of speech patterns does not occur and divergence may even obtain. In other words, people tend to talk like their recipients when they have the desires outlined above; otherwise they stick to their own patterns of speech or even exaggerate or intensify those patterns.

Whether women tend to speak more like their male counterparts during interaction is not clear. Some researchers argue that mixed-sex dyads encourage divergence rather than convergence of styles. For example, Golub and Canty (1982) found that women were less likely to assume leadership roles when paired with men than when paired with women. Men, on the other hand, were as likely to assume leadership roles with women as they were with men. However, Mulac et al. (1988) found that the language of male and female interactants is more clearly differentiated when the interactants are in same-sex rather than mixed-sex dyads. When women are speaking with women they use more gender-discriminating forms of speech than when they are speaking with men. This may be the case in business situations, where women do not want their gender to get in the way of conducting business successfully. They may consciously or unconsciously talk and act in ways commonly associated with males.

This reminds me of a situation I experienced recently. A male colleague told me that he wanted me to meet a woman who had recently taken a job at our university. He explained, "You'll really like her because she doesn't take any crap from anyone." I was left wondering why I would like someone who "doesn't take any crap from anyone." Perhaps that meant that I am like that too, and that she and I would be kindred spirits, tearing about the business school not taking any crap from anyone. Part of me liked the idea and found it more than a little amusing. Another other part of me thought I must surely be mistaken. On the other hand, it could mean that everyone likes a woman who doesn't take any crap, but research and personal experience don't support that conclusion. I finally decided that my male colleague admired women like that and since he also thought well of me, he thought I'd like her too. I did eventually meet her, and she does have a direct style. She is the kind of person you'd like to have on your side. She had learned over the years that always being sweet to everyone, including people who don't deserve it, is no way to conduct business. She stands out because most women do not have a direct style and many who do are not appreciated for it. She, however, appears to have found a balance of communication styles that suits her and is appreciated by most of her colleagues as well.

It may be that women must stand out in some way in order to be valued. Research indicates that while evaluations of men and women who have excelled in a task are very similar, male performance at a fair or poor level is often evaluated more favorably than female performance at the same level. Research indicates that stereotypes can carry over into task evaluations. On masculine tasks, ability is regarded as a more important determinant of success for men than it is for women. On feminine tasks, men and women are rated about the same (see Deaux & Emswiller, 1974; Deaux & Farris, 1977; Etaugh & Brown, 1975).

Recent research by Zahn (1989) offers some hope for women who wish to overcome the obstacles presented by their gender and gender-linked language. With undergraduate students as his subjects, Zahn found no effects for gender stereotyping on ratings of speaker dynamism and attractiveness and partial effects for gender-linked language. The stronger effects for gender-linked language occurred with dynamism. Encouraging is the finding that the effects of sex of speaker and gender-linked language were not as strong as those for within-sex differences (personal stylistic variations). Zahn's subjects were likely atypically high in education level, so it remains to be seen whether his results obtain with a broader sample. The study does suggest that women are not necessarily victims of their own gender and gender-linked language. Their own stylistic choices may be more important in creating a positive impression. What is needed are studies that assess the types of stylistic variations that enhance credibility (for example, perceptions of dynamism, attractiveness, competence) for women and men in a variety of contexts. Research has revealed that hedges ("sort of," "kind of"), hesitations ("um," "er"), intensifiers ("very," "really"), and tag questions ("They are, aren't they?") can affect perceptions of communicator authoritativeness, attractiveness, competence, dynamism, character, and power (Bradac & Mulac, 1984; Dubois & Crouch, 1975; Hosman, 1989; Hosman & Wright, 1987; McCroskey & Mehrley, 1969).

Research on the effects of gender stereotypes and gender-linked language use is important to persuasion study. A woman may be extremely competent and have strong evidence supporting her case and still fail to persuade merely because her language or actions suggest low power and influence to those with whom she is communicating. Could this be why so many people have argued that women must be especially competent to enter male-dominated positions? Could this be why American women have faced a "glass ceiling" in attempting to reach high levels in their organizations? These questions are worth considering, as affirmative answers might lead us to some clues as to how women might break down the barriers that prevent them from achieving the same goals as their equally competent male coworkers.

It appears that we need to keep abreast of the changing times when considering sex effects. As American women progress in their battle for equality, we should expect differences in persuasibility to diminish. As women enter the job force in increasing numbers, they, like men, will specialize in careers that provide them with demonstrable expertise.

Furthermore, we may find upon closer scrutiny of persuasibility research that questionnaire measures that suggest that women are weak-kneed responders may actually reflect an accommodating response style. Women attempt to integrate new or opposing information into their construct systems. Message reception is followed by a period of information integration during which women think through what they've learned. Women may ultimately reject as many messages as do men, but they take longer to do so. Thus the persuader who senses victory when addressing an all-female audience because audience members have not quickly taken a stand might be in for a big surprise later in the day, when they've made up their minds.

PERSONALITY AND CONTEXT

Persuasion texts abound with evidence that personality characteristics influence attitude change. Self-esteem (see McGuire, 1969, for an explanation of conflicting findings), anxiety and insecurity (Nunally & Bobren, 1959; Triandis, 1971), Machiavellianism (Christie, 1968; Guterman, 1970), and authoritarianism (Adorno, Frenkel-Brunswick, & Sanford, 1950; Triandis, 1971) are only a few on the long list. It is often difficult to know just how the findings of these studies can be used to facilitate our understanding of persuasion. In a nonlaboratory context it is usually considered gauche to administer a personality test to an audience prior to message preparation. Basically, then, these studies provide evidence that personality can influence attitude change, but in our search for predictor variables that can be manipulated by persuaders, they offer little hope. Personality cannot be manipulated in the same way as source credibility. Instead, we may find the information these studies provide useful in interpersonal encounters where persuasive messages can be adjusted to individual characteristics even in the course of their delivery. In fact, it may be possible to use the presence of those behaviors that researchers have considered reflective of personality types to determine the utility of consistency appeals in situation types.

Cooper and Scalise (1974) interpret the conflicting literature on personality trait effects as reason for considering the interaction of personality factors and situational variables. They suggest, "It may be that people experience dissonance when an action which they commit is inconsistent with a stable personality trait" (p. 566). They add that what may produce dissonance for one personality type may not do so for others. On the basis of Jung's definition of introverts and extroverts, Cooper and Scalise attempted to demonstrate that introverts who learn that they have conformed to the opinions of others instead of remaining their typical independent selves should experience dissonance due to the inconsistency of their behavior with their usual life-style. Extroverts, they assumed, should experience dissonance when they do not conform to the opinions of others. The results supported their hypotheses.

Although the Cooper and Scalise definition of "situational variables" is vague, their emphasis on the personality × situation interaction is important. Unlike much previous personality research, their study reflects a recognition of the multifaceted nature of human behavior. If human behavior were influenced solely by personality and were therefore free from all situationally imposed normative constraints, chaos would obtain. It is clear that human beings are neither totally self-operative nor robots driven by societal rules. This means that any research claiming to be reflective of the "real world" cannot dwell on personality variables alone but must also consider their interaction with situational expectations.

Some contexts of social interaction are highly formalized. In such cases, little room exists for personality influences. The rules are rigid and any violation of them elicits sanctions. The strongest influence on behavior here is societal rather than individual rule structures. The persuader wishing to alter the behavior of individuals in a formal context should focus on behavioral appropriateness rather than on consistency, since these contexts are usually characterized by high rule consensus (see Figure 6.1). In an organization with a formal rule structure, it may be enough to say, "That is the way things are done around here" when trying to persuade an employee to comply.

In less formal contexts, personality factors can exert more influence. The parameters of rule violation are wider, and individual idiosyncrasies are therefore given freer reign. A persuader finding herself in a flexible context may find appeals to inconsistencies between an individual's behavior and what she knows to be his personality (e.g., independence and extroversion) more effective than appeals to the inappropriateness of his behavior and what is expected of him in that context. Statements about "what is expected around here" may fall on

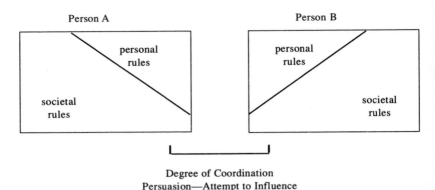

Figure 6.1. Formal Context

deaf ears, so to speak. In an informal organizational setting, it may be more effective to say something like, "We thought you'd want to do this because you have proven yourself to be an expert in these matters." As Figure 6.2 indicates, to the extent that a context is informal, agreement concerning expectations is reduced and therefore social rules become less potent tools of persuasion. In such contexts an individual can be persuaded to alter his or her overt behavior by appeals to inconsistency between his or her personal rules and overt behavior. Conversely, formal contexts allow the individual to violate personal rules with impunity by claiming that the context rules "made me do it." An extroverted person may refrain from telling his usual off-color jokes at a wedding because he respects the seriousness of the occasion. In such instances the formal context provides an excuse for not entertaining everyone all night long.

It has been suggested here that personality can be used to influence attitude and behavior change, but with less effectiveness in a formal context consisting of restrictive rules. Unless persuasion research focusing on personality includes situational variables, the results are likely to provide little useful information, because they will not reflect the interplay of societal and personal rules characteristic of real-life situations.

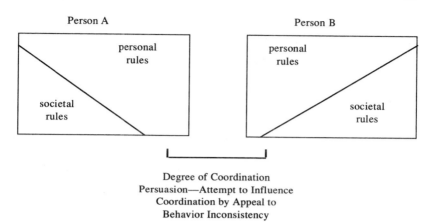

Degree of Coordination
Persuasion—Attempt to Influence
Coordination by Appeal to
Behavior Inconsistency

Figure 6.2. Informal Context

COGNITIVE COMPLEXITY

Intelligence has received much attention in terms of its relationship to persuasibility. Indices such as mental age, chronological age, and years of schooling have yielded only minimal support for the expected negative relationship between persuasibility and intelligence. Many studies indicate a positive relationship. McGuire (1973) has suggested that intelligence may make a person more susceptible to persuasion through the increased attention and comprehension it allows, but that it reduces persuasibility through increased resistance to yielding. He adds that we can expect an overall nonmonotonic relationship of the inverted U family, indicating that persons of moderate intelligence are more persuasible than persons of extremely high or low intelligence, with the level of intelligence at which maximum persuasibility occurs going up as the complexity of the communication situation increases.

This interpretation of intelligence effects on persuasibility lends some support to the position taken earlier in this chapter, that women may appear more persuasible when, in actuality, they may be more capable of integrating interpersonal information. If so, we should expect to find, through the use of more sensitive measures than those used previously, that women struggle to integrate novel or contradictory information into their cognitive systems before deciding whether to yield a former position. We may still find that women yield more often than men, but at least we will know that it is due to their greater tendency to weigh alternative perspectives.

That women are intellectually superior is not what is being suggested here. That is a research battle most of us would just as soon avoid. However, research has indicated that females are more interpersonally sensitive than males (Brierly, 1966; Dimitrovsky, 1964; Gollin, 1958; Livesley & Bromley, 1973; R. B. Rothenberg, 1970). Intelligence tests are insensitive to this phenomenon. The study of human communication requires the development of a measure to determine how effectively people deal with information conveyed in social interaction. The measure that meets this need and has been given much attention lately is cognitive complexity.

The constructivists have provided the most communication-relevant literature on cognitive complexity. Constructivists consider interpersonal sensitivity to be a function of the individual's ability to interpret social situations through the application of a personal system of interpersonal constructs or cognitive structures (Delia & Clark, 1977). We can expect that some individuals will surpass others in this, merely because they place more emphasis on communication. Brian Little (1972) suggests that different people specialize in different aspects of the environment and that their cognitive structures (constructs) will therefore be extended into a highly complex system only within the domain(s) of specialization. Knapp, Stahl, and Reardon (1980) have found that people integrate prior experiences into memorable messages that they can call upon to explain certain context-specific problems and to guide action in that context. These researchers suggest that memorable messages operate much like master rules that subsume more specific rules. They do so because, as limited-capacity information processors (Shatz, 1977), people are predisposed to find rules that allow their thinking to be more abstract and integrated rather than differentiated. For example, Knapp et al. explain that the memorable message "Never wait for a train or a lover because there will be another one along soon" is a master rule recalled by the subject who reported it because it integrated many past experiences into one overall, useful rule of thumb. It also serves to guide behavior in intimate relationships and thereby lends predictability to the individual's life. As you may recall from Chapter 2, it is Kelly's (1955) contention that we are always in the "business of prediction." Even if this is not totally accurate, we are predisposed to formulate logics or rules for our attitudes and behaviors. Master rules have the added advantage of associating disparate experiences with each other. They do so in terms of context. A lover and a train may have little in common, but in the context of a relationship rift, these two disparate objects come to be associated through the use of a master rule—a personal logic.

Schemata, constructs, rules, master rules, and the like are all methods of cognitive organization. They assist the individual in shaping expectations. They facilitate his or her attempts to deal with novel experiences. In short, they form the logic into which the individual integrates incoming stimuli. Delia, Clark, and Switzer (1974), Shroder, Driver, and Streufert (1967), Crockett (1965), Werner (1957), Reardon (1982), and others have agreed that the development of cognition involves an increased differentiation of elements and, simultaneously, an increased integration of them into a hierarchically organized system. Clark and Delia (1977), for example, support their contention that the more differentiated children's construct systems employed in person perception, the more effective they should be in adapting messages to others. In my own research, I found that cognitively complex children are better able to provide accounts for conversational rule violations, and are more adept at providing alternative endings for incomplete conversations in which a deviation has occurred, than are their less complex peers (Reardon, 1982). In that work, I introduced a computational model of cognitive complexity that, unlike previous methods of measurement, combines the dimensions of differentiation, abstraction, and integration. This approach emphasizes the quality dimensions of cognitive complexity (abstraction and integration) over the quantity dimension (differentiation). I also found high construct and predictive validity for my measure when studying children's ability to account for conversational deviations and provide cooperative alternative endings for these deviant conversations. The combined computational measure correlated more highly than any other single cognitive dimension measure with these two dependent variables and with age. However, since this measure did not produce a significantly higher correlation ($p < .05$), I concluded that this measure may not be a better indicator of cognitive complexity in very young children, whose integration abilities are not yet developed (Reardon-Boynton, 1978). The face, construct, and predictive validity, however, suggest that it is a strong contender with other cognitive complexity measures (for a review of other measures, see Sypher, 1980; Sypher & O'Keefe, 1980).

It appears, then, that cognitive complexity does play a role in human communication behavior. In terms of persuasion, complexity theory posits that more cognitively complex individuals can integrate reliable but inconsistent information into their current belief systems more readily than can less complex individuals. Herman (1977) explains that people with less complex cognitive systems may reject inconsistent information or distort it to fit their current belief systems. Cognitively complex individuals, on the other hand, can integrate inconsistent information without attitude or behavior change by further differentiating their belief systems. Borrowing from Sears and Freedman (1967), Herman adds that cognitively complex people can be regarded as "promiscuous information gatherers" who have high rates of exposure to persuasive communications, whether consistent or inconsistent with current beliefs.

More recent research suggests that cognitive complexity also influences the degree to which individuals attend to multiple aims or goals when constructing messages. O'Keefe and Shepherd (1987) have developed a message analysis system to determine the degree to which and manner in which multiple goals are pursued in messages. The three goals identified by these researchers are communicating cooperatively, maintaining coherent interaction, and protecting their own and partners' face. The concept of "face" is borrowed from Goffman's work on facework and politeness and consists of the desire to be valued by others and the desire not to be impeded by others. Requests are one way that people impede on others, since a request necessarily involves some degree of imposition (Brown & Levinson, 1978).

O'Keefe and Shepherd found that construct differentiation (one measure of cognitive complexity) does predict patterns of strategy use. The more complex people are, the more they tend to modify or elaborate their messages to serve face and interaction maintenance goals effectively. It appears that people vary in the extent to which they can focus on and serve multiple goals when constructing messages. You probably know someone who always seems to say the wrong thing. People like this don't seem to have "filters" for sifting out inappropriate or ineffective comments before they slip off their tongues and damage interactions. It may be that such people are unable to consider multiple goals when constructing messages. They may focus on the content and fail to recognize the need to frame that content in a fashion less likely to threaten the "face" of their interaction partners. Such myopia in message construction is likely the crux of many a persuasion failure. The effective persuader is capable not only of clarity but also of assuring that what he or she says keeps the channels of communication open by avoiding serious face threats to others.

It is apparent from this discussion that cognitive complexity is a variable that can influence the impact of persuasive messages. Although it is usually impossible to determine the cognitive complexity levels of members of a large audience, estimations of the general level of complexity may be accessible merely from premessage audience analysis typical of rhetorical perspectives. Scientific approaches may prove more useful in educational contexts, where an understanding of the cognitive complexity of the child can facilitate the development of more effective educational messages and methods.

COUNTERARGUING

Festinger and Maccoby (1964) and Osterhouse and Brock (1970) have suggested that when people are exposed to persuasive attacks, they subvocalize counterarguments. Much research has focused on the role of counterarguing in attitude change. Distraction occurring simultaneously with the persuasive attack message has been described as an inhibitor of counterarguing. According to Festinger and Maccoby, the inhibition of counterarguing facilitates attitude change because the individual is left vulnerable to the message appeals. While research contradicting Festinger and Maccoby's perspective exists (Haaland & Venkatesen, 1968; Vohs & Garrett, 1968), distraction is still considered an important variable in the study of attitude change.

Miller and Burgoon (1979) conclude from the conflicting research that distraction interacts with other variables to produce attitude change. Petty, Wells, and Brock (1976) provide support for this position. They state that

> distraction inhibits the dominant cognitive response to a persuasive appeal. If the dominant cognitive response is counterargumentation, then distraction will tend to inhibit this and result in increased persuasion; but if the dominant cognitive response is favorable thoughts, distraction will tend to inhibit this and result in decreased persuasion. (p. 883)

The nature of the message then appears to be one variable interacting with distraction to influence attitude change. Kiesler and Mathog

(1968) found that source characteristics can interact with distraction to influence communication acceptance. They observed a direct relationship between distraction and attitude change only when the source credibility of the message was relatively high. They explain their findings by suggesting that a low credible source requires less counterargumentation, since resistance to the message can be obtained by simply derogating the source.

Recent distraction studies do provide support for the idea that counterarguing can inhibit attitude change. What is needed now are studies that determine whether distraction alone can intrude upon the counterarguing process so that attitude change can be facilitated.

FREE CHOICE AND
FORESEEN CONSEQUENCES

Nel, Helmreich, and Aronson (1969) found that delivering a counterattitudinal speech made the speaker uncomfortable (dissonance) only when he thought that it was likely that the speech would convince his audience. Subsequent studies by Cooper and Worchel (1970), Goethals and Cooper (1972), Hoyt, Henley, and Collins (1972), Cooper, Zanna, and Goethals (1974), and others have indicated that aversive behavioral consequences are critical in determining the amount of dissonance-produced attitude change. For example, Cooper and Worchel had student subjects attempt to convince a waiting subject that a boring task was exciting and interesting. They were given either a low incentive (a half hour of extra research credit) or a high incentive (one full hour of additional credit). The results indicated that only when the attitude-discrepant speech was given for a small incentive and perceived to be accepted by the recipient did opinion change occur.

One of the most interesting results of these free choice/foreseen consequences studies is that, unlike much prior attitude change research, they give subjects some credit for evaluating their behavior. Nel et al. (1969) have suggested that dissonance is created by a discrepancy between an individual's self-concept and the knowledge that he or she has committed an indecent act. The subjects in the Cooper and Worchel study could have felt "indecent" because they lied. Since it is commonly held that decent people do not lie, dissonance was created. The need to feel decent again can be met by changing one's opinion about the lie object. In this case the dull task was perceived as more interesting than the initial opinion indicated. It is interesting to note that people feel indecent only if their lies are accepted as truths.

Cooper et al. (1974) found that the degree to which people like the individuals they mislead by lying is an important factor in attitude change. It appears that not only is a lie not indecent unless it is accepted, but it must be accepted by a liked rather than by a disliked person. We can see from this type of research that science, contrary to the claims of many humanists, can uncover the intricate workings of the human mind. It is true, however, that until recent years scientific studies of human behavior have avoided such concepts as "choice" and "responsibility," resulting in somewhat stilted conceptualizations of human cognition and behavior.

When a rather simple theory like cognitive dissonance becomes subject to qualification on the basis of whether the subject is free to choose, feels responsible, and is successful in convincing others, scientists must either discard the theory altogether (because too many factors have to be taken into consideration) or become more aware of the contexts in which they study human behavior. This text and much recent research indicates a trend toward the latter approach. The next section looks closely at a study that combines counterargument-distraction perspectives with a novel perspective on the importance of expectation violation, while also considering important contextual features.

EXPECTATION VIOLATION

As discussed in Chapter 1, much research points to the important influence expectations exert on behavioral choice. Miller and Burgoon (1979) examined the role of expectation violation in the process of persuasion. While they did not subscribe to the Kellyan perspectives introduced in Chapter 2, they pointed to the work of Brooks and Scheidel (1968), Brooks (1970), and Burgoon (1970), which concludes that the reactions of individuals to speakers may be a function of the contrast between speaker behavior and stereotyped expectations.

Miller and Burgoon (1979) based their research on a model of resistance to persuasion introduced by Burgoon, Cohen, Miller, and Montgomery (1978). According to Burgoon et al., inoculation theory alone is not sufficient to explain resistance to persuasion. Instead, they advance a communication-oriented model suggesting three primary factors that mediate ability to resist the appeals contained in a persuasive message: "(1) the amount of threat or motivation to counterargue the position being advocated in persuasive message, (2) the degree to which the communication fulfills or violates receivers' expectations of appropriate communication behavior, and (3) the context in which the persuasive communication occurs" (p. 301).

Burgoon et al. (1978) provide empirical support for the above predictions. Miller and Burgoon (1979) also offer a refinement of Burgoon et al.'s second proposition through the incorporation of explicit predictions concerning the effects of confirmation or disconfirmation of receiver expectations. Referring to the work of Burgoon, Jones, and Stewart (1974), Miller and Burgoon (1979) suggest that when expectations are violated in a positive manner the effect of the initial message should be enhanced, but when a source violates expectations in a negative manner, the effect of the initial message is inhibited.

MESSAGE VARIABLES

There is little disagreement among persuasion researchers concerning the importance of message style and appeals to attitude change. However, there appear to be very few simple answers to the question of what constitutes an effective message. Fear appeal research is a case in point. While it seems reasonable to assume that fear arousal should increase yielding to persuasive messages (fear-drive model), the research in this area does not support this perspective without qualification. Janis and Feshback (1953), for example, found that when fear is strongly aroused and no reassurances are included in the message, the audience is motivated to ignore or minimize the importance of the threat. While much research supports this finding, Leventhal and his associates found that fear-arousing communications do increase attitudinal acceptance when "effective" recommended actions are provided to the subjects as a means of reducing fear. For example, tetanus shots are generally considered more effective as a preventive measure against tetanus than toothbrushing is for dental disease (see Leventhal & Niles, 1964; Leventhal, Singer, & Jones, 1965). Weiss, Rawson, and Pasamanick (1963) suggest that the discrepancy among research findings could be attributed to the subjects' initial positions. In the Leventhal et al. (1965) study, the subjects were probably in favor of tetanus shots, but in the Janis and Feshback (1953) study, the subjects might have held an initial position opposing some dental hygiene recommendations. If so, the preferred procedure might have been strengthened by fear rather than by what was conveyed in the message.

Many other studies point to the complexity involved in fear appeal research (Berkowitz & Cottingham, 1960; Leventhal, 1970; Leventhal & Watts, 1966; Miller & Hewgill, 1964; Moltz & Thistlethwaite, 1955; Singer, 1965). McGuire (1973) suggests that while conflicting findings are discouraging because they indicate that the answers will not be simple ones, they are encouraging because complexities can serve to generate hypotheses about interaction effects. The Miller and Burgoon (1979) study attests to McGuire's insight. McGuire (1973, p. 234) points to the two-factor analysis as an example. It suggests that there is a nonmonotonic relationship such that some intermediate level of anxiety is preferable to no anxiety arousal or high anxiety arousal. Furthermore, it appears that the level of anxiety arousal that is most efficacious goes down as message complexity increases and also as the person's chronic anxiety level goes up (see Millman, 1968). Lehmann (1970) and Leventhal (1970), however, have found an even higher-order interaction with self-esteem.

In a review and critique of fear appeal research, Sutton (1982) argues that both monotonic views of fear (that persuasion increases with increased fear) and nonmonotonic views (that the effects of fear begin to wane as interfering effects increase at a faster rate than facilitating effects) have considerable shortcomings. He draws the following conclusions:

(1) Increases in fear are consistently associated with increases in acceptance (behavior and intentions).

(2) There is no evidence that fear and acceptance are related in a non-monotonic fashion.

(3) Increasing the efficacy of recommended action strengthens intentions to adopt that action.

(4) Providing specific instructions on how to perform a recommended action leads to a higher rate of acting in accordance with the recommended action.

(5) Greater similarity between communicator and recipient in terms of race produces more immediate behavior change without necessarily affecting fear.

(6) There is little support for interactions predicted by the fear-drive model.

Some researchers have also proposed that even clear recommendations and assurances of the efficacy of adopting them may not be enough
to elicit persuasive effects from fear appeals. Kirsch, Tennen, Wickless,
Saccone, and Cody (1985) argue that people may avoid situations
simply because they are afraid that they may become afraid in those
situations. The person who will not get up to give a public speech may
fear the disapproval likely to result if she does not do so, may know
how to follow recommended anxiety-reduction steps, and may realize
that giving the speech is likely to reduce her fear, but she may be so
afraid of feeling or appearing afraid that she will not even try to give
the speech. For such people, the anticipation of experiencing fear is
extremely punishing.

Basically, then, the research on fear appeals indicates that simple
answers are not forthcoming. Perhaps this is because the ways individuals handle fear vary across situations, more than early theorists be-
lieved possible. Also, what causes fear in one person may be ignored
by another.

A second message content variable is style. Bowers (1964) and
Bowers and Osborn (1966), for example, have found that metaphorical
(as opposed to literal) expressions may enhance persuasive impact
(see also Burgoon et al., 1978; Burgoon & Miller, 1971; McEwen,
1969). Intensity of language is another variable frequently associated
with receiver reactions to sources. Bostrom, Baschart, and Rossiter
(1973) and Mulac (1976) have focused on the effects of obscenity. The
former found that female sources using obscenity obtained more attitude change than did their male counterparts. Bradac, Bowers, and
Courtright (1979) describe this finding as "anomalous" in light of the
evidence that women use and are also expected to use little obscenity
(Kramer, 1974). Also, they explain that Bostrom et al. did not compare
the findings for females with a control group. Bradac et al. therefore
conclude that obscenity is inversely related to postcommunication ratings of source competence (p. 259).

Bradac et al. have also reviewed the literature on lexical diversity and
verbal immediacy. The former refers to the range of a source's vocabulary, the latter to the degree to which a source associates him- or herself
with the message topics. Strong evidence exists to support the inclusion
of these variables in persuasion research, since they influence receiver
perceptions of the source. However, the authors caution us to consider
one disconcerting flaw characteristic of the studies supporting their
generalizations. Researchers have rarely operationalized these vari-

ables in any precise way relative to the operationalizations of other researchers. This criticism is most applicable to intensity research. Bradac et al. suggest that this failure to agree on operational definitions has three important consequences: "(1) Within levels of a given variable, wide fluctuations may exist from study to study, such that one researchers' 'high' level may be another's 'low' range. (2) Degrees of effect are not amenable to analysis. (3) Effects that are apparently linear may in fact be curvilinear" (p. 266).

Earlier in their paper, Bradac et al. mention that most of the studies of intensity and lexical diversity are not grounded in theory and so the result has been a "proliferation of unintegrated data" (p. 257). Their integrations are thus a welcome change of approach, but little can be said of these variables with confidence until either agreement on operational definitions or reasons for differences are reached. Furthermore, as Bradac et al. suggest, this research would benefit from the inclusion in the design of context considerations. Other message style literature and research will be discussed in later chapters as they relate to interpersonal or noninterpersonal contexts.

A third message content variable is strategy. Specific areas include the treatment of opposition arguments, implicit versus explicit conclusions, order of arguments, and message repetition. In general, it is safe to conclude that the study of any variables in isolation from other contextual variables is likely to result in useless information. Research indicates that ignoring the existence of counterarguments when the audience is intelligent or initially hostile to one's view is counterproductive. Also, if the audience is aware of the opposition arguments, it is better to refute rather than ignore them. In terms of conclusions, some research indicates that explicit conclusions are more effective than implicit ones (Hovland & Mandel, 1952; McGuire, 1964). However, conflicting findings have resulted when the receiver's intelligence level has been taken into consideration.

Argument order has also generated much research effort. Zimbardo and Ebbesen (1970, p. 21) summarize this research by suggesting the following:

(1) Present one side of the argument when the audience is generally friendly, or when your position is the only one that will be presented, or when you want immediate, though temporary, opinion change.

(2) When opposite views are presented one after the other, the one presented last will probably be more effective. Primacy effect is more predominant

when the second side immediately follows the first, while recency is more predominant when the opinion measure comes immediately after the second side.

Research indicates that message repetition adds to the persuasive impact of a message (Staats, 1968; Stewart, 1964). McGuire (1973) explains that the most impressive finding of the repetition research is that this variable has so little effect. He explains this phenomenon as well as the differential effects found when one considers single versus samples of listeners: "An increase in impact usually appears for one or two repetitions but quickly reaches an asymptote beyond which further repetitions have little effect" (p. 235). It may be that with a captive audience comprehension is quickly maximized by the first several repetitions, so there is nothing more to be learned through further repetition. However, when one considers the initial step in the chain of behaviors leading to persuasion—namely, being presented with the message in the first place—repetition may well be efficacious up to a high level when one has a changing audience. In this case, while the effect of repetition on a given listener soon reaches its asymptote, repetitions at different times expose successive samples of listeners to the message. McGuire's explanation indicates once again that simple, concise generalizations that disregard the context of the communication are of little utility in persuasion research.

Another message content variable is that of issue salience. Functional perspectives suggest that people are concerned with the usefulness of information. Eagly and Himmelfarb (1978) point out that some people are concerned with maintaining or establishing social relationships with a communicator and that incoming information will therefore be judged on the basis of whether acceptance of it enhances that goal achievement. In short, sometimes the content is secondary to other contextual concerns. When these other concerns are not overriding in their influence, salience of the issue appears to be important to attitude change. Dissonance theory predicts that increasing initial attitude salience increases attitude change, because the counterattitudinal behavior becomes more dissonant. Self-perception theory, on the other hand, predicts that salience of initial attitudes decreases attitude change, because it increases the clarity of internal cues and thereby decreases reliance on external cues. Eagly and Himmelfarb (1978) suggest that current research findings favor dissonance theory.

EVIDENCE

Another variable important to the outcomes of persuasive inter-actions is evidence. Although evidence has been studied by communication scholars for decades, the jury appears still to be out with regard to its effects on persuasion outcomes. Reinard (1988) argues, however, that this may be due to the tendency to lump dissimilar evidence studies together as if they are comparable when they are not. The claims that evidence studies have produced inconsistent results is, according to Reinard, overstated. He argues further that researchers have not attended to the differences among studies in terms of how "evidence" and "no evidence" have been defined.

Evidence is the proof offered by communicators to support their claims. The elaboration likelihood model, described in Chapter 5, suggests that of the two routes information may take in influencing persuasion outcomes, evidence takes the central route, along with arguments and language. The peripheral route, you may recall, includes elements external to the message, such as credibility of the communicator, attractiveness, and social pressure. Petty and Cacioppo (1981) argue that preference for one route over the other is largely dependent on the message recipient's involvement with the subject and ability to process the information presented. If the recipient is not concerned with the topic or is unable to comprehend the message, he or she is likely to rely more on peripheral cues than on evidence and argument conveyed via the central route. So it follows that evidence is likely to have its strongest effects when the recipient of the message containing it is concerned with the topic and understands the message.

Evidence research has explored how types of evidence influence persuasion outcomes. For example, in courtroom settings jurors find eyewitness accounts compelling and tend to overestimate their accuracy (see Brigham & Bothwell, 1983). Other studies have found that biases of jurors can be ameliorated by unambiguous, reliable evidence (Kaplan & Miller, 1978; Kaplan & Schersching, 1980). Increasing the amount of factual evidence provided by expert witnesses may even offset defendant attractiveness effects (Baumeister & Darley, 1982) and racial prejudice effects (Ugwuegbu, 1979).

While evidence research is too extensive to report here, another group of studies provides information that may be of interest to those who base their arguments on statistical evidence. While considered "icons

of objectivity" in the Western world, statistics do not necessarily produce persuasive effects when compared with other modes of evidence
more familiar to the audience (Reinard, 1988). It may be that statistics
alone, without arguments that make the communication come alive, are
dull and do not encourage the central route processing likely to lead to
persuasive outcomes. Research has indicated that statistical evidence
tends to be more persuasive when reported along with a description of
the research from which it resulted (Cacioppo, Petty, & Morris, 1983;
Petty & Cacioppo, 1984). Perhaps an even greater effect results when
statistical evidence is explained in terms of audience experiences (e.g.,
what decreased birthrates mean in terms of future accessibility of
workers for the types of companies owned and operated by audience
members). Ruth Anne Clark (1984) demonstrates this principle in her
discussion of how a persuader might convince a young audience of the
importance of wearing helmets when riding motorcycles. She explains
that arguments for health promotion often fall on deaf ears with young
people because they feel invulnerable. One way to get the attention of
these people is to explain that 80% of motorcycle fatalities involve
people under 25 years of age. If your message is one of encouraging
audience members to change their diets, you might mention that one out
of every two people in the room will die of heart disease unless current
trends are reversed.

EMOTION

The final variable to be discussed in this chapter is emotion. No
theory of persuasion would be complete without it, because no human
being is complete without emotions. We are not purely cognitive beings,
despite our attempts to conceal that fact.

According to Schachter (1964), there are two interacting components
in emotion: peripheral physiological arousal and the cognitions associated with such arousal. If there is no cognitive element associated
with physiological arousal, people search the environment for arousal
explanations. Singer (1965) found that subjects with no ready-made
explanations for their arousal could be manipulated into euphoria or
anger.

Obviously, emotions can be a powerful ingredient in the persuasion
process, yet few of the theories introduced earlier in this book refer to
emotions, let alone give them a key role. For decades researchers have

treated persuasion as a largely cognitive activity in which people are pushed and pulled by inconsistency or reason about selections of strategies. One reason for this is the difficulty researchers have had in defining and studying emotions. Some believe that emotions are partly cognitive, consisting of physiological arousal and cognitive interpretations of that arousal. For example, observing a friend buy a new car when your are stuck with a junker may arouse in you physiological reactions that may be interpreted by you or someone observing as jealousy. In an effort to feel good about yourself, you might decide that the emotion you are experiencing is actually excitement resulting from your vicarious experience of your friend's emotional state.

Other social scientists consider emotion capable of effecting behavior without ever being interpreted. Fear, happiness, disgust, sadness, anger, surprise, and interest are basic emotions that manifest similar expressions across cultures. The surprised Indian looks like the surprised American (Buck, 1984).

Emotions can also be used purposefully to achieve interpersonal goals. Emotional behavior can be strategic in nature. It can be used to generate pity or guilt in the mind of the persuadee. People can feign emotions and use them in the service of their own self-deception. In short, some people can persuade themselves that they are actually experiencing an emotion suitable to the occasion or useful in eliciting a desired response from someone. As de Sousa (1980) writes, "Emotion attends self-deception. Vanity, grief, resentment, apprehension, all induce us to connive in the clouding of our vision" (p. 283).

So, contrary to common conceptions of emotional behavior, such behavior does not always represent a loss of control. Emotional behavior can be a spontaneous but reasonable response to an event or can be consciously used to elicit desired behaviors from others. Emotions can be natural barriers to persuasion if they prevent persuadees from attending to persuasive messages or heavily influence their interpretations of those messages. They can also be used by persuadees to discourage persuaders from further attempts to elicit desired responses from them.

Using McGuire's persuasion/communication matrix, described in Chapter 5, it is easy to see how emotions of the persuader or persuadee might interfere with the several steps leading to yielding (step 6). With regard to the persuader, if he appears nervous, the persuadee may not perceive him as credible and may tend to disregard his arguments. If the persuadee is nervous, he may be too distracted to attend to the message (step 2) even if it is presented in an otherwise effective manner.

Given that emotions can cloud reason or stand in the way of cooper-ative interaction, it is often important to deal with them early in the persuasion process. Sometimes people can be encouraged to reason about their emotional behaviors. Using the ACE model perspective, described in Chapter 5, they can be encouraged to see their emotions as somehow inappropriate to the situation, inconsistent given who they are, or ineffective given their goals. Another method for changing emotional behavior is to shift the person's attention away from the target of emotion. There is nothing like a little time away from a problem to encourage perspective. A third method of changing emo-tional behavior involves altering the beliefs with which they are asso-ciated. A person who is embarrassed is so because she believes that she has done something foolish. If she can be convinced that her actions were actually quite reasonable give the circumstances, her emotional reaction may dissipate. When emotional behavior is reduced to a level where attending to a message received from a persuader is possible, the likelihood of persuasion success is enhanced.

You might be wondering, however, about those times when persuad-ers try to increase emotional reactions rather than decrease them. Certainly more and more advertising involves emotional appeals. Be-cause people are bombarded by advertising, advertisers often use emo-tional appeals to capture attention. Advertisers even experiment with negative emotions.

So emotions may cloud vision and get in the way of what Petty and Cacioppo would call "central route processing" of persuasive messages or may interfere with steps in the McGuire model. But emotional reactions can also draw attention to subject matter that might otherwise pass unnoticed. Unfortunately, much work remains to be done in the study of emotion before we really know when emotion facilitates persuasion and when it inhibits it. We do know that researchers cannot continue to disregard emotion's impact, because persuasion is often an emotional activity.

CONCLUSION

This chapter has reviewed a number of variables that influence the effectiveness of persuasion. The chapter as a whole indicates the extent to which persuasion is a complex activity. How the source of the message is perceived, as well as his or her gender, personality, and rapport with the persuadee enter into the persuasion equation. In addition, message variables such as order of arguments, evidence, style of presentation, and salience of issues influence the outcome of persuasion efforts. Persuadee variables such as gender, emotional predispositions, cognitive complexity, expectations, and schemata contribute as well. Given the wide variety of persuasion variables and, as indicated in Chapter 5, the possibility that each might influence the central and peripheral information processing of persuadees on any specific occasion, it is easy to see why persuasion requires considerable skill.

The next several chapters move away from general theories of persuasion to take a closer look at how persuasion operates in a variety of contexts—interpersonal, organizational, mass media, and political.

7 Interpersonal Persuasion

Interpersonal persuasion occurs when two or a few people interact in a way that involves verbal and nonverbal behaviors, personal feedback, coherence of behaviors (relevance or fit of remarks and actions), and the purpose (on the part of at least one interactant) of changing the attitudes and/or behaviors of the other(s). This definition separates interpersonal persuasion from mass media persuasion, in which personal feedback and coherence are not present. Mass media messages are presented without interaction between the people involved. There are no surprises in the form of disagreement received from the persuadee. There is no pressure on the persuadee to act interested even if he or she is bored. No one's "face" is in jeopardy or on the spot.

The interpersonal persuader cannot be totally prepared for what might occur during interaction. Each person involved in an interpersonal encounter has the capacity to shift the topic, introduce new data, respond in a nonproductive emotional fashion, walk away, or engage in any number of actions that make it difficult for the persuader to convey a message effectively. The characteristic of unpredictability makes interpersonal persuasion particularly challenging. Any scripts prepared in advance of interpersonal interactions are temporary, since it is difficult to know what others involved might say or do to disrupt the plans. For example, while it is always useful to prepare for a job interview by practicing how one might respond to typical questions, it is impossible to prepare all that one might say during the interview, since the interviewer will interject his or her own agenda. The skillful interviewee may be able to bring the conversation around to his or her own agenda at points during the interview, but the topic coherence demands of interpersonal interaction make it difficult to do so abruptly. The interviewee must know how to create a "topic bridge" between his or her own thoughts and those of the interviewer. Sometimes a simple "That reminds me of the time . . . " is sufficient, but such obvious changes of topic cannot be used often in one interview. More subtle bridges, such as, "Yes, I had a similar experience once, which is why I think . . . " and "That is one story I will remember, it demonstrates why it is useful to . . . ," are often needed to assure coherence without losing total control of the course of the interaction.

Interpersonal persuasion is additionally complex because of the constant need to monitor the verbal and nonverbal actions of other interactants. As Petty and Cacioppo's (1981) elaboration likelihood model suggests, people may concentrate more on one channel than the other. When focusing on what Petty and Cacioppo call the "central route" of information processing, interactants may concentrate more on verbal arguments than on nonverbal expressions. But much valuable information is conveyed by nonverbal behaviors, so it is possible that an interactant relying solely on the logic of verbal arguments will lose much of the total meaning being conveyed. Skillful persuasion usually requires careful observation of how other interactants are responding both verbally and nonverbally to your arguments.

Another characteristic of interpersonal persuasion that makes it a complex activity is the fact that there is usually more than one persuader. Each interactant has the capacity to play both persuader and persuadee at any given time. You may start the conversation by attempting to persuade a colleague to work overtime on a project only to have him respond with efforts to convince you that longer hours are not as important as devoting full attention to the project during regular work hours. Here again, interpersonal persuasion defies extensive planning because anyone involved can take on the role of persuader and contribute to the direction of the interaction. The person who begins a conversation with an attempt to convince a colleague to work overtime may end up being convinced of the need to skip coffee breaks and avoid answering phones during regular work hours so that the project will be completed on time. Equally possible is a compromise outcome in which the two interactants decide to devote more attention to the project during work hours with the agreement to do overtime work if more attention does not prove sufficient to complete the task.

Many people are not good at interpersonal persuasion simply because they are not capable of attending to all the unpredictable events that occur during such interactions. They prefer to give speeches and perhaps respond to questions afterward. They assume that this approach affords them greater control. Unfortunately, it is not possible to maintain relationships with speeches. Coworkers, spouses, parents, and children must all rely on interpersonal persuasion throughout each day. To be effective on the job and at home, it is imperative that we learn how to engage effectively in interpersonal persuasion. This does not mean always winning; rather, it means being able to do such things as read verbal and nonverbal messages, create and convey appropriate responses, effectively interject one's own agenda, identify and explain creative solutions acceptable to the persuadee, and motivate the persuadee to change.

To facilitate the accomplishment of these goals, the remainder of this chapter will focus on theory and research that sheds light on the impact of relationship type on the course of interpersonal persuasion, strategies for gaining compliance, methods of maintaining some degree of control, and creative ways to shape outcomes.

THE IMPACT OF RELATIONSHIP

Research indicates that relationship type is an important consideration in the selection of persuasion strategies (Fitzpatrick, 1988; Miller, Boster, Roloff, & Seibold, 1977; Reardon, Sussman, & Flay, 1989). The level of intimacy in any relationship influences the choices available to the persuader as he or she formulates strategies. For example, acquaintance relationships are guided more by what Miller and Steinberg (1975) call "extrinsic rules." These rules are not unique to the relationship. They are widely shared prescriptions regarding what people should and should not expect of acquaintances. For example, it is usually considered inappropriate to expect an acquaintance to care for your dog without compensation while you are on a business trip. Yet it may be quite appropriate to expect this of your brother, depending on the relationship "intrinsic rules" you and he have developed over the years.

Just as expectations regarding appropriateness vary across relationships, so too do expectations regarding strategy selection. The better you know someone, the better prepared you are to select persuasion strategies likely to work. Unfortunately, many people do not use what they know about others to guide them in their strategy selections. They are stuck with a few overused strategies. When they want to be persuasive, they fall back on strategies they have used over and over. Such people do not benefit from knowing more about the people with whom they are interacting because they are unable or unwilling to learn. The person who always resorts to guilt when trying to persuade is an example of a myopic persuader. Fortunately, most people are not so limited; many do benefit from knowing more about the people with whom they are communicating. But most of us could become more effective persuaders if we were to develop better listening and observing skills. We could liberate ourselves from limited strategies by sensitizing ourselves to the expectations of our relationship partners.

INTERPERSONAL PERSUASION: A RULES APPROACH

People rely on rules of interaction to help them determine what to say and do during conversations. Their choices are based on their perceptions of the intrinsic and extrinsic rules operating in a particular context. To the extent that the predominant concern is with intrinsic (relationship) rules, the individuals are engaged in interpersonal rather than noninterpersonal communication. Miller et al. (1977) indicate that this reliance on psychological, rather than cultural and sociological, data in the determination of interpersonal message choices facilitates accuracy. Their perspective suggests that persuaders may use role expectations as a baseline from which the particular persuadee is expected to deviate. That deviation is governed by certain relationship rules and idiosyncratic rules, the latter of which the persuader may be unaware. Although this is not what Miller et al. explicitly state, it seems feasible that despite the predominant reliance on intrinsic rules in interpersonal communication, extrinsic rules may serve as a comparison level. Furthermore, they may be utilized when no relationship rule exists to govern a particular behavioral choice.

For example, if a man and woman have gotten to know each other fairly well in their work or classes but have never dated, we can expect that their first date may pose some difficult choices for each of them. They already have a relationship and some intrinsic rules, but it may be difficult for the man to determine whether or not he should pay for the movie, hold open the car door, help the woman on with her coat, and kiss her good night. He may find it necessary to rely on role expectations rather than relationship rules until such time as the two work all this out together. If he holds her coat for her and she smiles with obvious admiration and then launches into a 10-minute soliloquy on the positive virtues of chivalrous males, then the young man has been successful and is likely to assign chivalrous rules to the relationship. However, should he then proceed to pay for the movies because he assumes that it is the chivalrous thing to do, only to hear her respond with the statement, "I think that we should each pay for our own ticket. It's really very expensive otherwise," he will have to revise his role-guided behavior.

When persuasion is the goal in interpersonal communication, it may be useful to consider the importance rule maintenance has for a particular individual, since this may serve as a foundation for establishing dissonance. "It's the manly thing to do" is a common interpersonal strategy used by males in comradely exchanges and by females attempting to convince male friends to alter their behavior. It may be that doing the "male thing" is not as important to the persuadee as doing what is appropriate for the particular relationship, rendering the appeal to this role dysfunctional.

Below is a case that demonstrates how role prescriptions and relationship rules can come into conflict at work.

The Case of Acme Company's New Market Strategy

Mike and Frank have worked together at Acme Company for six years. They are good friends. They disagree once in a while, but it has never affected their relationship.

Recently, Mike was promoted to marketing vice president. He became Frank's boss. While Frank believes that he was equally qualified for the job, he doesn't begrudge Mike his success.

Over the years Mike and Frank have been quite candid with each other about their opinions of other workers. Frank has been especially vocal about his opinion of Jim. According to Frank, Jim has an unrelenting, undeserved superiority complex. He is rude and aggressive to a fault. Mike has always enjoyed listening to Frank's vivid descriptions of Jim's faults. His own view, however, has always been that Jim, though poorly socialized, is a competent worker.

Last week Mike learned that his first task as marketing head would be an important one. Acme was going after a competitor's market. The company would need all the strategies the marketing department could muster. Mike decided that he would need the most talented people working on this project. It might be difficult, but Frank and Jim would just have to work together. In order to avoid the appearance of favoritism, Mike did not give anyone the leadership role on the project.

In his characteristic manner, Jim took every opportunity to cut Frank off during the initial planning meeting in an effort to advance his own ideas. Some of those ideas were quite good. Mike was impressed with the background research Jim had done and the creative ideas he generated. If they were to get this market, they would have to work together, even if it meant occasionally tolerating Jim's boorish behavior.

It was all Frank could manage just to avoid an altercation with Jim. He knew that Mike wanted this project to work, but he felt somewhat betrayed by Mike's convenient lapse of memory concerning Frank's feelings toward Jim. This was only exacerbated by Mike's apparent appreciation of Jim's ideas and disregard of Jim's tactics.

In an effort to make things work, Frank arranged to meet with Jim. They talked about the project for a few hours and came up with a creative marketing strategy. It could honestly be said that both had contributed equally. Mike was pleased.

The next morning Jim arrived at work early. When Mike arrived, Jim presented him with his own revised version of the plan he and Frank had developed the day before. Mike assumed that Jim had cleared the revisions with Frank. The suggestions were good, and Mike told Jim to go ahead with the revised plan. Later that morning, Frank, Jim, and the staff met to go over the plan. Without warning, Jim announced that revisions had been made and okayed by the vice president. Frank was shocked.

What are the role prescriptions in this scenario? What are the specific relational rules for each person that conflict with role prescriptions? Given this conflict, what persuasive strategies might you use if you were in the shoes of each one of the people involved?

As this example demonstrates, it is important to determine what roles and rules parties involved in persuasion are using to guide their behaviors. Without this knowledge, all we have to work with is our own perspective, which may be far from the perspective of the others involved.

INTERPERSONAL PERSUASION STRATEGIES

The fluctuation between role and rule prescriptions characteristic of interpersonal exchanges renders persuasion in this context a complex task. Persuaders always operate on the basis of incomplete information.

Their perceptions of a particular interaction or a relationship are never exactly the same as those of the persuadee. Nevertheless, in an effort to simplify the task of predicting what strategies individuals will use to persuade others, a number of taxonomies have been developed.

One taxonomy has received much attention. Schenck-Hamlin, Wiseman, and Georgacarakas (1980) consider it the most comprehensive of those they reviewed. The Marwell and Schmitt (1967) taxonomy, which appears in Table 7.1, focuses on the availability of positive and negative sanctions for what can be categorized as either appropriate or consistent behavior. Of their 16 compliance-gaining techniques, techniques 9-13 appeal to self-image consistency, whereas the remainder appeal to the person's need for persuader (1, 2, 5, 7, 8, and 9) or general other (3, 4, 15, and 16) approval.

Miller et al. (1977) extended the work of Marwell and Schmitt by proposing a number of control strategies that can be used in interpersonal and noninterpersonal persuasion. These strategies may be considered means by which one person can convince another to suspend or reject a particular rule. Miller et al. reduced the Marwell and Schmitt strategies to five factors: I, rewarding activity; II, punishing activity; III, expertise; IV, activation of impersonal commitments; and V, activation of personal commitments.

Miller et al. (1977) used the Marwell and Schmitt taxonomy to determine what strategies are typically used in interpersonal and noninterpersonal situations with long- or short-term consequences. Their findings indicate that some strategies are more appropriate to intimate than to nonintimate communications. Also, some are used in long-term rather than short-term consequence situations. For example, they found that two strategies, negative esteem and aversive stimulation, are unlikely to be used in interpersonal situations. Long-term consequence situations appear to be marked by high-probability use of promises, positive altercasting, and altruism, whereas aversive stimulation is unlikely to be used in such situations.

The Miller et al. (1977) study indicates that persuasive strategies are situationally bound. The authors qualify this conclusion, however, by explaining that, as suggested by attribution theory, people tend to attribute their own actions to the situations in which they find themselves, while attributions to others are based on perceptions of personal proclivities and inferences concerning dispositional traits (see also Jones & Nisbett, 1971). Applying this perspective to their own study, Miller et al. explain:

Table 7.1 Sixteen Compliance-Gaining Techniques, with Examples from Family Situations

(1) Promise	(If you comply, I will reward you.) "You offer to increase Dick's allowance if he increases his studying."
(2) Threat	(If you do not comply, I will punish you.) "You threaten to forbid Dick the use of the car if he does not increase his studying."
(3) Expertise (positive)	(If you comply, you will be rewarded because of "the nature of things.") "You point out to Dick that if he gets good grades he will be able to get into a good college and get a good job."
(4) Expertise (negative)	(If you do not comply, you will be punished because of "the nature of things.") "You point out to Dick that if he does not get good grades he will not be able to get into a good college or get a good job."
(5) Liking	(Actor is friendly and helpful to get target in "good frame of mind" so that he will comply with request.) "You try to be as friendly and pleasant as possible to get Dick in the right frame of mind before asking him to study."
(6) Pregiving	(Actor rewards target before requesting compliance.) "You raise Dick's allowance and tell him you now expect him to study."
(7) Aversive stimulation	(Actor continuously punishes target, making cessation contingent on compliance.) "You forbid Dick the use of the car and tell him he will not be allowed to drive until he studies more."
(8) Debt	(You owe me compliance because of past favors.) "You point out that you have sacrificed and saved to pay for Dick's education and that he owes it to you to get good enough grades to get into a good college."
(9) Moral appeal	(You are immoral if you do not comply.) "You tell Dick that it is morally wrong for anyone not to get as good grades as he can and that he should study more."
(10) Self-feeling (positive)	(You will feel better about yourself if you comply.) "You tell Dick he will feel proud if he gets himself to study more."
(11) Self-feeling (negative)	(You will feel worse about yourself if you do not comply.) "You tell Dick he will feel ashamed if he gets bad grades."
(12) Altercasting (positive)	(A person with "good" qualities would comply.) "You tell Dick that since he is a mature and intelligent boy he naturally will want to study more and get good grades."
(13) Altercasting (negative)	(Only a person with "bad" qualities would not comply.) "You tell Dick that only someone very childish does not study as he should."
(14) Altruism	(I need your compliance very badly, so do it for me.) "You tell Dick that you really want very badly for him to get into a good college and that you wish he would study more as a personal favor to you."
(15) Esteem (positive)	(People you value will think better of you if you comply.) "You tell Dick that the whole family will be very proud of him if he gets good grades."
(16) Esteem (negative)	(People you value will think worse of you if you do not comply.) "You tell Dick that the whole family will be very disappointed in him if he gets poor grades.

SOURCE: Marwell and Schmitt (1967, pp. 357-358). Reprinted by permission of the American Sociological Association and the authors.

It may be, then, that the situational prominence revealed in this study was also a function of respondent orientation. Stated differently, given attribution findings, respondents faced with assessing the likelihood of their own choice of compliance-gaining strategies may have cued to situational differences in answering, responses not reflective of more stable (i.e., across situations) personal tendencies they might normally exhibit in their usual influence attempts. Subsequent research, therefore, will need to parse situational and personal characteristics affecting message choice more carefully. (p. 51)

It may be that the subjects in the Miller et al. study based their message strategy selections on role expectations rather than on relationship rule expectations. As suggested in Chapter 6, perhaps we need studies that look at the personal and situational characteristics affecting message choice as well as studies that look at relationship characteristics that might affect message choice. Miller et al. did examine the effects of relationship type to some extent by indicating whether the consequences were to be long or short term. However, we might benefit from breaking this dimension down into more specific categories, such as those offered by Fitzpatrick (1977) and applied in the work of Fitzpatrick and Winke (1979).

Fitzpatrick and Winke's (1979) work focused on strategies and tactics used in interpersonal conflicts between same- and opposite-sex persons. They asked subjects to indicate the nature of their opposite-sex relationship as "married," "engaged," "exclusively involved with this individual," "seriously involved with this individual more than others," or "only casually involved with this individual" (p. 6). They also asked subjects to indicate how satisfied they were with both their same- and their opposite-sex relationships. Using Kipnis's Interpersonal Conflict Scale, they asked respondents to estimate how often they used 44 conflict tactics.

One advantage to using this procedure is that asking subjects to consider a particular relationship in which they are currently involved, rather than a fictitious relationship, encourages them to consider rule expectations rather than situationally prescribed role expectations. If the subjects were asked to consider a person with whom they had an ongoing relationship (defined by using the Fitzpatrick and Winke typology) in a particular situation (such as those used in the Miller et al., 1977, study), we would expect to find intrinsic rules operating more frequently than extrinsic rules. To determine the extent to which rela-

compliance-resisting strategies. Nonnegotiation decreased with age in their sample. This finding is consistent with McLaughlin et al.'s (1980) claim that nonnegotiation is a high-risk strategy. As children become more aware of the feelings of others, it appears that they tend to use more prosocial strategies. Two prosocial strategies, justification and identity management, increased with age. This research also indicates that compliance-resisting strategies vary according to the type of strategy an individual is asked to resist, and the type of compliance-gaining agent.

Other research relevant to an understanding of compliance-resisting strategy choices focuses on rationales or accounts for resistance. Following a procedure developed by Howie-Day (1977), McQuillen and Higginbotham (1986) studied children's rationales for compliance-resisting. They found significant differences in subjects' use of rationales as a function of age, type of request, and gender of subject. Among tenth-grade subjects, they found differences between male and female rationales. For example, males used their highest-level rationales to respond to simple requests, and their lowest-level rationales in support of resistance of altruistic requests. Females used their highest-level rationales in response to incentive requests and their lowest-level rationales with simple requests. McQuillen and Higginbotham conclude that males at this age appear to honor, via increased levels of consideration, those strategies that are direct, whereas females are more attentive to strategies that emphasize social convention over those that stress overt control. These researchers also found that the extent to which subjects took the perspective of the persuadee when justifying their resistance varied as a function of the type of compliance-gaining strategy employed by the agent. They did not, however, find that level of perspective-taking varied as a function of the type of compliance-gaining agent.

McLaughlin, Cody, and O'Hair (1983), McLaughlin, Cody, and Rosenstein (1983), and Cody and McLaughlin (1985) have conducted research on accounts. They define accounts as the way in which "failure events" are managed in social interaction. Their focus is on how accounts work to effect repair in threatened communication episodes and/or relationships. Since compliance-resistance has the potential to threaten conversations and relationships, such work is highly relevant. For example, McLaughlin, Cody, and O'Hair (1983) and Cody and McLaughlin (1985) found that the nature of accounts, whether mitigating (e.g., excuses, concessions, and justifications) or aggravating (e.g., refusals), are influenced by the nature of the reproach. Cody and McLaughlin report that aggravated reproaches lead to aggravating accounts more consistently than mitigating reproaches lead to mitigating accounts. They explain the latter as possibly the result of the accounter resenting attempts by the reproacher to understand why the accounter engaged in the act in question, since he or she feels falsely accused of it in the first place.

Research on rationales and accounts examines the reasoning processes that accompany communication behaviors. Both compliance-gaining and compliance-resisting often involve encouraging or discouraging the target with reasoning. As discussed in Chapter 5, I have proposed that reasoned attempts to persuade may be classified into three broad categories: appeals to appropriateness, consistency, and effectiveness (Reardon, 1981, 1987). It is also my contention that preferences among these three categories vary with relationship and situational factors. Two studies provide consensual validation for the ACE model. In a study of tobacco use, Friedman et al. (1985) found that adolescents' refusal responses fell into three broad categories similar to those in the ACE model: fear disapproval (appropriateness), subject's personal convictions (consistency), and fear of the effects of smoking (effectiveness). Newman (1984) found that these same categories could be used to describe the reasons adolescents used to support smoking.

Health promotion and disease prevention studies constitute one area where compliance-resistance strategies have been studied fairly extensively. In an era when considerable emphasis has been placed on teaching young people to resist pressure to use drugs and to engage in unsafe sexual activities, compliance-resistance training has become a part of most high schools' curricula.

Recognition of the social nature of smoking has led to the development of a number of school-based interventions focusing on social pressure resistance skills. These interventions are based on the presumption that young adolescents smoke primarily as a result of social pressures to smoke, especially from peers. Social influence interventions have reduced the onset of smoking among young adolescents by an average of 50% (Flay, 1985). Teaching adolescents that cigarette smoking is harmful to health appears to be less effective than also teaching them what they can say to peers who invite or pressure them to smoke (Flay, 1985; E. L. Thompson, 1978; Tobler, 1986).

Despite the obvious importance of social resistance training to prevent smoking, little attention has been given to what adolescents are able to say to peers who pressure them to smoke. Interventions have been developed on the basis of what researchers believe adolescents should be able to say, rather than on the basis of what adolescents report they would say. Moreover, few studies have addressed the influence of relationship and contextual variations on adolescent smoking rejection strategies.

Hops et al. (1986) used the verbal refusal responses of adolescents to 26 audiotaped situations involving social pressure to smoke in an assessment of the effectiveness of an intervention designed to increase refusal skills. Their coding scheme contained nine response categories: refusals, health facts, conciliatory/supportive, excuses/change of subject, withdrawal statements, assertive, aggressive, external consequences, and acceptance. They found that adolescents who were favorably disposed to smoking and who were current smokers did worse than others in terms of use of refusal skills taught to them. They found a preference across subjects (control group and experimental group) for excuses. The researchers suggest, however, that this may be due to the fact that excuses are more effective for turning down offers of cigarettes without alienating friends. The researchers did not systematically vary the nature of the relationship between the refuser and the person exerting pressure, so this conclusion is tentative. They did examine influences based on the sex of the offender and the level of pressure exerted by the offer. The analyses revealed no significant effects.

Schinke and Gilchrist (1983, 1984; Gilchrist & Schinke, 1984) tested the effectiveness of a skills training component of their smoking prevention program. They used videotaped role-play assessments of refusal skills. Confederate peers offered subjects a cigarette. Students who received refusal skills training performed better on a composite index of behavioral ratings than did students who received no program or information only without skills training. Using a similar procedure, Rohrbach, Flay, and Reardon (1989) found that refusal skill training increases ability to resist pressure to smoke and self-efficacy regarding refusal.

The current absence of a clear understanding of what adolescents are likely to say when resisting pressure to smoke and how relationship and situational factors influence their strategy choices weakens our ability to train adolescents adequately in resistance skills. From smoking-cessation programs developed for adults, we have learned that the strategy must suit the individual or type of individual and situation (e.g., Benfare, Okene, & McIntyre, 1982), yet researchers often rely on their own perceptions of adolescent interactions to determine the types of resistance skills to be included in school-based smoking interventions (Sussman et al., 1986). We need to know more about what adolescents feel comfortable saying when they want to resist pressure to smoke or take drugs. For example, is it likely that adolescents will walk away or just say no to smoking if their relationships with the people offering cigarettes are important? Are high-risk adolescents, who often do not adhere to conventional school norms, likely to adopt strategies advocated in that environment by people who may not understand the pressures they experience daily? Are different resistance strategies likely to be used when there are several people present rather than a few?

A study by Reardon, Sussman, and Flay (1989) begins to answer some of these questions. This study of 268 adolescents was designed to assess the compliance-resisting strategies children use when rejecting pressure from peers to smoke. The participants were asked to indicate how they would respond to eight hypothetical situations varying in relationship type (friend offering a cigarette versus an acquaintance), number of people present (dyad versus a group), and amount of pressure (first versus second exertion of pressure by a peer or peers). We found that adolescents do vary their compliance-resisting strategies according to differences in relationship to the persuader, amount of pressure exerted, and number of people present. For example, the study participants were more willing to use assertive compliance-resisting strategies when pressured more than once and when confronted by a group of people rather than by one person. We also found that high-risk adolescents, those most likely to smoke in the future, are less likely to use assertive compliance-resisting strategies than those adolescents not at risk for future smoking.

Compliance-resistance research has a place not only in health studies but in studies of superior-subordinate relationships, child-parent relationships, and many others. Returning to the Acme case discussed earlier, we may ask, What compliance-gaining strategies might resolve the situation? The culture of the company or department, relationship rules, and role expectations will guide the selections. Just as there are married couple types, there are types of coworker relationships. Prior research suggests that different compliance-gaining and compliance-resisting strategies will be adopted by each type. The ground has only just been broken in this area. Much research work remains to be accomplished. The result will be a greater understanding of how variations in relationships and situations influence the choices people have when resisting persuasive appeals.

KNOWING THE RULES

Part of being persuasive is knowing what to expect from others and what they expect from you given the situation. People share expectations for how conversation should be enacted. Frentz (1976) tells us that persons engage in five conversational or episodic phases for which we can assume they have certain expectations. Frentz's episodic structure appears in Figure 7.1.

Some episodes require that we conduct all five phases appearing in Frentz's model. The following discussion is an example:

Jane:	Hi, Jim. How are you?	*Initiation*
Jim:	Fine.	
Jane:	I'd like to talk to you for a few minutes.	*Rule Definition*
Jim:	Okay, but make it short. I have to get to class.	*Rule Confirmation*
Jane:	I didn't get the notes from class yesterday. Do you think I could borrow yours?	*Strategic Development*
Jim:	Sure, no problem.	
Jane:	I guess I should let you get to class.	*Termination*
Jim:	Yeah. I'll call you later.	

In a conversation with a telephone operator, not all of the phases are necessary. The rules are implied by the purpose of the call and, unless the caller deviates from them, there is little need to confirm their existence. Effective persuasion requires that we recognize the rules operating in the episodes and episode phases in which we are engaged. Structural rules exist so that we can avoid having to deal with superfluous demands. For example, in the following conversation we can see that the rule for appropriate operator-client conversation is shared by both interactants, despite the client's deviant behavior.

Operator:	May I help you?
Kathy:	Yes, can you tell me what time it is?
Operator:	We are not allowed to give the time.
Kathy:	Yes, I know, but my electricity went off.
Operator:	It is 12:35.
Kathy:	Thank you.

Initiation	Rule-Definition	Rule-Confirmation	Strategic	Termination
Phase	Phase	Phase	Development	Phase
			Phase	

Figure 7.1. Episodic Structure

Despite her deviation from the consensually shared rule for operator-client communication, the client obtained the desired information. She appealed to another rule, which is that under certain circumstances operator-client communication rules are not binding. The client redefined the superordinate constructs influencing operator rule selection to include "emergency." The explanation, "but my electricity went off," was apparently a sufficient condition for rule 1 violation. It provided an account for the violation of that rule and an antecedent condition for the implementation of rule 2 (the rule for emergencies).

According to Toulmin (1958), the logical form of an argument includes data (evidence), a claim, and a warrant linking the data to the claim. Claims may be accompanied by a qualifier such as "sometimes" or "probably." A qualifier may also have attached to it some exceptions to the rule. Toulmin's model appears in Figure 7.2.

If we were to fit the operator conversation into Toulmin's model, the argument form depicted in Figure 7.3 would obtain. This argument is stated in an unequivocal manner. No qualifiers are included. It is offered as a fait accompli.

Figure 7.4 demonstrates how the client attempted to render the rule in Figure 7.3 inoperative by incorporating an exception to that rule. Essentially, the rule depicted in Figure 7.3 remains intact. Only its range of convenience is brought into question. The operator's willingness to provide the time indicates that she considered the rule-exception claim legitimate.

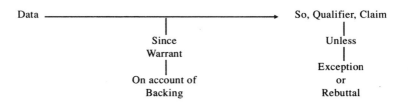

Figure 7.2.
SOURCE: Adapted from Toulmin (1958, p. 103). Reprinted by permission of Cambridge University Press.

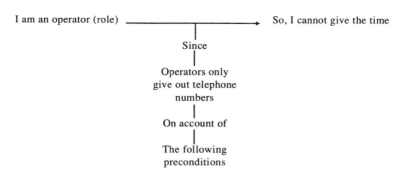

Figure 7.3.

From this example, it is apparent that knowing the rules is a precursor to using them as a means of persuading others. To the extent that an individual knows the rules and can create conditions rendering the strict interpretation of those rules inoperative, he or she can convince others to change their behavior.

Another example of how knowing the rules used by the persuadee facilitates persuasion follows. A valued employee may be unwilling to accept a transfer to another location because it would require removing his children from good schools and asking his wife to leave a good job. He may consider it appropriate for a good father and husband to think about the needs of his family before accepting a new position. His reasoning appears in Figure 7.5.

Assuming that you were this man's boss, how might you go about persuading him to accept the transfer? Some bosses would merely say,

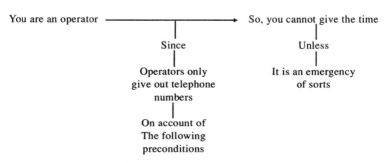

Figure 7.4.

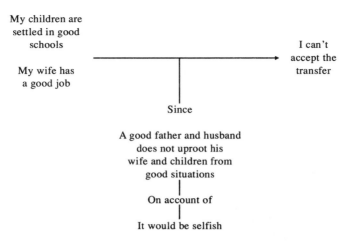

My children are
settled in good
schools

My wife has
a good job

I can't
accept the
transfer

Since

A good father and husband
does not uproot his
wife and children from
good situations

On account of

It would be selfish

Figure 7.5.

"Take the transfer or expect to go nowhere in this company." Others might try to find the weak point in the employee's reasoning. For example, a boss might argue that times have not changed that much, or he might attack the warrant by suggesting that good fathers also make sure they keep good jobs. A boss who is a compromiser might look at his employee's reasoning and find ways to assure that the children would go to good schools. He might call the other location and ask people where their children go to school. While talking with them, he might inquire into job opportunities for the employee's wife.

These are only a few of the ways that a boss might respond to the reasoning depicted in Figure 7.5. You may be able to think of several other alternatives. The value of knowing the data, warrant, and backing supporting compliance-resister claims is obvious from this example. It is one reason listening to persuadees and asking the right questions is so important in persuasion. These actions enable the persuader to see where the persuadee's reasoning is weak or where he might change some aspect of the request (e.g., delay the transfer until the wife finds a job in the new location) or add new data (e.g., inform the employee of the existence of private schools in the new location and offer him a salary increase to make it possible for his children to attend one of those schools). In the absence of insights into how a persuadee reasons about his or her response to a request, persuaders must rely on their own assumptions about why the persuadee is not complying. The results can be disastrous.

There are also times when the reason for compliance-resistance is not so much logical as it is emotional. There are times when a persuadee simply does not like a particular persuader. It is possible for people to respond emotionally to requests for change merely because they see such requests as implying that their current behavior is inappropriate or ineffective. It is also possible for people to be protective of some idea or behavior and thus unwilling even to discuss the merits of change.

Few compliance researchers have attempted to deal with the role of emotion in persuasion although it plays a fundamental role in the majority of interpersonal persuasion encounters. All the listening in the world and all the dissecting of persuadee logic can prove worthless if persuaders fail to consider emotional barriers in their path. According to Friedman (1979), social scientists have been negligent in their nearly exclusive concern with cognition over emotion:

> Part of this overwhelming concern with cognition in emotion may be due to the fact that emotional reactions are affected by interpretations of the situation. If you do not know that a jellyfish or a dynamite stick is dangerous, you will not be afraid of one. However, it may also be true that the role of cognition is overstated for historical reasons. First, because of a familiarity with cognitive approaches to other aspects of social psychology, cognition may be stressed when examining emotions. Second, cognition may be emphasized because of an underdeveloped methodology with which to study the expressive aspects of emotion. But the idea that the best (or only) way to find out how someone feels is to discover what he or she thinks strictly limits our approach to the emotional side of social life. The notion of nonverbal skill, however, opens up a new road to investigating questions of emotional reaction and expression. (p. 5)

While Friedman's explanation for our "overwhelming concern" with cognition may be accurate, it may also be true that our general disregard for emotional states is due more to the low value our society ascribes to emotional reactions. People spend most of their daily lives in structured environments where emotional reactions are treated as reflections of weakness and as dysfunctional to productivity. We prefer to think of ourselves as rational, not emotional. The truth is that we are emotional and that cognitions and emotions are intrinsically related. Buck (1975) explains:

The impact of the affective stimuli is felt at both a cognitive and a physiological level. On the cognitive level, the individual understands and interprets the stimuli on the basis of his past experience and present social role. On the physiological level, his nervous and endocrine systems work to adapt the body to the changed circumstances created by the affective stimuli. The cognitive and physiological responses interact with one another: the subjective experience of one's physiological reaction is an important source of information for the cognitive interpretation of the situation, and that cognitive interpretation itself may come to require bodily adaptation. (p. 7)

There is even some evidence to support the belief that when a person cannot cognitively comprehend the experience of another human, he or she can emotionally experience it. For example, people can experience a "sympathetic induction of emotion" (McDougall, 1908) in which they feel the emotions they perceive in others. Whether thought precedes or succeeds sympathy is very difficult to determine. Friedman's (1979) definition supports the latter interpretation: "Broadly construed, sympathy refers to the instinctually based ability of people immediately to experience the emotions of others" (p. 8). In this way Friedman differentiates compassion (the synonym for the common usage of the term *sympathy*) from sympathy, which he, following Darwin (1965), views as the basis for intimacy.

Given these important links among emotion, cognition, and behavior, it seems implausible that persuasion could occur in any face-to-face situation without some involvement of nonverbal communication. It is part of the perceived reality of both persuader and persuadee.

Perhaps one area of investigation that truly illustrates the importance of nonverbal communication to social interaction is the study of gender effects in decoding and encoding nonverbal behavior. An extensive review of nonverbal decoding literature by Judith Hall (1978) indicates a female advantage (unaffected by age), with the qualification that it "is not, however, a large difference" (p. 854).

Rosenthal and DePaulo (1979) examined literature on sex differences in social interaction and concluded that while women are superior to men in detecting intended, controllable nonverbal cues, they lose this ability as the cues become more revealing of true feelings: "As women mature, those who tend to focus on the positive or 'good' in the nonverbal cues of others may tend to become less accurate decoders of nonverbal cues and more especially so as these nonverbal cues become less intended, less controllable, or more leaky" (p. 97). Thus, while women are superior to males in their decoding of clear, nondeceptive behavior, they lose this advantage as ambivalence and deception increase. It appears that women interpret these cues as the deceiver wants them to be interpreted, suggesting that females are more interpersonally accommodating than males.

In some cases, the best way to deal with emotional impasses is to drop the subject and come back to it another time. If a persuader has the ability to listen effectively and respond with empathy, it can be useful to address the emotional issue. In any case, emotions cannot be totally ignored. They can be used to facilitate persuasion, as advertisers know so well, or they can stand in the way of reasoned arguments by distracting the persuadee.

Given the complexity involved in gaining compliance, there are a number of steps that should be undertaken to facilitate effectiveness. The following steps can guide persuaders in identifying issues that must be considered in the process of interpersonal persuasion:

(1) Identify your own and the persuadee's reasoning (claim, data, warrant, backing).

(2) Listen and identify similarities of reasoning as well as differences.

(3) Reduce emotional impasses by postponing discussion, expressing empathy for persuadee emotional reaction (e.g., "I reacted the same way when I heard . . . ") or by emphasizing similarities between your own and persuadee's emotions or logic, thereby creating a common ground.

(4) Locate weakness in persuadee logic or offer alternatives that make the proposal more attractive (e.g., as in the employee transfer example, locating good schools at the proposed transfer location).

(5) Select a strategy. Options include (a) discuss weakness in persuadee logic; (b) demonstrate inappropriateness, inconsistency, and/or ineffectiveness of the persuadee's current behavior; (c) demonstrate how persuadee logic is not very different from your own; and (d) compromise.

(6) Involve persuadee in the resolution.

(7) Select a style appropriate to the relationship and situation.

(8) Obtain commitment to change or to consider change.

(9) Follow up.

Step 6, involving the persuadee in the resolution, is important. Self-persuasion facilitates private acceptance of what the persuader is advocating rather than simple acquiescence. As research from counter-attitudinal advocacy suggests, it is possible for people to convince themselves to change if given the opportunity to consider and advocate views originally in opposition to their own. Simply telling people what they should do is not as effective as involving them in the decision.

Step 7, selecting an appropriate style, is also important to effective persuasion. As discussed in Chapter 6, it is possible to speak in ways that increase or harm persuader credibility and/or alienate persuadees. Bosses who speak in a paternal tone to all employees may find a good many of them unwilling to listen and even resentful. Some may find a paternal style comforting, but applying it across the board is likely to lead to many persuasion failures.

Step 8 recommends obtaining some form of commitment from persuadees. Quit-smoking training programs often require clients to sign written contracts committing them to a future without smoking. Of course, this type of commitment is not always possible. In such circumstances it may prove useful to encourage the persuadee to commit to one step. In the employee transfer example, the one step might be to commit the employee to holding back his refusal until he has considered all of the boss's arguments or until the boss has had enough time to determine whether or not a compromise is possible.

The final step is one frequently forgotten by persuaders. American business executives are notorious for forgetting to follow up on negotiations. They often treat the verbal agreement to accept a contract as the end of the bargaining process. This lack of follow-up can be just as serious between spouses attempting to negotiate child-care or home management responsibilities. If you do not follow up by reinforcing each other and refreshing each other's memories, the agreed-upon behaviors are likely to diminish with time. When people commit to some new behavior or to changes in their current behavior, they must be encouraged to continue to engage in that behavior in the persuader's absence. Persuasion maintenance was discussed in Chapter 1. Step 9 refers to persuasion maintenance and points to its importance in achieving long-term change.

CONCLUSION

Interpersonal persuasion is a complex activity. The research, models, and strategy tips presented in this chapter merely scratch the surface of what it takes to engage effectively in interpersonal persuasion. When each of the people involved is capable of playing the roles of persuader and persuadee at any juncture in the interaction, it is difficult to plan ahead. This does not mean that there is no value to entering an interpersonal persuasion encounter armed with strategy options and prepared for the strategies likely to be used by the persuadee(s), but flexibility is required.

Researchers continue to study how relationship and situational factors impinge on compliance-gaining and compliance-resisting behaviors. This chapter has described some of these findings while recognizing that much remains to be done if we are to have a good understanding of how persuaders and persuadees select their strategies.

8 Persuasion in Organizations

A 1989 Columbia University graduate school of business study, involving 1,500 senior executives from 20 countries, focused on the ideal CEO in the year 2000. Following are some of the results:

(1) Of the respondents, 89% saw communication as a primary trait of effective CEOs of the future.
(2) A total of 98% considered "conveys strong sense of vision" a dominant trait of the successful CEO.
(3) "Communicates frequently with customers" was viewed as likely to double in importance by 2000.
(4) Persuading the best people to stay with the company was described as vital to protecting investments as competition intensifies.

The ability to communicate effectively is key in distinguishing between effective managers and ineffective managers. As discussed in Chapter 2, people are guided by their own schemata or constructs. The effective manager recognizes that people differ not only in how they view the world but in how they view assignments, rewards, reprimands, promotions, and their day-to-day responsibilities. The effective manager knows that his or her task is to manage employee perceptions. Doing so requires the ability to communicate and persuade. It means recognizing the existence of conflict and knowing how to deal with it. It means recognizing the importance of rewards and knowing how to use them. Add to these the ability to motivate employees to excellence and to encourage each employee to see him- or herself as an ambassador to the customer.

For those who deal with customers, effective persuasion includes identifying appropriate markets, developing effective messages, locating appropriate vehicles for conveying messages, and keeping ahead of the competition in terms of developing and maintaining customer loyalty. These are some of the areas of organizational persuasion to be covered in this chapter. It is impossible to do justice in a single chapter to the extensive research conducted in these areas; this discussion will skim the surface and attempt to provide an understanding of the important role persuasion plays in effective organizations. An examination of three models of organizational goal integration is presented first. Each model presents a different view of how managers and the people they manage interact.

THREE MODELS OF
ORGANIZATIONAL GOAL INTEGRATION

Organizations enter into relationships with their employees characterized by varying levels of goal integration. High goal integration exists when an organization creates conditions that allow its members to meet both organizational and personal objectives. It follows that to the extent goal integration is valued by an organization, self-autonomy will be valued. Moreover, to the extent that self-autonomy is encouraged, persuasion is likely to be reciprocal. Individuals will influence the organization and vice versa.

The Exchange Model

Barrett (1977) proposes the existence of three models of organization-employee interaction. The first of these he calls the exchange model. Organizations operating according to this model provide incentives to employees to increase productivity. They exchange money and social outlets for work. Barrett explains that this is an extrinsic reward model characterized by very little goal integration. What the organization does for the employee makes no direct contribution to the organization, and what the employee does for the organization makes no direct contribution to the employee. In the terms introduced in this text, the type of persuasion manifest in such climates is acquiescence. The employee relinquishes his or her own personal rules in favor of the organizational rules for at least the eight-hour workday. He or she experiences little encouragement to question the status quo. Any attempts to change the goals of the organization are not welcome; a relationship of mutual tolerance with unidirectional persuasion obtains. Certainty is valued over creativity.

In organizations using this model, the employees may engage in what McKelvey (1969) calls passive idealism or passive cynicism. Merton (1957) describes passivity as a preference to change one's expectations of the organization rather than vice versa. Idealism is characterized by positive sentiments toward the organization and a sense of control over one's career advancement. Cynicism is characterized by negative sentiments toward the organization and a belief that it controls career advancement.

If personal rules are important to an individual, having to relinquish them even for 40 hours a week can create cognitive inconsistency unless the employee engages in some form of rationalization. If the organization operating under the exchange model were to offer some hope for employee participation in the shaping of organization rules, such rationalization might be unnecessary. It does not. Therefore, employees are likely to justify their personal rule relinquishment by strongly disliking the organization but reasoning that the job provides the money they need to enjoy their weekends. This is an example of passive cynicism. Another possible rationalization takes the form of feeling very loyal to the organization. The incentives offered may be interpreted as indications that promotion is possible if the employee wishes to work. This is passive idealism.

The Socialization Model

The second organizational model introduced by Barrett is the socialization model. Organizations following this model operate from the premise that people can be persuaded to value activities that help the organization achieve its objectives. Departing a bit from Barrett's perspective, we may interpret this to mean that employees are expected to relinquish or revise those personal rules that are incompatible with the organizational rules. The persuasion characteristics of this model, then, are acquiescence and accommodation. Persuasion, as in the case of the exchange model, is primarily unidirectional. The organization is the persuader, the employee the persuadee. This does not mean that employee acquiescence and accommodation are devoid of the potential to persuade superiors that the employee is concerned about the organization and therefore worthy of promotion. On the contrary, research indicates that the extent of communication influence is usually related to perceived homophily (Alpert & Anderson, 1973; Byrne, 1969; Falcione, McCroskey, & Daly, 1977; Rogers & Shoemaker, 1971). Thus if an employee wishes to be promoted, his or her emulation of superiors loyal to the organization's objectives is likely to be of some assistance.

Barrett explains that the socialization model involves leadership by example. The superior who stresses the importance of organizational objectives, and with conviction calls for them to be pursued with diligence, can accelerate the socialization process. To the extent that superiors are successful at encouraging employees' private acceptance of organizational rules, they are likely to create conditions conducive to peer socialization. In this case peers also persuade each other to adopt organizational rules and so employee socialization becomes a vertical (superior-subordinate) and horizontal (peer-peer) process.

Reardon-Boynton and Fairhurst (1978) attempted to identify the rules operative in a military organization characterized by a socialization perspective in dealing with officers. The subjects in this study were U.S. Navy submariners of four ranks: ensign, lieutenant junior grade, lieutenant, and lieutenant commander. The researchers were interested in determining which message types these officers used in responding to a subordinate's, a peer's, or a superior officer's request for some time on an extremely busy day. It was assumed that consensus on the type of response in each condition would indicate the operation of an implicit rule provided by the formal context. As expected, these officers demonstrated greater rule conformity when responding to superiors and subordinates (the latter were students at the submarine school who were there to learn and get the attention that would make them good naval officers). In the peer condition, the officers felt comfortable calling upon their own rule structures to guide their behavior rather than any guidelines provided by the organization. It appears that the military organization accepts greater self-autonomy in peer communications, manifested in wider variations in response choice.

The Reardon-Boynton and Fairhurst (1978) study indicates that, at least in formal organizations, rules exist to guide behavioral choices. However, the focus on rules to some extent obscures the difference between roles and rules. The use of rank as a variable does account for role to a certain extent, but just how much that contributes to the behavioral choice is not clear. In short, a question that has rarely, if ever, been addressed in organizational research is the extent to which roles and rules interpenetrate to influence behavioral repertoire development and behavior selection from that repertoire.

The term *interpenetrate* is used here in a manner similar to Cronen and Pearce's (1978) treatment of it. They contend that to the extent two persons' rule sets interpenetrate (in the sense of being a "good fit"), coordinated management of meaning is facilitated. It seems likely, then, that role and rule expectations can also interpenetrate in the job context, to facilitate or inhibit job satisfaction. For example, if people's personal rules conflict with the role expectations their companies have for them, problems are likely to arise. Most people alter their rule sets to at least some extent to accommodate the job demands. The extent of that alteration defines the degree of rule-role interpenetration.

The following scenario describes a case in which your rules as an employee conflict with the role expectations you have for someone in your boss's position. In this case rule-role interpenetration was not established.

The Case of the Disgruntled Employee

Chris, your boss for over two years, has been seriously negligent regarding a response to your request for a raise. Several weeks ago, during a private luncheon, you and Chris discussed your dissatisfaction with your salary. It was one of several topics discussed at that meeting. Chris looked surprised when you told him of your dissatisfaction, but promised to "look into it as soon as I can." He also promised to get back to you soon.

Now you think those must have been idle words. You feel that Chris thinks you should be satisfied with the 10% merit raise and 3% cost of living raise you received a few months ago. The problem is that you were underpaid when you received those raises and you believe that your work should place you higher on the pay scale than the top one-third of employees. After all, the job is often monotonous and requires long hours. You never complain and your work is always on time and well done.

You realize that Chris became quite busy with a special project from the CEO shortly after your last meeting. You and other employees received a memo some time ago indicating that Chris would make time for each of you on an "as-needed basis." You consider your request to be exempt from this as-needed requirement because you made it prior to the time when Chris took on the new assignment. You have given him the benefit of some additional time, and you have not bothered him with additional requests.

Patience may be a virtue, but six weeks is a long time to wait for an answer. Yesterday you decided to take matters into your own hands. You wrote a memo to Chris's boss, a senior VP who reports directly to the CEO. In the memo you explained how offended you are by the fact that you are underpaid in comparison to others in the company performing similar tasks. You explained that Chris's lack of responsiveness to your request is an indication that the company does not intend to take any meaningful action to assist you. You sent a courtesy copy of the memo to Chris and to the CEO.

You have never gone around your boss before, but you believe that Chris had ample time to respond. You can't wait forever. Now Chris wants to meet with you to discuss your memo.

What are some of the rules and role expectations you have that led you to write the memo? What might be some of Chris's rule and role expectations that led him to delay in responding to your request? How might these rule and role expectations be made more compatible during the meeting with Chris? Is there hope for you in this company? If you were Chris, how would you start the meeting? What can companies do to avoid incidents like this one?

Some organizations facilitate rule and role alignment through training sessions and other less formal reminders of the importance of conformity. When this occurs, persuasion is mostly one-way, selling the idea that the job comes first and personal considerations second. In the case described above, Chris may choose to do this.

When employees see themselves behaving in ways consistent with job expectations, they may decide that such behavior is reflective of their own rules rather than those given by the company. To the extent that an individual does this, little demarcation exists between the self he knows on the job and the self he knows in other contexts. Perfect role and rule interpenetration is thus obtained, and this individual becomes very predictable, and, furthermore, vulnerable to persuasion by those who know the messages that will create in his mind the perception of inappropriateness or ineffectiveness.

Although most individuals do not totally sacrifice their rule sets for the good of the organization, it is true that employees like to know what is expected of them. Role ambiguity (Hamner & Tosi, 1974; Locke, 1968; Miles, 1975) and role conflict (Gross, Mason, & McEachern, 1958; Kahn, Wolfe, Quinn, Snoek, & Rosenthal, 1964;

Reardon, Noblet, Carilli, Shorr, & Beitman, 1980; Schuler, 1975; Tosi, 1971) literature and research indicate that job satisfaction depends on both knowing what others expect (role ambiguity) and agreement among those others (role conflict).

My colleagues and I have proposed a theoretical model of rule invalidation, a condition exacerbated by role ambiguity and role conflict (Reardon et al., 1980). We contend that a new job creates an uncertain situation in which old rule sets may prove inappropriate. We explain that people interpret the new environment and determine appropriate rules on the basis of that information. If the interpretations or rule sets are incompatible with the novel context in which the employee finds him- or herself, new constructs and new rules may have to be generated. This task is facilitated by a clear understanding of what is expected.

People who do not know what is expected of them are vulnerable to persuasion, since they have no baseline for comparison of information input. Also, such people have not established what my colleagues and I have described as the "rule invalidation threshold" (Reardon et al., 1980). People who have been at a particular job for some time establish comfortable sets of rules. The invalidation of those rules requires more evidence than the invalidation of newly developed rules. In Toulmin's terms, the data, warrant, and backing used to create rule-role discrepancy must be substantial when low levels of both role ambiguity and role conflict exist and toleration thresholds are well established. Under such conditions, people are relatively certain of what is expected. Convincing them that role or rule discrepancy exists is no easy task.

It follows from this discussion of rule and role expectations that one means of determining how effective a campaign to increase employee motivation might be is, first, to determine the extent to which employees perceive their personal rules and occupational roles to be compatible. The second step would be to close that rule-role gap through (a) providing accounts for its existence (e.g., "To get the job done right we sometimes have to put personal preferences aside"), (b) increasing incentives for role-consistent behavior, or (c) developing a program of workshops and seminars in which rule and role differences are diminished through employer role-expectation accommodation to employee personal rule expectations. More attention will be given to the relationship of roles and rules later in this chapter. For now, it is important to recognize their relationship as growing increasingly close as organizational socialization succeeds.

On the surface, this socialization of employees to conform with company policy appears quite useful. After all, a degree of certainty is valued in organizations, the very existence of which discourages self-autonomy. However, Alpert and Anderson (1973) caution that too much similarity can be dysfunctional to organization objectives. They consider certain dissimilarities to augment persuasion, and so they introduce the concept of "optimal dissimilarity" or "optimal total heterophily."

This preference for some dissimilarity over total homophily suggests that organizations that encourage only acquiescence and accommodation characteristic of the exchange and socialization models may actually inhibit progress. Perhaps these models are best utilized at some, but not all, levels of the organizational hierarchy. Organizations must locate their own balance of flexibility and rigidity. They must discover the optimal level of employee self-autonomy they can or must allow in order to function efficiently. The dilemma is one of balancing rigidity with flexibility to encourage innovation, an objective that the concept of organization discourages (J. D. Thompson, 1967).

The conclusion to be drawn here about the socialization model is that it is very useful for establishing the homogeneity organizations typically prize, but it can, if taken to an extreme, militate against innovation. The nurturance of certainty, and thereby prediction, is not always in the best interest of the organization. Instead, organizations might encourage high levels of communication competence so that they may deal constructively with uncertainty. Farace, Taylor, and Stewart (1978) describe competence skills as relating to "the employee's understanding of the communication rules of the organization, and his or her ability to work with (and around) the rules" (p. 287). They add that "competent individuals know how to 'cut the red tape.' "

The Accommodation Model

The third model introduced by Barrett (1977) steps beyond the unidirectional persuasion perspective of the two previous models to give employees some say in the shaping of organizational rules and goals. This is the accommodation model. The organization adopting this model operates as follows: "The needs and motives of the individual are taken as a given, and the organization is structured and operated in such a way that the pursuit of organizational objectives will be intrinsically rewarding and will provide for the simultaneous pursuit of the individual's existing goals" (p. 11).

This model encourages greater self-autonomy than the other models and thus creates a climate conducive to cooperation and coadjuvancy. Since the employees are included in much of the problem-solving, objective-setting, and decision-making activities of the organization, reciprocal rule revision (cooperative persuasion) and the generation of mutually satisfying new rules are overtly encouraged.

It is difficult to imagine an efficient organization operating under this model at all levels at all times. However, it is possible for organizations to be responsive to the personal needs of their employees. Herzberg (1966) advocates designing job roles to meet individual needs. And Argyris (1964) suggests the use of personality theory in the determination of job design. This high-level goal integration, while encouraging some uncertainty, discourages stagnation. The apparent risk here is that uncertainty generates communication (Huber, O'Connell, & Cummings, 1975) and thus increases the potential for conflict (Huseman, Logue, & Freshly, 1977). However, Weick (1969) suggests that uncertainty provides members with the motivation to engage in organizing behaviors. It appears that people tend toward certainty when confronted with high levels of uncertainty, and move to maximize uncertainty when too much certainty exists (Danowski, 1975). This perspective suggests that those large, conglomerate organizations that encourage management by confrontation between top-level executives from each subsidiary may actually generate organizing behavior through fostering conflict uncertainty.

Barrett's (1977) research indicates that the goal integration found in socializing and accommodating organizations generates positive results:

> Organizational units that rank high in goal integration also tend to rank high with regard to the amount of communication that occurs within them, the amount of influence exercised over the unit's activities by all levels of employees within the unit, the adequacy of coordination within the unit and between it and other units, and the number of innovative ideas that are generated for solving work problems. In addition, individuals who rank high in the extent to which they see their personal goals as being integrated with the organization's objectives also tend to rank high in their motivation to come to work and work hard, in their satisfaction with the organization and their job in it, and in their feelings of loyalty to the organization and commitment to its success. (pp. 98-99)

The research findings discussed above have some far-reaching implications for the development of organizational incentive programs and training. For example, if it is true that low levels of uncertainty and complete allegiance to a company's objectives, or what McKelvey (1969) refers to as "crusading idealism," are dysfunctional to creativity, then organizations that attempt to make the job both the core and the fruit of employee life may be doing themselves a disservice. In the mid-1950s, Robert Dubin (1956) addressed this issue. From his work he concludes that attempts to center primary human relationships in work are at odds with social reality. He points to Weber's (1947) position that impersonality and efficiency can exist together, provided there are other places in society where the primary social relations can be experienced. This suggests that organizations might spend less time attempting to persuade employees to become full-time participants in the "company team" and instead support community affairs and the nonwork activities of employees. This, Dubin suggests, might be a "more significant way to enhance attachment of employees to their company" (p. 141).

In terms of training, organizations relying on innovation should train their employees to deal constructively with uncertainty and the large amounts of communication it generates. Argyris (1962) considers interpersonal competence the best communication predictor of organizational success. Yet, many upper-level managers are not trained to deal with out-of-role behavior. For example, several managers with whom I have communicated indicate that they discourage any display of emotions. This preference for "rational" behavior may actually result from an inability to deal with emotions. Certainly our organizations cannot function efficiently if employees are encouraged to scream and cry at will, but such extreme emotional outbursts are usually the result of continually refusing to accept one's emotions as a natural and profoundly positive indication of being human.

The organization has long been the province of men, and men in our society are expected to suppress emotions on the job—a fact probably responsible, in part, for the longer life span of females. Some organizations have begun to respond to the emotional needs of their employees by employing counselors, but few companies actually train their employees to accept emotions as a natural way for humans to signal the existence of problems, rather than as a threat to organizational efficiency. More is lost in a blanket refusal to address the realities of human emotion than is lost in the small amount of time it would take to train managers to deal effectively with emotionality. If McGuire (1973) is correct in his belief that "we notice any aspect (or dimension) of ourselves to the extent that our characteristic on that dimension is peculiar in our social milieu" (p. 244), it is likely that employees who perceive their own emotions as "peculiar" in the job environment will spend much precious time attending to and controlling them. If they are free to accept them and even assisted in dealing with them, productivity should increase.

Research indicates that female leaders stress interpersonal relations, are more receptive to the ideas of others, and encourage effort more than their male counterparts (Baird & Bradley, 1979). Some managers have seen female sensitivity as an advantage on which to capitalize. Marion Woods (1975) found that male managers are discovering that women have a unique sensitivity that can be put to good use with important clients. Whether sensitivity and other "feminine" character-istics are actually exclusive to women, whether male-female differ-ences are innate, immutable, or merely the residue of social learning (Mischel, 1974), and whether these differences can be put to use in organizations is still unclear. However, considering that the number of women entering the work force continues to increase, and that organi-zations are likely to find themselves dealing with women as clients or as employees, we cannot afford to devote too much more time to research that tells us only that male managers have difficulty commu-nicating with females. It should come as no surprise that they do. Questions organizational researchers can answer for managers include these: How can the qualities that are uniquely male or female be utilized by the organization to achieve its objectives? How can the organization assist males and females in dealing with the stereotypes that encroach on their potential productivity?

MODELS OF POLITICAL RULE IN ORGANIZATIONS

An alternative to Barrett's method of categorizing organizations focuses on the political climate developed and maintained within them. Morgan (1986) argues that many organizations create conditions of political rule that conflict with the democratic society in which many employees live. In a democratic society, people are supposed to be free to express their opinions and be treated as equal. Many organizations encourage behaviors quite opposite to the democratic ideal. They are more autocratic than democratic. In such organizations power is held by an individual or small group. Persuasion occurs, but there are clear rules concerning who may endeavor to persuade whom.

Decision making is often reserved for the powerful, those who control decision agendas and processes. These people control what is talked about, who talks about it, and how it is talked about. They have the ability to avoid subjects or redirect attention so that issues threatening the status quo do not receive attention. Persuasion is difficult in such organizations unless one's persuasion purpose is in line with the needs of the people in power.

Persuasiveness within organizations where power is not widely shared requires an ability to become trusted by the people in power so that one can provide input in the form of written reports, verbal presentations, and/or informal expressions of opinion. When the people in power do not share one's value systems or fail to recognize the contribution one might make to the decision-making process, it may be better to find another job than to spend a lifetime engaged in fruitless attempts to have influence.

Some people obtain power by virtue of their valued expertise. For example, someone who writes excellent speeches may be valued by senior executives whose jobs require frequent public appearances. Such valued people develop webs of dependency around them. Others, even quite senior people, may come to them to obtain advice. To the extent that experts become indispensable, they also become powerful. Some experts retain power by refusing to share their knowledge with others. A computer expert, for example, might refuse to share some important knowledge with subordinates. In time, if experts also acquire the trust of senior management, they can exert considerable influence on decision making within their organizations.

Perhaps the best way to obtain an influential position when expertise or family ties do not provide it is the "friends in high places" approach. Few of us have been spared the surprise of seeing someone who is not particularly productive obtain a high position in an organization. "How did he do it?" people ask. He did it by being in the right place at the right time. He did it by nurturing relationships with people in power and forming informal alliances and networks. By trading help today for promises of reciprocated assistance tomorrow, experts and nonexperts alike raise their chances of holding power within their organizations.

Morgan (1986) explains that much network and alliance building in organizations occurs through chance encounters or planned informal meetings such as lunches. Others, however, are formed through project teams or advisory boards. Employees who gain influence by nurturing relationships are usually quite skilled at identifying opportunities that may lead to contacts with people in power. If they are equally adept at maintaining those relationships even as they move on to make new ones, they are even more likely to succeed. Too frequently people are not as adept at relationship maintenance as they are at relationship formation. When this occurs, the people who are no longer being courted begin to feel as though they were used. They may then use their power to make sure that those who used them never get power.

These are only a few of the ways that people obtain positions of influence in organizations. It is important to point them out because influence is not merely a function of knowing persuasive strategies. It is a function of how one is positioned with an organization and what one does to enhance that position. Persuasion is certainly not just "who you know," but skillful persuaders know that organizations are composed of people who have power. It is wise to know some of them and to have their trust.

NEGOTIATION

No matter what model of political rule an organization ascribes to, its people engage in negotiation within the organization and often between cooperating organizations. Negotiation is a popular means of making decisions and settling conflicts within and between organizations. Another term used in the research to describe some forms of negotiation is *bargaining*. Bargaining, like negotiation, involves attempts by two or more people to determine what each shall bring to and take away from a transaction between them (see Rubin & Brown, 1975).

Some researchers look at bargaining from a micro level. They explore how sequential behavior between negotiators contributes to conflict escalation or deescalation. For example, if both negotiators begin with cooperative styles and then one changes to a sequence of competitive moves, conflict is likely. The noncompetitive negotiator may perceive her partner to be untrustworthy and may respond with her own competitive behaviors. Competitive moves tend to elicit competitive responses even from negotiators who would prefer to be cooperative.

Putnam (1985, 1989) argues that treating bargaining as a series of strategic moves can falsely dichotomize cooperation and competition. The two may occur together in the same negotiation; in fact, they often do. Putnam argues for treating distributive orientations, which aim to maximize self-payoffs, and integrative orientations, which aim to maximize common goals or to increase total payoffs to each party, as complementary processes. The two processes work together to recast goals, redefine issues, and influence outcomes. In short, Putnam (1989) advocates an interdependence model of bargaining that treats bargaining development as the transformation of disputes through argumentation and debate on the definition, scope, and feasibility of proposals. At any time during negotiation the parties may focus on their own payoffs or mutual payoffs without sending the entire negotiation off in a positive or negative direction. Putnam (1989) argues for more research that clarifies how integrative and distributive orientations interact in the process of bargaining, since it is this "merger of opposites" that propels the process. Each negotiation outcome reflects degrees of integrativeness and degrees of distributiveness.

Pruitt (1983) has developed a category scheme of integrative and distributive outcomes. The following hierarchy is a modification of that category scheme, containing four levels ranging from most to least integrative (Putnam & Wilson, 1989, p. 122):

(1) *Bridging:* the creation of a new proposal. This consists of the addition of information claims, or interdependence, to the proposal that shift the focus and transform the initial issues, expanding the pie or increasing available resources and options for reformulating problems.

(2) *Sharpening:* meeting the demands of one party while reducing the costs and burdens of the other party. This involves using redefinition or language clarification to reduce opposition to the initial proposal and to reduce the opponent's costs; highlighting, clarifying, or redefining the original proposal to make it acceptable to the opponent.

(3) *Trade-offs:* merging concessions to create a package that would be acceptable to both sides. This often involves exchanging low-priority items for high-priority gains, logrolling, splitting the difference, finding some middle ground.

(4) *Win-lose:* adopting an issue as initially proposed or dropping an item from the settlement. Minor alterations could be made on the issue, but the settlement represents win-lose through acceptance or through rejection of the issue.

Like outcomes, specific strategies (e.g., being tough versus soft or problem solving versus competitive) and tactics (e.g., threats, information exchange, compliments) can be categorized as more or less integrative or distributive. For example, integrative outcomes are often linked with use of positive affect statements, initiations, agreements, exploratory problem solving, and other-supporting statements and conciliations, whereas distributive outcomes are linked to such tactics as putdowns, threats, irrelevant arguments, and negative affect statements (see Putnam & Wilson, 1989, for an overview). However, it is possible for each of the above tactics to serve both integrative and distributive functions. Too much conciliation or too many concessions can lead to low joint outcomes (Ben-Yoav & Pruitt, 1984). Threats, usually considered a distributive tactic, can force a bargainer to pay attention (Pruitt, 1986). Future research may provide more information regarding when and how strategies and tactics that appear to be integrative or distributive actually contribute to opposite outcomes.

The difficulty inherent in trying to place strategies and tactics in either distributive or integrative categories points to the complexity of negotiation. Negotiators differ in their adeptness in such things as providing support for their claims, understanding other negotiators' needs, listening to arguments and responding on the spot, recognizing how what they say contributes to the overall course of the negotiation, and knowing when to be tough and when to acquiesce. These are only a few of the skills that separate effective negotiators from mediocre ones. Each of these skills takes years to develop, and many organizational negotiators come to the table knowing what their companies or departments have to offer but bereft of the ability to convey that information persuasively. Graham and Sano (1984) see poor preparation as the root of American business executives' negotiation weaknesses:

> We don't teach our students how to ask questions, how to get information, how to listen, or how to use questioning as a powerful persuasive strategy. In fact, few of us realize that in most places in the world, the one who asks the questions controls the process of negotiation and thereby accomplishes more in bargaining situations. (p. 9)

In cross-cultural negotiations, Americans make a number of mistakes. They often go to the negotiation table alone. This is fine in some regions of the world, but in Japan being outnumbered or, worse yet, being alone is a severe disadvantage. Moving quickly to a first-name basis is another faux pas that can set negotiations on the wrong path. Americans like to downplay status differences and to become friendly. In Japan, status dictates how one should act at the negotiation table, what is said, how it is said, and who says what. In Saudi Arabia the seemingly harmless question, "How's your wife?" is viewed as an insult, because wives are not considered an appropriate topic of conversation as they are in the United States, where asking about a business counterpart's wife and/or family is courteous.

Add to these problems the fact that Americans tend to think that everyone should negotiate in English. While even the European Economic Community uses English as its negotiation language, there is something presumptuous about a foreigner who *expects* that to be the case. The American who apologizes for his limited French, German, or Italian, for example, may find her negotiation counterparts more receptive than if she merely launches into a negotiation in English.

Another cross-cultural negotiation problem for Americans is their tendency to want to get to the point as soon as possible. In most countries, negotiations begin with social talk and perhaps a little tea or coffee. In some countries there is a ritual exchange of gifts (Reardon, 1986), and in others there may be days of simply getting to know one another before serious talks begin. Negotiators who make round-trip airline reservations may find themselves scheduled to return home long before negotiations have even gotten under way. It is not unusual for a Japanese negotiator, for example, to ask an American counterpart when he intends to depart. Armed with such knowledge, the Japanese negotiator can postpone decision making until just before the American negotiator's departure. At that point the American negotiator is so anxious to make a deal before his plane leaves that he will agree to less than he might otherwise get from an extended bargaining process. The wise negotiator does not tell his counterpart when he is leaving, but says, "When our business is complete, I will make my plans to return. I hope to spend some time enjoying your wonderful city before my departure."

There are many more skills an effective cross-cultural negotiator must develop. Perhaps most important is a willingness to listen and learn, to put one's own schemata on hold, and to explore how differently one's negotiation counterpart views the world.

STRATEGIC CHANGE
WITHIN ORGANIZATIONS

Most companies find themselves at one time or another faced with having to convince their employees of the need to change philosophy, mission, values, rules, image, or some other aspect of the organization. Research on strategic change within organizations is a fast-growing area. Some researchers have focused their work on the differences between deliberate and emergent forms of organizational change (Mintzberg & Waters, 1985). Others have observed how changing organizations succeed or fail at realigning themselves with their environments (Ginsberg & Grant, 1985; Gray & Ariss, 1985; Snow & Hambrick, 1980). Still other researchers have sought to identify environmental and organizational conditions that restrict or expand opportunities for strategic change (Aldrich, 1979; Child, 1974; Hannan & Freeman, 1977).

In an overview of theory and research, Greiner and Bhambri (1988) integrate a number of perspectives in their definition of strategic change:

> Strategic change involves a shifting interplay between deliberate and emergent processes that receive their relative emphasis under certain environmental and organizational conditions, leading radically or gradually to major changes in strategy (e.g., mission, product/market mix), and/or organization (e.g., structure, systems, culture, people), and which result in a realignment between the firm and its environment. (p. 3)

Greiner and Bhambri focus their discussion on deliberate strategic change involving a planned intervention by senior executives. They argue that the main initiator of deliberate organizational change is and must be the CEO. When CEOs are not predisposed to lead major change efforts within their organizations, the result is often failure of those efforts. Research indicates that externally recruited CEOs are more likely to initiate and lead change efforts than CEOs selected from within the ranks of the company.

Aside from a willingness to lead change efforts, a CEO must have power attributed to him or her by subordinates as well as by the board of directors. If the CEO is new to the company, this may mean bringing in a new team of senior executives. The downside of this route, however, is that none of them knows very much about the company. Another route is for the CEO to demonstrate his or her ability to take the reins of the company. He or she might improve profitability of the company or respond to employee needs.

In a recent study, my colleagues and I developed a schema for bringing about culture change in troubled companies (Reardon, Greiner, & Leskin, 1989). While working with one company (Company Y) in dire need of a change in values and strategic vision, we developed a "values implementation plan" that demonstrates what it takes to persuade an entire company to change its way of doing business. The following segment of that plan focuses on starting the persuasion process with senior management. This top-down persuasion style has proven useful in many successful culture change efforts (Greiner & Bhambri, 1988).

VALUES IMPLEMENTATION PLAN

This plan focuses on the initial stage of a "shared values" implementation plan for Company Y. Stage 1 involves working with the CEO and the senior executive team (a) to derive consensus on Company Y's strategic vision, (b) to develop a credo articulating a strong values-oriented vision for the company, and (c) to identify action plans for implementing these two interrelated visions throughout Company Y.

Issues of Concern

- A clear shared value system does not exist among employees at Company Y. At present there are numerous conflicts between stated rules and what is actually rewarded.
- Many employees perceive the existence of a "double standard" with regard to rewards and punishments. A lack of consistent guidelines results in different interpretations of the rules and who is expected to abide by them.
- Many employees have not received adequate training regarding their roles and responsibilities. Moreover, training has not kept pace with changing environmental demands.
- Company Y has suffered significant attacks on its credibility by the press, specific customers, and government representatives. The perceived need to be silent in the face of these attacks has resulted in a perception among employees and the public that the company has something to hide.

Company Y has enjoyed 50 years of accomplishment. It is now faced with an ongoing crisis not likely to pass with time. The public credibility of the company is at stake, which in turn threatens a strong relationship with its customers. At the heart of this crisis is the absence of a shared sense of core values that guide every aspect of the company's activity. The circumstances described above suggest that Company Y must create and adhere to a living credo that not only expresses a set of values but becomes the essence of everyday behavior among Company Y's employees. Preliminary reports indicate that the company intends to commit time and resources to the process of developing and communicating a set of shared values.

One key to success in values change is commitment of senior management. At the heart of this approach are two important perspectives: (a) Effective change must build on Company Y's existing culture, and (b) success depends on active involvement of all Company Y employees, beginning with senior management, who must establish role models for others to follow. As James O'Toole (1987) explains in his book, *Vanguard Management,* "A group will reject a foreign system of values the way a healthy body rejects a virus." A revolutionary change in Company Y's values could be disruptive, painful, and counterproductive. Company Y needs evolutionary change in values and in the way they are communicated to employees. It will be important to preserve aspects of Company Y's culture that are fundamental to its success. The proposed approach does not impose a foreign set of values but assists Company Y in creating its own value system—one that employees can live with and by at every level of the company.

Methodology

Interviews with Senior Management

The first step must be the gathering of data to be fed into the first retreat. Interviews with the CEO, all members of the senior executive team, and selected members of middle management and the Board of Directors are key. These interviews allow Company Y to accomplish the following:

- Assess perceptions of Company Y's current strategic vision and what it might become.

- Consider the existing value system as described by employees and reasonable expectations for change.
- Identify distinctive competencies possessed by Company Y to be considered in the development and dissemination of a system of values.
- Identify competencies that Company Y should develop to assure that values become a fundamental part of decision making.
- Examine the advantages and disadvantages of current reward systems.
- Determine the likelihood that team members are truly committed to changing the value system at Company Y.
- Explore perceptions of how executive team members might *visibly* demonstrate their own commitment to values.
- Identify obstacles to change at various levels of the company.
- Describe the communication climate at Company Y.
- Identify the type of leadership that can bring about needed changes.

Interviews of this type provide a number of benefits:

- The advisory team becomes acquainted with the leadership team to determine potential problems more accurately.
- The executive team is drawn into the change of values process even before the scheduled retreat.
- Time is saved. Prior to the retreat, areas of consensus, areas for further discussion, and areas likely to threaten progress are outlined.
- Key elements of a potential strategic vision and set of values can be brought to the retreat rather than using retreat time to start from scratch.
- Executive team members can begin to consider the roles they will play in disseminating a value system throughout the company.

Planning the Retreat Design

Prior to the first retreat, the advisory team should meet with the CEO. He is then provided with a chart of his team's perspectives on strategic vision and implementation of a value system. The design of the first retreat is then proposed and discussed with the CEO.

Using data from the interviews, the retreat begins with the development of a strategic vision statement. Values must be set in the context of the strategic vision. The question, What do we want to become? is a natural precursor to the question, How do we achieve our goals? Past research clearly indicates that it is simply not enough to educate people about values. They must understand how these values apply given their own goals within a business context.

It is important to articulate Company Y's strategic vision so that values are made a part of achieving it right from the beginning. If these processes are treated as separate, they continue to be so. A division between goals and process (values) threatens to undermine efforts to make values a part of everyday decision making.

First Retreat

A two- to three-day retreat should to be attended by all senior executives reporting directly to the CEO. The goal of the retreat is to develop a draft statement of strategic vision and a credo of values.

The retreat is introduced by the CEO, and the advisory team guides and facilitates the meeting. This permits the CEO to devote his time to being an active member of the team rather than having to focus on managing the process.

Company Y does not have a tradition emphasizing teamwork, so initial efforts must focus on achieving a willingness among team members to be a part of the values change effort. Progress during the retreat is judged according to how effectively the team reaches consensus on the statements of vision and values.

Everyone must be listened to in a collaborative atmosphere. All must be involved in drafting the strategic vision and the credo. Dividing the group into two or three "think tanks" to work with a first draft of the strategic vision is the first step. Each think tank then presents important elements that should be incorporated in a vision statement. These elements are synthesized by the total group into a working draft statement. After a strategic vision has been developed, a discussion follows, focusing on the implications of such a vision for development of a value system. Examples of how other companies succeeded or failed in their efforts to develop strong credos are explored. The think tanks reconvene to develop a Company Y credo. Each group reports its views to the entire team. A preliminary draft of a credo complementary to the strategic vision follows.

Group Meetings of Middle Managers

Selected members of the senior executive team take the statements of vision and values to three or four groups of middle managers, who read and discuss them. The groups assess (a) whether the two statements are ones they would like to see implemented, (b) whether additional changes are necessary to make implementation successful, and (c) whether the company currently falls short on the values described in the credo. Representatives from these second-tier groups may be invited to the second retreat to report their groups' reactions. In this way, two additional levels of management are already involved in the process and communication between levels has been initiated.

Second Retreat

The purpose of this retreat, to be attended by all members of the senior executive team, is threefold: (a) to report findings from the middle management group meetings, (b) to draft the final strategic vision statement and credo, and (c) to plan an action agenda for companywide dissemination of the vision and values. The following are questions that may be used to meet these goals:

- How will the company disseminate these views to the next level of managers?
- What changes must be made in the current communication system?
- What will convince employees that top management is committed to the new vision and values?
- What actions will encourage managers to feel a part of the change rather than recipients of it?
- Should there be retreats at the division level?
- To what extent is the top team still open to feedback? Are the new vision and credo etched in stone?
- Are the vision and values statements sufficiently concrete for employees to convert them to action?
- Is there a need for change in the structure of the company to assure congruence with the company vision and values?
- What leadership role will each member of the team assume to assure successful implementation of the new plan?
- When will the senior executive team meet again to check progress?

Management of Retreats

Between the two retreats and after the second retreat, the CEO is debriefed. Debriefings allow sharing of impressions, shifts in focus, and/or discussions of techniques for handling problems. After the second retreat, the debriefing focuses on how actually to carry out the goals defined and any additional efforts that might be needed to secure the cooperation of team members.

A task force of selected executive team members should be assigned responsibility for moving the process of strategic vision and credo dissemination to the next level of management. In preparation for this move, the task force brings the statements of vision and values to focus groups of middle managers. The focus groups assess the statement of vision and credo in terms of the likelihood of implementation throughout the company, obstacles to implementation, and methods for facilitating implementation.

Expected Benefits

After working through the phases described above, the following goals and benefits should be achieved:

- greater consensus and commitment of the senior management team to a strategic vision for the company
- agreement on the basic management and employee values that senior management will emphasize in behavior on the job
- preliminary testing of strategic vision and values with middle management
- clearer understanding of certain key aspects of the organization (e.g., reward, policies) that will need to change if vision and values are to be implemented successfully
- development and commitment to an action plan for implementing the strategic vision and credo

The values change proposal for Company Y demonstrates the level of commitment that must be obtained from senior management to achieve companywide changes in behavior. The persuasion process is, in such cases, incremental. Change does not occur overnight. At each level, from senior management to line workers, there must be a concentrated effort to obtain belief in the need for change and commitment to change.

The willingness of CEOs to take leadership positions in any companywide change process varies considerably. In a study involving 60 corporate leaders and 30 public sector leaders, Bennis and Nanus (1985) pursued leaders "who have achieved fortunate mastery over present confusion—in contrast to those who simply react, throw up their hands, and live in a perpetual state of 'present shock' " (p. 21). CEOs who achieve "fortunate mastery" share certain characteristics. One of these is a focus on outcomes, a vision to which they are so committed that others are influenced to get on the bandwagon. The second shared characteristic is the ability to communicate one's vision. As Bennis and Nanus explain, "Many people have deep and textured agendas, but without communication nothing will be realized" (p. 33). Effective leaders have the ability to organize and manage meanings for employees. They realize that good ideas do not sell themselves. They are unlikely to respond to a crisis with silence or to expect other people in the organization to do all the work in bringing about change. Leadership involves managing employee schemata about the company and creating shared schemata that encourage commitment.

Organizational Style

It is possible for leaders to desire effective communication with employees but to meet resistance from the system itself. Companies differ in the extent to which communication is encouraged. Courtright, Fairhurst, and Rogers (1989) explored two systems of communication within organizations. The first of these, mechanistic systems, involves a managerial "command style" in which communication tends to be one-way or "top-down." In such systems, great emphasis is placed on setting direction and defining limits to action; feedback and negotiation are less important (Weick, 1987).

In mechanistic systems, influence flows from the top of the organization downward. Mechanistic systems are also characterized by high levels of conflict. Competition for resources creates rivalry among the managerial ranks. Top management is expected to sort things out. According to Weick (1987), arguing is the main thing that goes on in mechanistic systems.

In organic systems the center of control depends upon where the expertise resides. There is no designated top management other than that defined by the task at hand. All knowledgeable employees contribute to decision making, and there is considerable emphasis on discussion and negotiation (Burns & Stalker, 1961; Weick, 1987). Self-management teams are often part of organic systems. Self-management is a form of participatory management involving employees in such things as selection of work procedures and work standards (see Manz & Angle, 1986; Manz & Sims, 1984). Communication in such systems involves much two-way interaction and greater use of advice by managers rather than commands (see Courtright et al., 1989; Manz & Sims, 1987).

It is easy to see that leadership in mechanistic and organic types of organizations can be very different. In fact, the entire process of bringing about change in culture, values, strategic vision, or policy is by necessity different in mechanistic organizations than it is in organic organizations. The change guidelines described above for Company Y were developed with a mechanistic environment in mind. Most companies in the United States are more mechanistic than organic, although attempts to blend the two systems occur. So the Company Y plan for bringing about a change in values is relevant for most companies. Bringing about such change in organic systems requires involving employees at all levels right from the start. Top-down persuasion might fall on deaf ears, so to speak, in companies where employees are used to a high degree of self-management. Such tactics as identifying opinion leaders within divisions and developing change-focused teams are likely to be more effective in organic systems.

There is one thing, however, that can be said about both mechanistic systems and organic systems with regard to effective change. Borrowing from Bennis (1989):

> The best-run and most successful companies in America do not think in terms of victories and defeats, or shining moments, or last-minute saves, and do not count on regulations or referees. Instead, they think in terms of staying power, dedication to quality, and an endless effort to do better than they have done . . . and they see change as their only constant, count on their own ability to adapt to the world, rather than expecting the world to adapt to them. (p. 100)

THE SKILL SIDE OF
PERSUASIVE LEADERSHIP

Bringing about change of any type within organizations requires attention to leadership. This includes leadership at various levels within the organization. Research indicates that leadership is a skill that is learned through actual experience and that the most critical aspect of this skill is interpersonal competence. McCall, Lombardo, and Morrison (1988) found that some of the toughest leadership situations are those that require getting others to do things when they do not have to and may not want to do them. Three general project/task force assignments were described by the executives in their study as particularly challenging: trying out new ideas or installing new systems, negotiating agreements with external partners, and troubleshooting a problem-filled situation such as a major accident or plant closing. Such challenges teach executives how to handle ignorance (which is often difficult for a technical or functional expert) and how to get others to cooperate when one has no authority over them.

McCall et al. (1988) also found that effective managers tend to learn during the early phases of their careers that, while they may need to be tough, they also need to be persuasive. Research by Bies, Shapiro, and Cummings (1988) supports this view. These authors found that bosses who provide subordinates with accounts or excuses for refusing a request often mitigate conflict-inducing responses from them. Of course, bosses vary in their abilities to provide reasonable and credible accounts for their actions. Bies et al. found that the boss's sincerity in communicating the causal account and the adequacy of the reasoning supporting the causal account influenced the emotional responses of subordinates. When a boss and subordinate disagree on the "real reason" behind a boss's actions and cannot negotiate a shared understanding of the situation, causal accounts may actually exacerbate an already negative situation, although employees may appreciate an attempt at providing an adequate causal account over no attempt at all. In any case, such research suggests that bosses who rely solely on their superior status as sufficient reason for refusing a request may be inviting defensive responses from subordinates, including complaints to the boss's boss.

Considerable research attests to the need for bosses to recognize the value of employees. This does not necessarily mean that they must be warm and nurturant. It does mean that subordinates must sense that they are not easily replaced. Bennis (1989) points to Louis B. Mayer, the head of MGM studios during Hollywood's golden era, as a man who, while known for his tyrannical habits, knew the value of his people. He once said of his talented directors, writers, and actors, "The inventory goes home at night." He recognized that MGM's primary resource was its people.

Bennis (1989) points out that American business has traditionally seen its workers in an adversarial light, "as mere cogs in the corporate machine: necessary, perhaps, but anonymous, replaceable, and greedy" (p. 86). He argues that successful companies are not run like feudal estates in which workers are to be seen but not heard, but like round tables in which workers are expected to speak out and are assured of a receptive audience. To Bennis, the 1980s were not a good decade for American business because of the "elevation of obedience over imagination." By discouraging input from their employees, companies fail to instill commitment and discourage the kind of ingenuity that improves products and customer relations.

Persuasive leadership does not have one face. It comes in many shapes and sizes. The strategies that work for one leader may prove dysfunctional for another. But all effective leaders take an interest in their subordinates and provide them with something positive. They are not only willing to listen, but want to do so. They tend to learn from experience that *telling people what to do is not as effective as persuading them that it is the best thing to do.* They are not afraid to be persuaded themselves and value the skillfulness of employees who are able to make that happen. The persuasive leader is not necessarily the most articulate of his or her peers, but certainly one of the more attentive to the reasoning behind the actions of others and facile at using that reasoning to advance his or her perspective.

THE BUYER-SELLER RELATIONSHIP

We have all heard the phrase "The customer is always right," but rarely are customers treated as if they are right. Most companies treat their customers as if they are engaged in what has been described as a discrete relationship. Discrete relationships are manifested by money on one side and an easily measured commodity on the other (Dwyer, Schurr, & Oh, 1987; Macneil, 1980). In such relationships, there is nothing between the seller and the customer other than the transaction itself. There is little communication and nothing that could be called a relationship in the traditional sense. The customer in such an exchange is not compelled to return by the pleasantness of the experience or by some feeling of having been treated well. The only satisfaction derived from a discrete interaction is the successful completion of the transaction.

A number of researchers have argued that treating customers as if the exchange of money and goods is the only part of the relationship that matters is a good way to assure the absence of a stable customer base. Macneil (1978, 1980) describes more enduring relationships with customers as "relational exchanges." Relational exchange participants develop a history over time with regard to their interactions. This history becomes the basis for future collaboration. More than one party may be involved, as in a negotiation. Obligations and promises may be involved as well, and efforts are made to develop trust and to deal constructively with conflict. As Dwyer et al. (1987) explain, "Relational exchange participants can be expected to derive complex, personal, noneconomic satisfactions and engage in social exchange" (p. 12). They add that such relationships can provide a competitive advantage. The potential for joint and individual payoffs is often significant. The seller benefits by having a reliable customer whose relationship with the seller is a disincentive to switch to another source of the seller's product. The buyer has someone he can trust to do right by him, and both derive social satisfaction from the association.

If relational exchanges provide a competitive edge, why is it that more sellers do not embrace this philosophy as a way of doing business? One reason is that the maintenance of relationships of any sort requires time and resources. Some sellers are simply not skillful at developing long-term relationships. Others do not see that the rewards outweigh the costs. Moreover, the characteristic emphasis on the "bottom line" discourages some sellers from taking time to focus on the future rather than on short-term profits.

Just as it is impossible, to say nothing of undesirable, to establish friendships with everyone you meet, it can be said that it is unnecessary for sellers to invest time and energy in every customer relationship. The decision to invest in one's customers may require an analysis of long- and short-term benefits. Customers might be grouped according to the advantages they bring to the seller. After all, American Express does not offer everyone a platinum card. Or sellers may decide how each group of customers might be treated well, with special incentives for long-term relationships given to customers who clearly bring more benefits than costs. In this way all customers are treated well while special customers are given even greater incentives to continue doing business with the seller.

The McKay Envelope Company trains all of its salespeople to learn as much as they can about their customers. They are encouraged to keep notes on each customer's interests and to show regard for those interests. For example, if a salesperson knows that one of her customers likes tennis, she might take a few minutes to send him a copy of a program from a tennis tournament that he was unable to attend. There is no doubt that such attention to customers takes time and effort. There is also no doubt that such efforts have payoffs. The McKay Envelope Company is quite successful, and the CEO attributes much of that success to paying attention to customers (McKay, 1988). In persuasion terms, there are few things as powerful as a favorable history when attempting to influence someone in the present.

CUSTOMER INFLUENCE STRATEGIES

Chapter 7 discussed interpersonal persuasion strategies and the research currently being conducted to increase our understanding of how people select among them. A similar body of research exists in marketing. It focuses on the coercive and noncoercive strategies used by company representatives (salespeople or dealers) to influence customers to purchase products or dealers to sell more products. This research is of particular interest in an era when the ethics of typical business conduct are frequently questioned.

In a study of how manufacturers of automobiles influence dealers, Frazier and Summers (1986) attempted to determine whether the powerful position of these manufacturers encourages them to use coercive or noncoercive strategies. Most research supports the view that power corrupts and leads to exploitation (Dwyer & Walker, 1981; Robicheaux & El-Ansary, 1975; Wilkinson & Kipnis, 1978). Other research suggests that power can facilitate coordination in exchange relationships (Blau, 1964; Stern, 1969; Stern & Heskett, 1969). Frazier and Summers identify six influence strategies used frequently by manufacturers' sales representatives. Among these are both coercive and noncoercive strategies:

(1) threat strategy
(2) legalistic plea strategy
(3) promise strategy
(4) request strategy
(5) recommendation strategy
(6) information-exchange strategy

The researchers found that the manufacturers in their study tended to avoid coercive strategies. They used them only when other types of influence strategies failed. They found that dealers were less satisfied with coercive manufacturers and more likely to be considering switching suppliers or going into a different type of business when manufacturers were coercive. Moreover, dealers reported that manufacturers who resorted to coercive influence strategies were less accommodative. On the other hand, use of noncoercive strategies such as information exchange and request are related to increases in dealer satisfaction and positive perceptions of manufacturers.

Training employees to use effective strategies with dealers and other customers can be accomplished by internal marketing of a customer orientation (Enis & Reardon, 1989; Reardon & Enis, 1990). Internal marketing involves encouraging each employee to define his or her job in terms of how it serves customers. Sometimes customers are other organizations, other departments within the same organization, or people who purchase the product made by the company. In all cases, each employee focuses on what improvements he or she might make to enhance customer satisfaction.

American companies are often criticized for their lack of attention to customers. They focus on the bottom line, often forgetting the people most responsible for raising or lowering it—customers. Many scholars argue that the Japanese have outpaced American companies because they attend to customer needs. Companies that focus on customers, set up reward systems that encourage employee attention to customers, and train employees to serve customer needs may have become rare in the United States, but this philosophy is still what separates quality-oriented companies from simply profit-oriented ones. It is also, in most cases, a philosophy that leads to profits.

CONCLUSION

This chapter has focused on a number of persuasion-relevant aspects of organizational life. Whether the focus is on individual change or on changing an entire organization, the person or people to be changed must choose to do so. The role of the change agent is to find ways to elicit the desire to change—to make change rewarding. The typical American organization is not well suited to this challenge. Most U.S. firms are mechanistic in orientation and committed more to the illusion of participative management than to its actuality, and employee motivation is hard to come by in these organizations. This lack of motivation often translates into nonchalance about quality and inattention to customer needs. Perhaps the 1990s will not be characterized by what Bennis describes as the "elevation of obedience over imagination" that was prevalent during the 1980s. Time will tell.

9 *Persuasion and the Mass Media*

It is obvious from the discussions in previous chapters that all forms of communication influence and even shape who we are as well as what we wish to be. The mass media, however, are our most pervasive forms of communication. For this reason they have been the target of much criticism, both deserved and exaggerated. Common complaints are that the media do not reflect our lives accurately, that they degrade the taste of the masses, and that they encourage people to do things they would otherwise not consider.

Horace Newcomb (1979a) suggests that this negativism, toward television in particular, has restricted the development of a critical climate. Very few careful descriptions of television programs exist. Instead, most serious commentaries focus on the audience and thus deny television properties of its own. Furthermore, television is usually condemned for what it is not rather than for what it is, or, Newcomb adds, for what it might become. Television is therefore perceived as an intruder in our culture.

According to Newcomb, the result of unquestioned negativism and fear is a mass audience that has little of the respect for television that it has for books. Because there is little if any disagreement among audience members concerning the negative attributes of television, there is little if any need to develop counterarguments. The mass audience, then, is an uncritical audience and, as such, is left at the mercy of those who are willing to manipulate it.

Researchers have done little to contradict this negativism. They, like the mass audience to which they belong, have already passed sentence on television. Certainly, there are studies that indicate that television can make positive contributions, but assumed negativism predominates in this arena too. It would appear, then, that when it comes to television humankind has shirked its responsibility through an uncritical acceptance. What we need are critiques of the cultural or contextual milieu of television. Perhaps, like books, television is to become a repository of cultural heritage, whether respected or abhorred. In any event it is necessary that we attempt to integrate mass communication theory and research in a fashion that will facilitate the active analysis of television. Its popularity alone supports this proposition. For all the negativism, television is one of the most popular communication media ever experienced by our culture.

THE MASS AUDIENCE

The concept "mass media" has been accused of being misleading and pernicious because it implies that the audience is an "undifferentiated, inert aggregate, and thus ignores the varied and specific forms of social interaction" (Corner, 1979, p. 27). Corner summarizes these criticisms as follows:

(1) The concept unquestioningly inherits the notions concerning large-scale, homogeneous groupings from the mass society theorists.
(2) In doing so it also and necessarily assumes that the masses are "inherently stupid, unstable, easily influenced."
(3) It limits communication studies to "a few specialized areas like broadcasting and the cinema and what it miscalls popular literature."

Corner contends that these criticisms are addressed to the weakest meaning of *mass,* and he is convinced that this weak meaning has not "overtaken us or prevented our attending to variation and complexity" (p. 28). He points to the "uses and gratifications" approach (which specifies why people use mass media) as one that, while maintaining "mass" in its formulations, has stressed the activity of audience members rather than their passivity. The most cogent of Corner's arguments is his interpretation of the adjective *mass* as applying to the communication system rather than to the audience. He explains that "such a usage importantly differentiates 'mass communication' from 'mass culture,' a notion which is harder to defend in terms of a specifiable process."

Mass media infrequently require of us immediate responses that are visible to other people. Behavior can be postponed. Advertising, for example, may not create a need or generate a response for weeks after the initial message is delivered. The demands that media place on us, then, are much less immediate than most interpersonal forms of communication. Also, if we do not like what we are reading or viewing, termination of our interaction with most media can occur without anyone being the wiser. In this sense there is more choice involved in our relationships with media than in our interpersonal relationships. It is gauche, at best, to walk away from a conversation. An account, such as "I have to run. My meeting is in five minutes," is usually required. This perspective stands in opposition to the argument that media shape us without providing us a means of escape. Even in our interactions with media we are choice makers, and one does not need "50 ways" to leave a media relationship. Merely walking away often suffices.

Despite this apparent freedom to leave the media relationships we have established, it appears that most of us prefer to remain in those relationships. Functional theories, such as uses and gratifications, suggest that we do so to meet a variety of needs. Mass media can provide company to the lonely, vicarious pleasure to the overworked, compliments to the person with a low self-image, otherwise unobtainable knowledge to the curious, and simple entertainment. They are less demanding than most of our friends and colleagues and are more easily accessible. Is it any wonder, then, that so many people rely on the media? On the contrary, one might wonder how they ever tear themselves away.

Michael Novak (1977) suggests that television is "the molder of the soul's geography" (p. 41). He explains that it builds incrementally a psychic structure of expectations. If this is true, the lack of a demand for immediate response from the audience does not in any way indicate that it is not being influenced. The influence may be just as far-reaching as that of interpersonal communication, although the effects may not become obvious for some time. While it is true that interpersonal communication episodes, if repeated over and over, have the potential to shape the attitudes and behaviors of interactants, the reciprocal nature of such interactions requires that the participants verbally or nonverbally commit themselves to some position in relation to the subject at hand. As discussed in Chapter 6, when people are opposed to a certain perspective and realize that they may be required to make some statement, they will create counterarguments. What of media participants, who know that they will not be required to respond in any overt manner? They are uncritical participants. Thus they are vulnerable to persuasion.

THE CHALLENGE OF
MASS COMMUNICATION

In Chapter 7, interpersonal interactions were differentiated on the basis of whether intrinsic or extrinsic rules were the primary force governing behavioral choice. As Corner (1979) indicates, the mass media audience consists of individuals who negotiate meanings just as interpersonal communication interactants do. The primary difference is that the mass audience members have what Schramm and Roberts (1972) refer to as a greater "latitude of interpretation and response":

> Characteristics of the mass communication situation, such as the receiver's freedom from many of the social constraints which operate in interpersonal communication, greatly attenuated feedback, and lack of opportunity to tailor messages for specific people allow any individual receiver a good deal more latitude of interpretation and response than he has when speaking face-to-face with friend, colleague or acquaintance. (p. 392)

Goffman (1967) considers every face-to-face interaction a situation that places the interactants in jeopardy. They risk losing "face." Each time we open our mouths to speak with others we risk possible rejection of our messages and/or ourselves. Because of this, most of us pay very close attention to the image we are conveying and protect ourselves from undesirable attributions by using disclaimers, aligning actions, accounts, and so forth, to lessen the impact and thus the impression imparted by our message. We choose our behavioral responses with the understanding that they will not pass unnoticed or uninterpreted.

Novak (1977) contends that television speeds up the rhythm of attention, thereby training the viewer to expect a certain fast-paced, multiple-logic activity in his or her interactions. Watt and Krull (1976) have demonstrated that the form or structure of media messages can have serious effects on the aggressive levels of adolescents. Their research indicates that "one could predict as accurately the aggressive levels of adolescents by considering only the form of the programming which they view as by considering the degree of violence in the programming which they view" (p. 107)

In terms of our relationship expectations, Novak (1977) holds that television portrayals of interpersonal relationships only "whet the appetite," in contrast to what real-world interactions provide, because television cannot tap certain depths of experience. As a result, it gives us a superficial perspective on human emotion. Furthermore, Novak explains, television does not represent the nation in terms of accents, cultural patterns, and so on. It is thus a biased medium. This bias, Novak adds, is exacerbated by the fact that television, as an industry, is run by intellectuals. As such, it represents the "educated class's fantasies about the fantasies of the population" (p. 50). To attract the attention of the population, these intellectuals celebrate two mythic strains in American character: the lawless and the irreverent. Novak suggests that this consistent celebration of the transgressing of inhibitions could actually lead to the collapse of inhibitions.

Before joining Novak in his indictment of television, let us take a few moments to consider Leo Rosten's (1977) perspective on this issue. Rosten suggests that we look not only at the medium as the source of evil, but at the masses as well. He explains that the deficiencies of the mass media are a function, in part at least, of the deficiencies of the masses. While it may be true that the media do not create an unlimited number of plots to entertain us, life itself has a limited number of plots. In terms of the lack of fresh talent, Rosten states that talent is scarce (p. 5). He adds, "Our land has produced few first-rate minds, and of those with first-rate brains, fewer have imagination; of those with brains and imagination, fewer still possess judgment."

Concerning the lack of first-quality material, Rosten replies, "To edit is to judge, to judge is, inevitably, to reward some and disappoint others" (p. 6). It is important to remember, Rosten implies, that the aesthetic level of the mass media is not geared to the tastes of the intellectual. As adverse to admitting it as the intellectual is, he or she is not a member of the masses. There is, Rosten explains, an "inevitable gap" between the common and the superior. The intellectuals, guilt ridden by the awareness that they are not members of the masses, do themselves great disservice because they dismiss those attributes of character that set them apart and make intellectualism possible.

Thus, while it may be true that mass media, and television in particular, could improve stylistically and respond to the needs of the population they serve, it must be remembered that they are money-making enterprises selling what the people want. This perspective implies that media are only half the reason for any problems they appear to create. The audiences that buy or view them are the other half.

The next section looks at the most popular models of television effects and their contributions to the negativism described by Newcomb.

MODELS OF
TELEVISION INFLUENCE

Newcomb (1979b) may be accurate in his contention that the negativism surrounding television has restricted the development of a critical climate, but the inescapable fact that mass communication research is characterized by a very low level of theoretical integration may also deserve some blame. McQuail (1979) suggests that this obvious neglect of theory is due to the demands placed on researchers for quick answers. He explains that research on the effects of television has been stimulated mainly by policy concerns. Broadcasters, educators, parents, and others have sought evidence to justify actions to protect "defenseless" audiences such as children. Theoretical integration has been sorely neglected.

McQuail also tells us that legislators, parents, teachers, and other interested parties regard themselves as experts able to see for themselves the influence of television and other media on the audience members. Under these circumstances, the scientist is reduced to a technician or fact producer. To please the self-appointed experts, he or she is often forced to work within a theoretical framework simple enough for the lay "expert" to comprehend.

Finally, television has the dubious honor of being one of the few social influence processes that appears to lend itself neatly to cause-effect explanations. Attempts to explain the effects of family, friends, school, or other interpersonal aspects of the socialization process are complicated by the realization that such experiences are personal and highly variable. Television, on the other hand, is viewed simultaneously by people across the county. It is thus one of the few sources of common experience and is often naively assumed to be interpreted in the same manner by all those who share in the experience. It has been difficult for those in a rush for answers to realize that people develop relationships with television characters in much the same way that they develop interpersonal relationships. The television character constitutes only one of two sources of relationship definition. In their attempts to identify the common source, researchers have often neglected the relationship. As McQuail (1979) explains, "The world of what happens between sender and receiver is too often regarded by the empirical researcher as terra incognita, dealt with mainly in terms of type of effect and conditions of content and viewer characteristics associated with such effects" (p. 347).

McQuail holds that there is no need for this vagueness. He adds that we do know enough to account for the effect processes we observe. We can get at the "why" of effects. A first step in this process is to recognize the difference between effect and influence. The latter refers to the intentional exertion of power over others, while the former refers merely to reaction or response of audience members. Since this book is about persuasion, the primary focus here will be on the intentional exertion of power.

McQuail describes four models of influence: information processing, conditioning or associational, functional, and relational. The relational model focuses on the relationship between the sender and the receiver of the message. This model is the most generally useful for explaining the effects of television on the "defenseless" as well as on more "prepared" audiences.

McQuail places considerable emphasis on the role of power in the relationship between sender and receiver. He explains that while the concept of power has restricted application in mass communication, given that the material rewards, physical force, and other motivational factors operative in interpersonal contexts are not available, its influence is not seriously attenuated. McQuail (1979) indicates that the essential point concerning power is that "the would-be sender of influence must have some 'assets' relevant to the needs of the receiver, while the latter must actively co-operate if the influence is to succeed" (p. 353). The first segment of this definition of power reflects the functional view of influence. As you may recall from Chapter 4, functional theories explain attitude change as a "function" of personal needs. Instrumental, ego-defensive, value expressive, and knowledge are the four functions discussed by Katz (1960). Certainly, having something that someone else wants or needs can be considered a position of power. However, it is the second part of McQuail's definition that separates the relational view from the functional view of influence. The sender and receiver must cooperate in this power relationship if influence is to succeed. People can and often do reject power. There must be sufficient motivation to cooperate. It is in the unveiling of this motivation to cooperate that the "why" of television effects lies.

Kelman's (1961) social influence perspective provides a rationalization for audience cooperation with the media. He suggests that there are three basic processes of influence: compliance, identification, and internalization. Compliance occurs when an individual accepts influence from another person or group because he or she hopes to obtain a favorable reaction from the other. Kelman explains that this person may be interested in attaining certain specific rewards or in avoiding some type of punishment. The particular behavior is not adopted because the individual believes in it, but rather because its adoption is instrumental in the production of some satisfying social effect.

Identification occurs when an individual adopts a particular behavior because it is associated with a satisfying self-defining relationship to the other person or group. In this way the individual defines his or her own role in the relationship in terms of the role of the other person(s). Pearce (1976) describes four modes of negotiation used in interpersonal communication that reflect Kelman's notion that an individual will adopt a particular behavior in order to participate in a relationship. Pearce's four modes of negotiation are invocation, ingratiation, creating shared experiences, and metacommunication. He describes these as means whereby coordinated management of meaning is attained. Like Kelman, Pearce assumes that the individual participates in a role relationship with another not necessarily because of some belief in the particular role content but because he or she wishes to meet the expectations of the other. This assures the continuation of his or her relationship with the other person or group. Unlike compliance, however, identification does involve both private and public acceptance of the role.

Kelman's third process of social influence is internalization. This occurs when an individual accepts influence because the behavior is congruent with his or her value system. Unlike compliance and identification, internalization occurs when the content of the behavior is rewarding. The behavior is adopted because it is seen as somehow integrated with the individual's particular orientation with regard to his or her world.

Kelman's perspective is introduced here because it is possible to construe mass media influence as a function of the types of relationships people establish with media. Often the media attempt to define the relationship, or at least set the parameters for its development. For example, some advertising has as its primary goal the compliance of its target audience. According to Kelman's social influence typology, the advertiser should attempt to link the product with the social needs of the persuadee. If, instead, the advertiser wishes to convince the persuadee that participation in successful relationships with, for example, the opposite sex involves the use of a particular perfume, then identification is the goal. The acceptance of this product is seen as prerequisite to the persuadee's adoption of a preferred role. If the advertiser has a product that can be seen as value supportive, or can demonstrate that the absence of this product somehow conflicts with the persuadee's orientation toward his or her environment, then internalization is possible. Kelman considers credibility of the change agent a necessary element in internalization. If the product is endorsed by someone the persuade perceives as possessing a value system similar to his or her own, internalization is facilitated. The credible source revises the persuadee's conception of a particular means-end relationship by suggesting that the endorsed product will lead to the desired end, or at least will function to increase its likelihood.

Kelman's (1961) summary of the distinctions among the three processes appears in Table 9.1. This table suggests that persuasion depends on the ability of the persuader to create (a) conditions that bring into question the persuadee's perceptions of what is socially rewarding, what constitutes a satisfying relationship role definition, or the means whereby he or she is adhering to a particular value, and (b) acceptable methods to solve this problem.

Kelman's model provides guidelines for the creation of appropriateness and consistency appeals. His social influence typology is actually quite consistent with the perspective on persuasion introduced in Chapter 5. For example, Kelman's "basis for the importance of the induction" is, in the terms used in this text, the persuadee's constructs, which together elicit an orientation that is primarily situation focused, role focused, or self-focused. Kelman does not discuss the rules such orientations generate, but his emphasis on antecedents, consequents, and behavioral choices implies their existence.

Kelman recognizes that certain conditions render appeals to context or role prescriptions potentially more effective than appeals to personal values. The conditions for change in Table 9.1 suggest that, should the persuader's goal be internalization (self-orientation) rather than compliance (context or other orientation), he or she must create means-end inconsistency in terms of the persuadee's values (or rules) rather than in terms of his or her desire for social approval.

Also consistent with the perspective in this text, Kelman's model implies the need for some familiarity with persuadees and their environments. For example, even if the persuadee is under surveillance by others, compliance may not obtain. Also, if the persuader refers to role relationships that are not salient or values irrelevant to the persuadee, identification and internalization will not occur.

Table 9.1 Summary of the Distinctions Between the Three Processes

	Compliance	Identification	Internalization
Antecedents			
(1) Basis for the importance of the induction	Concern with social effect of behavior	Concern with social anchorage of behavior	Concern with value congruence of behavior
(2) Source of power of the influence agent	Means control	Attractiveness	Credibility
(3) Manner of achieving prepotency of the induced response	Limitation of choice behavior	Delineation of role requirements	Reorganization of means-end framework
Consequents			
(1) Conditions of performance of induced response	Surveillance by influencing agent	Salience of relationship to agent	Relevance of values to issue
(2) Conditions of change and extinction of induced response	Changed perception of conditions for social rewards	Changed perception of conditions for satisfying self-defining relationships	Changed perception of conditions for values maximation
(3) Type of behavior system in which induced response is embedded	External demands of a specific setting	Expectations defining a specific role	Person's value system

SOURCE: Kelman (1961, p. 67). Reprinted by permission of Elsevier North Holland, Inc. Copyrigh 1961 by The Trustees of Columbia University.

The Kelman model is a relational model of influence. It does not appear to be power oriented. However, McQuail's (1979) definition of power as having some "assets" relevant to the receiver is implied in the model. It is the task of the persuader to convince the persuadee that some product or behavior will meet needs for social approval, social relationship anchorage, or value congruence. In this sense, a power relationship can be said to exist between the persuader and the persuadee. Mass media create this type of relationship with their audiences. Advertisements provide the receiver with information for facilitating social acceptance. Program content can teach people how to play roles that will allow them to participate in satisfying relationships with others. The news can teach people not only what to value, but also when and how to shift those values to make them congruent with those of significant others.

Cartwright (1971) has introduced a perspective on mass persuasion that, like Kelman's, focuses on the antecedent conditions and desired consequences perceived by the persuadee. Cartwright's approach constitutes one of the few attempts to understand what happens psychologically when someone attempts to influence the behavior of another person—the "why" of effect. Cartwright suggests that influence requires a chain of processes that are both complex and interrelated, but that in broad terms may be characterized as (a) creating a particular cognitive structure, (b) creating a particular motivational structure, and (c) creating a particular behavioral (action) structure (p. 429). These processes are comparable to the antecedent conditions, desired consequences, and behavioral repertoire of the rule model.

According to Cartwright, personal needs provide energy for behavior and contribute to the establishment of goals in a person's cognitive structure. These goals are achieved by appropriate choices from the individual's behavioral repertoire. Cartwright describes this relationship between goals and behavior as one the mass media can use for persuasion by showing that a behavior can bring about the desired goal. The role of mass media then becomes one of modifying or creating needs as well as providing the means by which those goals may be attained:

> It follows from these general observations about the nature of human motivations that efforts to influence the behavior of another person must attempt either to modify needs (and goals) or to change the person's motivational structure as to which activities lead to which goals. This means that a person can be induced to do voluntarily something that he would otherwise not do only if a need can be established for which this action is a goal or if the action can be made to be seen as a path to an existing goal. Little is known at the present time about the establishment of needs, but it appears unlikely that any single campaign via the mass media can actually establish new needs. (p. 438)

Although Cartwright does not specify inconsistency production as the means whereby goals and/or the ways of attaining them can be changed, he does suggest that a given action will be accepted as a path to a goal if it fits into the person's larger cognitive structure. If the persuader can demonstrate that the persuadee's typical behavior just does not "fit" with the expectations society has for him or her (appropriateness) or with some other more important personal rule (consistency), persuasion is facilitated. The next step is to convince the persuadee to adopt the persuader's proposal.

On this issue Cartwright provides some rules of thumb: The greater the number of goals attainable by one path, the more likely it is that a person will take that path. Second, the more specifically defined the path of action to a goal, the more likely it is that the particular motivational structure that would lead to the goal will gain control of behavior. Third, the more specifically a path of action is located in time, the more likely it is that the motivational structure will gain control of behavior. Finally, one way to set into action a motivational structure that has lain dormant is to place the persuadee in a position where he or she must decide whether to accept or reject the persuader's proposal.

Another model of media influence is media system dependency theory. According to DeFleur and Ball-Rokeach (1982), people are problem solvers seeking information to attain specific personal goals. They may need information to help them deal with problems of daily life or with specific problems, such as serious illness. People develop dependencies on media to the extent that they perceive those media as providing information relevant to their goals (Ball-Rokeach et al. 1984). Media dependencies influence the extent to which people allow themselves to be exposed to certain media or actively seek that exposure.

Media dependency varies in intensity as a function of personal goals, social environments, ease of access to media, and expectations regarding their content. People with strong social support networks who are seeking information about their own illness may find it unnecessary to develop intense dependencies on media for information about that illness. Friends, doctors, and other medical professionals may provide all the information the patient wishes to obtain. The extent to which the patient is an information seeker by nature also influences the intensity of his or her dependence on various media.

Kelman, Cartwright, McQuail, DeFleur and Ball-Rokeach, and others have suggested that we consider mass communications media as partners in relationships with individual receivers whose cognitive structures and motivations differ. This perspective places part of the responsibility for influence on the audience members. It shifts us away from the negativism that Newcomb considers dysfunctional to the development of critical viewing. It suggests that while media may have the power to "shape our souls," as Novak suggests, they do so only if we perceive that what they propose "fits" our cognitive and motivational structures. This does not mean that media cannot create needs. On the contrary, they probably do so quite often. However, they do so only if we choose to participate in relationships with them. The succeeding sections of this chapter look closely at our relationships with advertisements and programs and why they have the potential to influence our everyday behavioral choices.

ADVERTISING:
THE BLATANT PERSUASION

As indicated previously, it is somewhat unduly pessimistic to view ourselves as the unwitting pawns of mass media. However, just as the interpersonally competent individual has an edge when attempting to influence others, certainly advertisers, whose entire careers are devoted to determining what we value, have an advantage. They study our rule systems and develop messages that will convince us that what we desire can be obtained if we purchase the products they advertise. When our rules and values do not provide a path for such persuasion, they create for us what LaPiere (1954) refers to as "fugitive values." This term refers to the high priority or desirability we give to objects or behaviors because of their newness. Just as a disc jockey can make a song a hit by choosing to play it frequently, advertisers can convince us that some behavior is valued by society merely because we are repeatedly exposed to it in the context of a "fun" commercial. Nietzke (1977) suggests that Americans are obsessed with fun, that they need to have it or to experience it vicariously. Advertisers know this and realize that the association between a product and fun in the minds of audience members can create a market where no market previously existed. It is not necessary for advertisers to state explicitly, "If you want to be appreciated by gorgeous members of the opposite sex, use this product." Instead, they create for the audience an "array of cues" (Cox, 1962). These cues refer to price, color, scent, the opinions of others, and so on. The consumer is expected to use these cues as a basis for making judgments about the product. In this way the mass media create contexts for us and then tell us how to respond appropriately.

Cox (1962) has shown that the information value of a cue is a function (but not a simple function) of the predictive and confidence values assigned to the cue by the consumer. The predictive value of a cue is a measure of the probability with which that cue seems associated with (i.e., predicts) a specific product attribute. For example, if a consumer can be convinced that a particular car has high-quality internal components, he or she will most likely believe that there is a high probability the car is of good quality. This cue, then, has high predictive value. Confidence value is a measure of how certain the consumer is that the cue is what it appears to be. For example, even if consumers realize that high-quality internal components are indicative of a good-quality automobile, if they are unable to determine to their satisfaction that the automobile actually has such components, the confidence value of the cue is likely to be low.

Cox's perspective on how people evaluate products is consistent with interpersonal communication studies indicating that people will use the "best" information available to them when formulating impressions of others. Cox explains that perceiving information value as a function of two different and independent dimensions indicates not only that it is not a simple additive or multiplicative function of predictive value, but that often highly predictive value information will not be used merely because the consumer has low confidence in it. On the other hand, low value information (in terms of prediction) may be overutilized because its confidence value is high. Eagly, Wood, and Fishbaugh (1980) conducted a study in which one group of subjects was given information only about the sex of an individual, while another group was given information about both the sex and the job position of the individual. The group receiving only sex information used that information to judge the individual, but the group that had what one would assume to be higher predictive and confidence value information ceased to use sex information. It appears that sex does function as a status characteristic because in real life it correlates with status. It therefore has sufficient predictive and confidence value to be used as a status cue unless higher value information is available.

It seems feasible to assume that similar cognitive functions occur when an individual is attempting to judge a product instead of another individual. Persuaders must determine what constitutes high predictive and confidence value cues for their target groups, given the particular product.

Cox (1962) suggests that the marketer's ability to change the image of a product or brand depends on how well he or she uses two main strategies:

> He may alter the characteristics of dominant cues, and/or he may alter the information value of the cues in the array in order to make some cues more (or less) dominant or to alter the nature of cue-attributed associations. To the extent that he can (a) identify dominant cues, and (b) specify the factors which will alter the information of a cue, his job will be that much easier, and his efforts that much more effective. (p. 421)

Cox focuses on an approach to persuasion similar to that introduced in Chapter 4: demonstrating the inaccuracy of superordinate constructs. For example, altering the dominance of cues in the array is actually fiddling with the consumers' construct systems. If, as Cox points out, the consumer interested in purchasing a high-quality speaker for a new stereo system still considers size of the speaker to be the dominant cue, the persuader must determine which approach might alter that anti-quated cue hierarchy. He or she might decide to appeal to the "common knowledge" that "good things come in small packages," or might demonstrate that technology has advanced to the point where small calculators are even more efficient than their larger predecessors, and the same is now true of speakers. In essence, the persuader must show the consumer that his or her present construct system for the evaluation of speakers is inaccurate. Once the persuader has successfully con-vinced the potential buyer of the superior predictive value of factors other than size, it becomes necessary for him or her to increase the confidence value of those cues by comparing speakers that lack what the persuader considers dominant cues with those speakers possessing those attributes. If the persuader then recognizes that the desired con-sequences of the consumer are good sound quality and a fair deal, he or she can imply or explain that buying the less expensive brand would constitute the application of an inappropriate rule, given the new con-structs and these desired consequences.

This does not appear difficult until one considers that, in contrast to the one-on-one sale of a product, the mass media disseminate informa-tion to large audiences whose members may be at different points in the process of influence. What is meant here by the term *process of influ-ence* is similar to what marketers refer to as the *hierarchy-of-effects model.* Advertising messages, for example, can influence one or more of several response stages. The typical sequence is awareness, comprehension, conviction, and action (Ray, 1973). Ray suggests that these stages can be subsumed under one of three major levels: cognitive, affective, and conative. He contends that the important question is whether cognitive precedes affective and conative or some alternative formulation is appropriate. Ray points out that there is sufficient evidence in marketing research to indicate that learning or cognitive response is often not a measurable precedent to either affect (evaluation) or conation (behavior). Similarly, as discussed in Chapter 4, the affective-conation (attitude-behavior) relationship has received much criticism over the last 50 years of attitude research.

Ray suggests that, in lieu of discarding this hierarchy-of-effects model altogether, we consider the possibility that all marketing situations can fit one of three response orders: (a) the learning hierarchy (cognitive-affective-conative), (b) the dissonance-attribution hierarchy (conative-affective-cognitive), and (c) the low-involvement hierarchy (cognitive-conative-affective).

Ray indicates that the learning hierarchy occurs when the audience is involved in the topic of the campaign and when there are clear differences among alternatives. He suggests that diffusion of innovation research provides the best illustration of this type of situation. Exceptions to this order, which often occur because of varying availability of the mass media, demonstrate behavior change prior to affective or cognitive changes. These situations are explained by the dissonance-attribution hierarchy. This hierarchy assumes that a choice from among undifferentiated alternatives is made through some nonmass media source, followed by attitude and cognitive responses to that choice. Finally, the low-involvement hierarchy is based on the notion of almost unlimited effect on the cognitive variable because audience members either do not care or are not involved. In such situations there is very little perceptual defense against advertising messages, and so, after much repetition of the message, the advertiser can alter the conative and later the affective responses of the audience members (see also Krugman, 1965).

It is often difficult for advertisers to determine which hierarchy level best reflects a particular audience. The amount of interpersonal interaction with respect to a particular type of product prior to a new message about that product is often impossible to determine. In such cases, the best bet is to assume that the relationship between the product and the buyer is practically nonexistent. All levels must then be considered. Awareness, comprehension, conviction, and action must be addressed in such advertisements. Once the product has received sufficient exposure and been a focus of conviction, action is feasible. This is similar to those interpersonal episodes in which past interactions serve as the rule-definition and rule-confirmation phases. Once a product has developed a relationship with its buyers, much of the effort that once went into the definition of the relationship can go into the continuation of it.

The next section looks at the relationships advertisers attempt to develop with children, and the steps that have been taken by the Federal Communications Commission (FCC) and other groups to prevent advertisers from becoming the more powerful party in that relationship.

CHILDREN AND ADVERTISING

Much research attention has been given to children's perceptions of television advertising. Children constitute the most "defenseless" of the uncritical audiences that participate in a media relationship with television. The natural propensity for parents and educators to protect children from harm has made the question concerning just how much power television has over children a very important one.

In terms of advertising, two of the major questions being asked by researchers are whether children can separate program content from commercial content, and whether they realize that commercials are attempts to persuade them to buy particular products. In 1974 the FCC determined that all licensees must ensure that a clear separation be maintained between program content and commercial messages. This requirement identifies television as a substantial contributor to the child's conceptualization of reality. However, just how prepared children are to distinguish between those messages whose sole purpose is to shape their perceptions and those intended to inform or entertain has not been determined. To protect children from the possibility that advertisers might take "unfair advantage" of them, the FCC has recommended the implementation of methods that facilitate children's ability at least to separate persuasive content from program content.

The FCC has suggested that commercials be "clustered" at the beginnings or ends of programs. This is one method of compensating for the young child's egocentric or private thought processes, which are characterized by an absence of reflexivity or criticism of his or her own thinking. Imprisoned by limited, nonreflexive processes, the child must rely on outside sources to provide separations, integrations, and critiques of new information that will, through the processes of assimilation and accommodation, become part of his or her conceptualization of the "real" world (Kohlberg, 1966, 1969; Piaget, 1962).

Unlike other audiences addressed by the mass media, children do not bring to the relationship the cognitive capacities necessary to recognize subtle persuasion, nor do they possess past experiences that would caution them against accepting, without question, attempts to influence their behavior. In terms of Cox's (1962) predictive and confidence value criteria, children are learning what to value and, should their favorite television character tell them that a toy possesses attributes they have learned are important, their confidence in that cue will be enhanced. Unable to construe their relationship with the television episodically (behavior-pattern identification), young children are incapable of recognizing where they are being led.

The controversy over what advertisers are doing to children has frequently taken on the appearance of a monkey-in-the-middle game, in which the responsibility for children's responses to advertising is passed back and forth between parents and advertisers. Considerable concern has been expressed by consumer advocates and social policy decision makers about the effects of advertising on family relations (Robertson, 1979). Of primary concern is the potential strain that may be imposed on parent-child relations by children's consistent consumption requests. Many advertisers respond to this negativism by suggesting that advertising can provide positive interaction between parent and child, since it represents an opportunity for consumer learning. The low level of parental concern about children's commercials reported in several studies (Atkin, 1975a; Bauer & Greyser, 1968; Feldman, Wolf, & Warmouth, 1977) suggests that even if this opportunity exists, parents are not likely to take advantage of it. Robertson (1979) contends that what appears to be parents' abdication of responsibility for the mediation and regulation of child viewing may be explained by the pressure parents may feel not to interfere with other socialization objectives met by television viewing.

Low parental concern about advertising does not mean that parents are not offended or upset by it. Feldman et al. (1977), for example, found little relationship between parental dissatisfaction with commercials and parental monitoring of children's television viewing. It appears that parents are aware that commercials increase parent-child conflict and that commercials may persuade children to want things they do not need (Culley, Lazer, & Atkin, 1976). These two problems can be explained in terms of the regulative rule model. If a child learns to expect certain behaviors from parents as a result of watching television commercials, to the extent that those expectations are violated, family conflict potential is increased. The following model depicts the rule violation children may be perceiving when parents refuse to buy something they want:

Antecedent conditions: Mothers and fathers love their children.

Desired consequences: Mothers and fathers want their children to be happy.

Behavioral choice: Because my mother and father love me and want me to be happy, they will buy what I want.

Although the National Association of Broadcasters Code prohibits directing children through commercials to purchase a product or service or ask their parents or other adults to buy the product or service for them, advertisers can still succeed in conveying this message implicitly. When, in a commercial, Johnny hugs his mother and tells her that she is the greatest mom in the whole world because she bought the product he and his friends wanted, the implication is that great moms conform to their children's expectations in the purchase of items. The child whose parents refuse to conform to such expectations may begin to believe that they do not wish to make her happy or, even worse, that they do not love her. Both advertisers and parents recognize that this logic can be created and nurtured in the mind of the child and thus can place annoying pressure on the parent to purchase what the child wants. Perhaps the best way for parents to combat this pressure is to help their children revise their logic as follows:

Antecedent conditions: Mothers and fathers love their children.

Desired consequences: Mothers and fathers want their children to be happy.

Behavioral choice: Because my mother and father love me and want me to be happy, they will buy me what I need and things that are good for me.

Research is needed that focuses on the effects of parental attempts to revise television-generated modes of logic. In essence, parents could be trained to inoculate their children against persuasive messages that have the potential to influence family life negatively. If parents thought that they could succeed in monitoring the influence television has on their children's perceptions of parental concern, they might be more willing to make the attempt.

It is likely that the battle over the potentially negative effects of advertising on children will go on for some time. The extent of child disappointment in not receiving advertised products (Atkin, 1975a; Greenberg & Gorn, 1978; Robertson & Rossiter, 1977; Sheikh & Moleski, 1977), influence of product-choice strategies used by children (Wartella et al., 1979), developmental stages of consumer information processing (see Brown, 1976; Capon & Kuhn, 1978; Robertson & Rossiter, 1977; Wackman & Ward, 1976; Wartella, Wackman, Ward, Shamir, & Alexander, 1979), and form complexity as a factor in attention to commercials (see McEwen, Watt, & Shea, 1977; Wartella & Ettema, 1974; Watt & Krull, 1976) are only a few of the issues that have captivated researchers. While many of the findings may have contributed to the negativism Newcomb (1979b) views as an inhibitor to critical viewing, they have also contributed to our understanding of the unique relationship between children and the mass media.

ADVERTISING AND
THE PORTRAYAL OF MINORITIES

Few mass media experts would disagree with the position that television has influenced the values of this country. The extent of that influence, however, is difficult to determine. Loevinger (1979) has introduced a theory of mass communication that places some limitations on the potential influence of mass media. His reflective-projective theory postulates that mass communications are best understood as "mirrors of society that reflect an ambiguous image in which each observer projects or sees his own vision of himself and society" (p. 252). Recognizing the diversity among audience members, program producers have often settled for creating homogenized versions of Americans. The result is an extensive mosaic of inaccurate reflections of society that many persons begin to believe is the real world. As Cummings (1979) has explained, "Hollywood has provided us with cultural fantasies and reinforcing reveries; the icons of our age, creating and defining ourselves for us, are celluloid chimeras which, like those incredible walking-talking-wetting dolls, come closer and closer to being the real thing" (p. 78).

Cummings believes that distinguishing between illusion and reality has become increasingly difficult because of the mass media's influence on our perceptions. He adds that cultural ambiguity increases individual anxiety because, while persons may know more, they are less sure of that knowledge. As a consequence, critics, commentators, and media personalities in general become the interpreters of complex reality for the befuddled spectator.

Most people are aware that this ambiguity discussed by Cummings is very apparent in sex role stereotypes. Sex role stereotypes impose limitations on behavioral choices. When these stereotypes undergo changes, people become unsure about which behaviors are masculine and which are feminine. If Cummings is accurate, then we should expect to find these confused individuals looking to the mass media for some behavioral guidelines. For women, those guidelines are likely to reflect some noncomplimentary messages. The first major message is that women are not as important to society as men. This message is conveyed implicitly through the low percentage of women, as opposed to men, appearing in television advertisements. This consistent imbalance is a symbolic annihilation of women, because their role is trivialized (Tuchman, 1978).

Absence is not the only mode of symbolic annihilation experienced by women in the media. Gerbner (1978) postulates the existence of three main tactics used in television to resist the changing status of women: discrediting, isolating, and undercutting. Discrediting is manifested in the selection of the most bizarre or provocative aspects of the threatening movement as the primary focus for television coverage. For example, Gerbner points to television's focus on supposedly "typical women's libbers," who are seen as hostile, aggressive, unappreciative of men, and unwilling to listen to reason.

The second form of resistance is isolation. The tactic here is to segregate women, to put them "in their place," such as the kitchen or the bathroom. Toilet paper commercials are an excellent example of this type of tactic. Men appear to care very little about the type of toilet paper they use, whereas women often appear to spend their days worrying about the potential embarrassment involved in selecting the wrong roll.

Undercutting is what Gerbner (1978) describes as "basically the tactic of terror" (p. 48). The "institutionalization of rape" or the treatment of it of as "normal crime" is one form of undercutting the changing image of women. A second form is seen in the acceptance of pornography as a "liberating force" rather than as a mode of exploitation. Advertising is frequently a culprit here. Sometimes the insult is conveyed by subliminal messages, messages sufficiently subtle to be deniable if advertisers were asked to justify their inclusion in the ad. Most advertising pornography is more obvious. However, our society has become accustomed to seeing partially nude women traipsing across the television screen.

The rules being conveyed to the "befuddled" spectator are ones that perpetuate condescending behavior toward women. For instance, women appear to be totally incapable of experiencing the camaraderie so characteristic of men in beer commercials. Conflict literature indicates that women are more competitive toward each other than they are toward males (Frost & Wilmot, 1978). They have never learned to disguise their competitive emotions with the verbal battles characteristic of male camaraderie. Television does much to feed this damaging image. The only time we see a woman competing in advertisements is when she wishes to have her husband's shirts designated as the cleanest or her home as smelling better than the homes of other women. The backslapping verbal dueling of males appears to allow no place for a woman unless she is the subject of the exchange. The male has cornered the market on this type of humor.

Gerbner (1978) paints a dismal picture for the future concerning changes in these negative depictions of women on television. Until the structure of social relations between the two sexes becomes intolerably insulting to women, it is likely that advertisers will continue to portray women in insipid roles. Since very few women appear to be sufficiently incensed by their trivialization in media advertising, advertisers are at liberty to perpetuate images that should have met their demise years ago. The desired consequences of a clean toilet bowl, soft toilet tissue, and shirts without spots separate the women from the men, whose desired consequences are usually focused on issues of insurance, liquor, sports, and other "more important" matters. Until advertising begins to respond to the inconsistencies between the media reflection of what women consider important and their real interests, people will continue to derive behavioral guidelines from distorted images of women.

Women are certainly not the only segment of our population unfairly portrayed on the television screen. The elderly are consistently devalued as consumers by their underrepresentation in commercials (Gantz, Gartenberg, & Rainbow, 1980). Damaging as this problem is, underrepresentation is not nearly as damaging as the one-dimensional, undeveloped character images of the elderly. Korzenny and Neuendorf (1980) provide support for the positive role television can play in enhancing the self-images of elderly persons. They, like women, are attempting to accommodate their rule systems to changing societal expectations for elderly persons. Certainly, negative stereotypes linger and are perpetuated by youth-oriented mass media, but as their increasing numbers become too obvious to ignore, the elderly are beginning to emerge as an important segment of our society. If, however, the elderly look to the mass media for guidance concerning appropriate behavior, they are likely to experience the same devaluation that women experience through the mass media.

Another segment of society suffering the effects of underrepresentation in the media are minority groups such as Blacks and Hispanics. Research in this area has focused on the effects of symbolic annihilation on the minority child. Comstock and Cobbey (1979) explain that all children share general needs for information. However, they perceive the minority child's relationship with the television as somewhat special. They conclude that what sets minority children apart is their relative isolation from other sources for the satisfaction of information needs. They add:

> This circumstance arises in part from their ethnicity, but more from the socioeconomic disadvantage that is frequently associated with minority status. Thus the evidence suggests that minority children share with children of lower socioeconomic status generally a particular reliance on television—because it brings information that is not otherwise readily available. (p. 110)

The special dependency relationship between ethnic minority children and television defines this mass medium as the creator and disseminator of societal expectations for these youngsters. To the extent that those images consistently viewed by children are distortions of reality, their rule repertoires will be insufficient to meet their needs in the real world. This does not mean that the only source of influence for the minority child is television, but it certainly appears to be a primary source.

The emphasis given to television advertising as an important source of role information has excluded from discussion the less obvious forms of persuasion prevalent in television. The next section looks at how television programs contribute to our social expectations for self and others.

THE TELEVISION PROGRAM
AS A SOURCE OF PERSUASION

In previous sections of this chapter the mass audience was described as a collection of individuals who, while sharing many rules, differ in their perceptions of events. Emphasis was placed on the relationships these audience members establish with the mass media. It was suggested that we recognize that individuals, perhaps even more so than in interpersonal relationships, can choose to participate in episodes of reciprocal influence with the media. There is no need to apologize or account for one's rudeness toward a mass medium.

Despite this perspective on mass media as selected participants in our everyday communications, it could be argued that some media allow for greater choice than others. For example, a book is a private medium. Television, on the other hand, is a public medium that many of us view in the company of others. Frequently people find themselves viewing programs they have not truly chosen, but to continue interpersonal interactions with family and/or peers, they participate in the media event.

Television advertising and program content can be separated in much the same fashion. It is probably safe to assume that few persons select the programs they view on the basis of what advertisements they can expect to experience. However, their interactions with advertisements are usually the result of having selected particular programs. In this sense there is more choice involved in program viewing than in advertisement viewing. We can conclude that the program viewer is comparatively more responsible for his or her media relationship than is the advertisement viewer. When program viewers flip the dial to a particular program, they are indicating some preference for a particular type of relationship.

What does this perspective mean in terms of television criticism? It that despite the abundance of journal and magazine articles ing the negativism toward television that Newcomb (1979a, ls unhealthy, television program relationships are more a hoice than most other relationships in individuals' daily lives. Viewers' complaints about the sex and violence that they "must" be exposed to are little more than a sour-grapes philosophy if they continue to participate in these supposedly unpleasant interactions. The television viewer is a willing persuadee who has found a subject for condemnation and whose negative opinions will bring little disagreement from fellow viewers, who also define themselves as unwilling participants in a relationship where divorce is out of the question.

Be this as it may, the prevalent perspective is still one describing the television viewer as a victim of much that is evil in our society. Victims are those with an excuse for passivity. Their mental set does not predispose them to search for a way out. Vandenberg and Watt (1977-1978) provide some support for this perspective. Their survey of Connecticut television viewers indicates that despite high subject preference for audience member and industry, rather than government, regulation of sex and violence in programming, few parents monitor the viewing patterns of children. Vandenberg and Watt found that almost half of the children under 18 had no time restrictions on viewing, and almost two-thirds had no content restrictions.

Our perception of ourselves as victims of mass communications media has allowed us to relinquish our right to choose our media relationships. Our behavior fits Ray's (1973) low-involvement model. Because we either do not care or are not involved in the media relationship choice, almost unlimited effect on the cognitive variable is afforded. Little perceptual defense exists, and so, after much repetition of the same themes, the programmer can alter the conative and later the affective responses to sex and violence. They become a fact of life.

The high tolerance for mass media biases indicates that people do not seek to resolve minor inconsistencies with any predictable regularity. Viewers who complain frequently about the content of the programs they watch but refuse to do anything about it might be convinced that their behavior and desired consequences are inconsistent. However, unless they can also be convinced that there is something they can do about this inconsistency and that it constitutes a problem of greater magnitude than they previously imagined, the inconsistency is likely to remain unchallenged. This is the anatomy of the negativism Newcomb (1979b) perceived as a roadblock to developing an effective critical attitude toward television.

The general malaise characteristic of the television viewer places viewers in the position of contributing less to the media relationship definition than programs and advertising contribute. They are thus relegated to a position of little power in McQuail's (1979) terms. They are consistently the persuadees, rarely the persuaders. They have defined themselves and, as the Atkin (1975b), Feldman et al. (1977), and Vandenberg and Watt (1977-1978) studies indicate, their children as victims in a potentially damaging relationship.

FACING THE MEDIA

Given the potential power of the media to influence, it is important for companies to manage how they are portrayed in print and electronic messages to their customers. There is some controversy surrounding the training of executives to respond effectively to journalists. Some take the view that the truth will never be known if executives become too skillful at handling journalists' tough questions. Of course, that depends on how good the journalist is as well. Given the stakes, the best response to this criticism is that it is unwise to go into any interview unprepared for tough questions. So, given that a good part of this chapter has been spent focusing on theories of media influence, some space will be devoted in this section to practical applications and consideration of what people need to know if they are to deal effectively with media interviews.

It is important for interviewees to know how to respond to tough questions. Below are some tips that should prove helpful.

(1) *Anticipate questions.* First and foremost, put yourself in the listener's shoes and ask yourself the questions you would ask if you were in the audience.

- Look for contradictions, arguments lacking sufficient evidence and gaps in logic.
- Consider your various options and determine which one is the strongest.
- Keep responses concise and to the point. Don't meander around the point, providing the questioner with more information than called for by the question.

(2) *Stay cool, calm, and collected,* even if you don't think you know the answer.

- Never look panicked or bewildered. Appear contemplative.
- There's no shame in saying, "I don't know" if you don't say it too often. Indicate that you will check on the matter, or refer the questioner to sources that might provide the answer.
- Consider saying, "That's a good question. Let me tell you where we are on that . . . ."
- If you are unsure of the meaning of a question, repeat it slowly or ask the questioner to repeat it or restate it in different terms.
- Do not respond to multiple questions in one question. Separate the issues and respond first to the one you can answer best.
- If you are unable to answer the question directly, relate it to a similar issue that you feel more confident addressing.

(3) *Always address the question, not the questioner.*

- Don't become emotional, or you will lose credibility, to say nothing of your train of thought.
- Discuss the words, information, facts, or logic contained in the question, but never get into a shouting match over the questioner's or your own personality, qualifications, attitudes, personal values, or the like.

(4) *Dissect the question and its foundation.*

- Listen carefully to determine the questioner's purpose.
- Consider the data, warrant, and backing behind the questioner's claim.
- You might respond, "Your question presumes that A causes B. That is not the case according to . . . ."

The above tips are not easily implemented. It is difficult to remain objective when a journalist is pressing for answers on a controversial issue. However, the likelihood of the print, radio, or television story being favorable to the interviewee is more likely if these tips are followed.

While many companies would just as soon not bother facing journalists' challenges, the chances of avoiding them are becoming slimmer and slimmer. An article in the *Los Angeles Times* referred to 1989 as the "Year of the Corporate Attack." The article told of an instance where two people hired by a company tiptoed around a hotel in the middle of the night distributing copies of a magazine article to executives attending a trade conference. The article, slipped beneath the doors of the 500 slumbering executives, described the company's archrival as arrogant and ineffective. While corporate smears have been around forever, they appear to have increased significantly in recent years. According to the *Los Angeles Times*, "Executives locked in life-or-death corporate struggles are skillfully using take-over lawyers, public relations aides, private investigators and others to unearth the opposition's most embarrassing secrets, then publicize them to inflict maximum damage."

In the late 1980s, a beer distributor passed along rumors that a rival's beer was contaminated with urine. A lawsuit ensued, but was dropped when the distributor agreed to say publicly that the beer was not tainted with urine. Another company fought rumors that it was tied to devil worship, an accusation that originated with two competitors. A telephone company won a libel judgment against a company that claimed its slumping sales were due to customers being unable to get through on the phone company lines (*Los Angeles Times*, 1989).

Mudslinging abounds in corporations. Add to this the type of problem experienced by Johnson & Johnson when tampered-with Tylenol capsules led to several deaths, and it becomes clear that no company can be sure that it will not have to face the media. Johnson & Johnson decided to respond to media questioning quickly when the Tylenol-linked deaths occurred, and that readiness paid off. Had the company tried to hide from media inquiries, the loss of credibility it would have suffered with customers would likely have resulted in far greater losses than were experienced.

If the media exhibit a preference for the negative, it pays for companies to be prepared to counterpersuade those who would believe untrue, costly stories. Knowing how to do this takes valuable time, but, as Johnson & Johnson learned, it is time well spent.

CONCLUSION

Jay Jackson (1966) refers to that condition in which persons agree about some sentiment toward a person or object (high consensus) but few sanctions exist to encourage or discourage relevant action (low intensity) as one of "vacuous consensus." This characterizes the general negativism toward television that Newcomb describes as responsible for our lack of concerted effort to bring about positive changes. This societywide malaise is the result of a victimization myth that immobilizes us further. A victim is someone who has an excuse of passivity. By defining ourselves as such, we have given up the self-autonomy we could elicit in defining our relationships with television and mass media in general.

Moreover, our general acceptance of deception in media, and particularly in advertising, reflects a set of superordinate constructs that we pass from generation to generation (Wolf & Hexamer, 1980). The effects of this mental set are reflected in the prevalence of sexual, age, and ethnic stereotypes pervading mass media messages.

If the possibility exists that mass media "shape the soul's geography" or even contribute to it, then children should be encouraged by schools and parents to take responsibility for their media relationships. Miller and Burgoon (1979) have clearly demonstrated that people prepare counterarguments when they expect intensely persuasive messages. Without such expectations message recipients are more vulnerable, since the self-autonomy that often serves to check and balance "borrowed rules" in interpersonal exchanges is absent.

The main point is not that mass media messages are without virtue. On the contrary, they have contributed greatly to our education. Even advertising, generally viewed as the most overt form of mass media persuasion, has opened our eyes to products that have made life more comfortable. What is needed is greater persuadee responsibility in media relationships. Without it, some mass media messages will continue to enjoy undeserved credibility.

Besides describing mass media relationships, this chapter has also introduced models of mass persuasion that support or extend the perspective advanced in this text. Kelman's model suggests the use of persuasion strategies paralleling the accuracy, appropriateness, consistency, and effectiveness appeals described in Chapter 5. While appropriateness is the most commonly used marketing appeal, Kelman's perspective does not preclude the use of accuracy, consistency, and effectiveness in mass media persuasive messages.

10 Political Persuasion

This chapter's emphasis is on factors that influence the positions voters take on both political candidates and political events. The questions to be addressed are as follows: What mental processes influence the course of political decision making? How are past events used to influence choices in the present? What characteristics of political candidates influence the course of voter decision making? What impact do various information sources have on political decisions?

THREE THEORIES OF POLITICAL DECISION MAKING

Most elections are conducted in a political environment that is ambiguous, where information is unclear, contradictory, open to a variety of interpretations, and hard to get (Conover & Feldman, 1986). Sometimes ambiguity is the result of an unwillingness on the part of candidates to take firm stands on the issues relevant to their campaigns. Ambiguity also results from media coverage of campaigns. In place of issues, the media often focus on the "game" aspects of a campaign—strategies for winning, logistics, and who is appearing where with whom (Graber, 1980; Patterson, 1980).

During the 1988 presidential race, the media were frequently criticized by the two candidates for diverting attention from the real issues of the campaign to focus on such questions as whether Michael Dukakis had ever received psychiatric treatment and whether vice presidential candidate Dan Quayle had engaged in or even considered engaging in an affair while married.

With so much ambiguity surrounding political campaigns, the average voter is faced with a considerable challenge. How does the voter sort through the barrage of issue-irrelevant information to select a candidate? In an effort to respond to this question, political scientists have borrowed theoretical explanations from social psychologists. Three theories have emerged as the most popular explanations of voter decision making: cognitive consistency, rational information processing, and a cognitive schema perspective.

Cognitive Consistency Theory

Cognitive consistency theory, as discussed earlier in this book, suggests that people strive to avoid imbalance in their judgments of people and events. In terms of political choices, people find uncomfortable inconsistencies between their prior actions and current candidate preferences. When such inconsistencies occur, voters are motivated to change. They may change their current preferences, revise their views of past actions, or change their views on the issues that make the inconsistency obvious.

Cognitive consistency theory explains why it is so difficult for voters to change their party loyalties. Party identification obtained early in life and reinforced for years afterward can be a powerful source of inconsistency for adults experiencing a change of heart regarding party affiliation. Voters faced with this dilemma may project their own preferred issue positions on the candidates representing their families' parties rather than deal with the inconsistency. Another alternative is for voters to allow themselves to be persuaded that their party's candidate really does have a better position on the issue (see Conover & Feldman, 1986).

Rational Choice Approach

While cognitive consistency has been the most popular explanation of voter behavior, some political scientists have adopted the rational choice approach. This approach describes people as making decisions on logical bases. People are seen as behaving according to how they attribute causality. For example, if a voter notices that having a Republican president regularly covaries with his being laid off from his job, then he may attribute his unemployment to Republican economic policies and come to dislike Republican candidates (Lau & Sears, 1986).

Following this model of political behavior, it would behoove a candidate to determine the associations voters might make between such characteristics as the candidate's party, age, region of birth, and religion and the voters' good and bad experiences. With this knowledge the candidate is better prepared to emphasize favorable associations and to deemphasize or dispute those contradictory associations not in her favor.

Case in Point

During the 1990 campaign for the governorship of California, opposing candidates Pete Wilson and Dianne Feinstein attempted to associate each other with the savings and loan crisis that was costing the country billions of dollars. Feinstein used television ads to accuse Wilson of using his influence in Congress to help S&Ls. Wilson retaliated with televisions ads accusing Feinstein and her husband of ownership in an S&L that the country had to bail out. Both ended up in a mudslinging match that clouded a number of other issues while they argued about which of them was more intimately involved in the S&L crisis.

Cognitive Schema Perspective

A third perspective on how people make political decisions rests heavily on the contention that people use cognitive schemata to make such decisions. A schema is a knowledge structure, derived from experience, that organizes a person's perceptions of the world. Lau (1986) argues that "political schemata" include some combinations of issues, group relations, party identification, and/or candidate personality factors. These political schemata guide the formation of personal schemata for specific politicians. When a person is confronted by political information, he or she tries to "fit" that information into a preexisting political schema. Schema-inconsistent information may receive added attention at input, if task conditions allow it (Fiske & Taylor, 1984; Hastie, 1981). Given adequate time, people elaborate and explain inconsistencies, thereby strengthening them in memory. Research also indicates that inconsistent information requires more time at encoding (interpreting meaning) than irrelevant or consistent information. This added attention at input may account for its tendency to be remembered. Candidates who wish to have people sit up and take notice of their views may want to consider an occasional inconsistency to get people thinking and remembering. Too much inconsistency is threatening to people, but occasional inconsistency appears to be memorable.

Conover and Feldman (1986) propose that schemata vary in accessibility—the ease with which they are cued in the mind. Level of accessibility is determined by such factors as expectations and motivations of the individual and salience of an issue to that individual. If an ideological clash is expected, some voters will have ideological schemata accessible. They will be ready to refute attacks on their candidates or party perspectives. When voters view the confrontation along party lines, their party schemata are likely to be accessible. With regard to motivation, those voters more involved with campaigns are likely to have their political schemata readily available. Finally, voters who focus much of their attention on a particular issue or issues are likely to interpret much information in light of relevant schemata. Conover and Feldman point to the feminist voter as an example. Feminists tend to perceive candidates in terms of women's rights schemata (Conover, 1984) and are therefore likely to draw candidate inferences on the basis of such issues as equal rights and abortion rights rather than, say, inflation.

To the extent that voters are cognitive misers, the best strategy for a candidate may be to take a highly visible position on those issues highly relevant to a majority of voters rather than try to cover every possible issue. For instance, if a large percentage of the voters are elderly, then issues involving their well-being may have to be high on a candidate's list. If another large portion of the voters are "baby boomers" with small children, then work-site child care and parental leave may be targeted as important issues.

APPLICATION OF THE ACE MODEL TO POLITICAL SCHEMATA

The ACE model of reasoned behavior proposes that people organize their thinking around three predominant criteria: appropriateness, consistency, and effectiveness. How does this view of human reasoning fit with the perspective just discussed? As indicated earlier in this text, people do not always use all three criteria in determining their views or behaviors. Each situation, each issue, and individual traits tend to enter into the ordering of criteria. It is also possible for a persuader, interpersonal or media, to encourage focus on one criteria over the other two.

The ACE model can be used to categorize certain types of schemata. For example, Conover and Feldman (1986) argue that "social group" schemata likely play a significant part in guiding the inferences voters make about candidates. Such schemata fit into the "appropriateness" category of the ACE model. Lane (1986) suggests that consistency in arguments (compatible schema) is often valued for the appearance of self-consistency. For example, people who see themselves as liberals must believe in minority rights. Thus these two types of schemata become linked. When voters feel the need to be or to appear consistent, what has been described as the consistency criterion for reasoning becomes paramount and guides inferences made about a candidate or issue. Finally, there is the motivation to bring about the best conse-quences—the effectiveness dimension of the ACE model. Such an emphasis would lead to the accessibility of schemata providing guid-ance in achieving goals.

The ACE model provides a means of categorizing schemata and a potential guide for developing political campaigns. As voters read the situation at hand, they decide on some level whether social consid-erations, consistency considerations, or goal considerations are more salient or whether some combination of the three is important. This de-termination makes some schemata more accessible than others, thereby influencing the course of voting behavior.

CREDIBILITY

Among the many schemata people have available to them when deciding which candidates to favor, a number pertain to their overall impressions of candidates' credibility. The extent of a candidate's expertise and trustworthiness are two dimensions of credibility that likely have an impact on voters' impressions of him or her.

It would be useful to have a list of behaviors that encourage voters to see candidates as credible. Research indicates, however, that the effects of credibility are, in part, a function of the predispositions of the person receiving the candidate's message. For example, it appears that credibility strongly affects people who are relatively uninvolved. Peo-ple who are involved in an issue pay more attention to the message being conveyed than to the communicator. They are inclined to create coun-terarguments, especially if the person speaking is a highly credible source. The involved persuadee invests cognitive activity in protecting his or her views on the issue and thus resists the persuader's arguments (Petty & Cacioppo, 1981).

Despite the fact that the effects of communicator credibility are dependent, to some extent, on the level of the message recipient's involvement in the issue at hand, there are certain characteristics that appear to predispose Americans to think well or ill of a president. For example, according to Kinder (1986), people demand of their president such traits as competence, leadership ability, integrity, and empathy. In general, the more educated the individual observer of presidential behavior, the more critical he or she tends to be. Of course, the political sensibilities of the critic influence his or her decisions. Democrats are typically more generous in their evaluations of Democratic presidents, whereas Republicans are more generous to Republican presidents.

Research on presidential popularity indicates that, with few exceptions, such popularity declines after a president takes office (Sigelman & Knight, 1983). There appears to be a "presidential unpopularity cycle." One explanation for this phenomenon is that there is an "inevitable disjuncture between presidential promise and performance" (Stimson, 1976). Few presidents can live up to all the promises they made while campaigning for office. In fact, presidents who have taken office surrounded by the grandest expectations have suffered the worst popularity declines.

Case in Point

During his campaign for the presidency, George Bush told voters that there would be no tax increases if he were elected. He told voters, "Read my lips. No more taxes." In 1990 the savings and loan crisis, a growing deficit, and other problems caused President Bush to reconsider his promise of no more taxes. The newspapers were full of attacks on Bush's credibility. He had made a promise to the American people during his campaign and was showing signs of reneging on that promise. His detractors were saying that Bush's new slogan was "Reread my lips." Bush was well into a decline in credibility, which Stimson describes as the "inevitable disjuncture between presidential promise and performance."

Sigelman and Knight (1983) contend that while expectations and popularity may indeed be tied together, their relationship may not be one of cause and effect. Rather, the two are "joint outcomes" of the effectiveness with which the president is seen to be handling the job. The more presidents fail to accomplish, the less they are expected to accomplish. If this is true, then expectations are not causally prior to evaluations, except at the outset of a new president's term.

The six months following a new president's inauguration constitute an important transition period. During this time people formulate
expectations. President Bush's decision to insist that John Tower become his secretary of defense came during this six-month period. When
Tower's nomination was voted down by Congress, in part because of
Tower's extramarital affairs, President Bush's credibility was damaged.
He quickly nominated Richard Cheney, who some reporters described
as a man who, unlike Tower, had been "married forever," since he had
married his childhood sweetheart and had remained loyal to her. Moreover, he had never been involved in activities that made him anything
less than an ideal candidate for secretary of defense. History will tell
whether President Bush's defense of John Tower and his subsequent
loss to Congress on that matter set up expectations of him as a weak
president or whether his immediate selection of Cheney after Congress
refused to accept Tower saved him from that fate.

Within that same six-month transition period, President Bush also
faced a major environmental issue. In March of 1989, an Exxon oil
freighter spilled millions of tons of oil off the coast of Alaska. The spill
threatened the livelihood of Alaskan fishermen and took a considerable
toll on the sea life of that region. Environmentalists claimed that the
spill demonstrated that oil could not be safely shipped from Alaska and
that all planning to increase drilling there should be halted. President
Bush resisted such protests. In so doing, he risked appearing inconsistent with his preelection claim that he would be an "environmental
president." This contradiction so early in his presidency and coming as
it did on the tail of the John Tower affair was another threat to presidential credibility. During this six-month transition period, people still
remember the promises made by a presidential candidate. They judge
the president's success to some extent on the degree to which promises
are met. Success or failure in the first six months of a new administra-
tion can lead to reduced expectations—something a president would
have to offset by impressive successes not long into his or her tenure.

Most scholars who examine media treatment of presidents argue that
the media shape how presidents are perceived. Some even argue that
presidential newscasts "are presidential only in the sense that the chief
of state provides the 'news peg' upon which the show hangs" (Hart,
1987, p. 120). The president merely provides reporters with an opportunity for dramatic conflict. As Hart (1987) points out, much media time
is spent setting up ferocious struggles between presidents and their

adversaries. If the two are not sharing the same physical space during the battle, images of them can be spliced together so that they appear to be in direct confrontation.

Presidents are not exactly pawns in the media game. A number of presidents have used the media to create dramas of their own. The president who can creatively manipulate the emotional climate of his or her presentations has a considerable advantage. Emotion is central to presidential politics. A presidential candidate may be extremely intelligent, but if he or she is incapable of grabbing the hearts of the American television viewer, making it to the White House is not in the cards. Vice President Mondale and Governor Dukakis are two examples of what the absence of emotional appeal can do to what may initially be promising presidential candidates.

Presidents and presidential candidates are carefully advised in their selection of audiences. The last thing presidential candidates want is to have the entire nation watch them as they speak to a hostile audience. The well-chosen audience sends a message of approval to the American public. When the president cannot choose the audience but must face a press conference, he or she has a rare opportunity to tell what he or she truly thinks and feels. Some presidents do this quite well. But even the president who glides through a press conference becomes the source of extensive postconference debates among reporters.

One can only marvel at how poor reporters have become at finding experts who are not reporters to comment on presidential presentations and press conferences. The American public usually finds two or three reporters interpreting what the president said in an address, rather than experts on politics, economics, foreign policy, and other areas covered in the talk. If reporters deserve criticism, surely it is for this state of affairs. Reporters who sit before the American public interpreting the president's word without assistance from experts are far too enamored of their own expertise. In their failure to see their own limitations, they become interpreters of American politics rather than reporters of it. When they do this they threaten their own credibility even as they sit and disparage or praise the credibility of the president. But worse, they deprive the American public of the opportunity to hear a variety of views, especially from experts whose entire lives have been devoted to the study of the topics discussed in presidential press conferences and presentations.

PERSUASION AND POLITICAL ISSUES

The preceding sections of this chapter have been devoted to how candidates for public office and their adversaries use persuasion to win elections. Another important area of political persuasion involves persuading the public to adopt particular political perspectives. Of course, the first question that must be answered is, Just what constitutes a "political issue"? In the broadest sense, a political issue can be any issue that generates conflict between people affiliated with each other in some fashion. The affiliation may be one of colleagues in the same department of a company, residents of the same neighborhood or voting district, or residents of the same country. If these people with some common affiliation hold diverse opinions regarding some plan of action relevant to their community, the plan of action may become a political issue. This section will focus on those issues that become topics of public debate between members of the same society (e.g., abortion, foreign investment in U.S. property, child care, medical care for the elderly, AIDS, cancer, the homeless, gun control).

Like political candidates, how political issues are perceived by members of society is a function of how they are portrayed by the media and how people make sense of what they see in the media. Dervin (1989) argues that information is not conveyed so much as it is constructed. She describes two models of communication: the "information-as-description" model and the "information-as-construction" model. The former implies that information can be transmitted or conveyed. The observer is privy to specialized observations and is responsible for transmitting these to a receiver, who, like an empty bucket, receives them without interpretation. The latter model suggests that information is created by the people who observe it and that their own self-interests enter into how they interpret what they observe. Dervin (1989) subscribes to the latter perspective and has proposed a model of "sense making," or how people make sense of their worlds.

Political issues are subject to the sense-making activities of those engaged in the debate. Prior to his election to the presidency, George Bush probably did not foresee the extent to which abortion would become a political issue in 1989. Even if he was aware of the likelihood of abortion becoming a major political issue so soon after his election, he may not have foreseen how personally female voters would interpret his actions with regard to this issue. It became clear in 1989 that the issue of abortion was not going to be fought in back rooms. It was the issue that led to the defeat of many candidates that year and an issue that would loom large for years to come because the American public was drawn into the struggle. A barometer of how the American people were making sense of the abortion issue was being erected in every political office. In 1989, many candidates began waffling and even changing their minds from total antiabortion positions to compromised positions as they interpreted American sense making to be on the side of women's right to choose.

How one issue becomes a major political issue and others remain dormant is a fascinating study. In 1989, Americans were drawn into a conflict over the appropriate penalty for desecration of the American flag, while issues such as the fact that 40,000 children die daily from starvation around the world and that foster care in America is in such deep trouble that children are suffering had not made the big time, so to speak. Sometimes an event occurs that draws such media attention that an issue is thrust into the limelight. In such cases, people who did not feel the need to make sense out of a particular issue are drawn into interpersonal discussions or influenced by the media to begin to care about it and to develop opinions. Sometimes exposure for a particular issue comes from what Boorstin (1961) calls "pseudoevents" and Robinson (1981) calls "medialities." Both are events that take place primarily so that they can be shown on television. They are events planned and literally performed by political organizations to get television exposure. The media themselves sometimes also create pseudoevents when there appears to be an opportunity for a good story. Unfortunately, to make a story interesting and to keep it within the time constraints imposed by the media, only parts of the full story are told and shown. Whether one calls this media bias or just the facts of life, it is often the way events stimulate major political issues.

POLITICAL AGENDA-SETTING

Most people receive a sizable percentage of their information about the world from television news. According to the agenda-setting hypothesis, problems that receive prominent attention on the national news become the problems the viewing public regards as those most important to the nation (Iyengar, Shanto, & Kinder, 1987). The more time given to a story, the more important it is perceived to be.

Television news has a major impact on political perceptions as well. Research suggests that this is especially true for less educated people. Those who rely solely on television news for political information are also influenced greatly by that medium (Iyengar et al., 1987).

One theory explaining the agenda-setting effect of the media contends that the complexity and abundance of political information cloud actual message content. The result is confusion. The only detail people retain is the fact that they received information about a particular subject. As Taylor (1981) argues, people are cognitive misers. They look for cognitive shortcuts to simplify the vast amounts of information they receive from newscasts. Even when actual content is lost, they remember the frequency and relative importance given to a topic by the media.

This may explain why recent research on the inoculation effects of political direct mail turned out as it did. A study by Pfau, Kenski, Nitz, and Sorenson (1990) looked at the influence of direct mail as a form of inoculation. You may recall that inoculation theory posits that forewarning people of possible arguments and providing them with counterarguments can motivate those people to resist the arguments they have been prepared to refute (McGuire, 1961). In fact, research suggests that inoculation promotes resistance to both same and different counterarguments. So Pfau et al. expected that people who received inoculation regarding attacks on a political candidate would resist those attacks more than people who did not receive inoculation. Also, those who received the inoculation would refute more than just the issues covered in the inoculation message. As these authors explain, inoculation can "spread a blanket of protection against opponent's attacks." It is as if once the recipient of a direct mail inoculation begins to protect the candidate on issues covered in that inoculation, he or she expands that protectiveness to other issues as well.

Pfau and his colleagues found that inoculation using direct mail during the 1988 presidential campaign did result in deflection of the persuasiveness of political attacks, whether the attacks were the same as or different from the inoculation issues. It appears that it pays for political candidates to warn voters of the attacks their opponents may make on their character and/or positions on issues. The cognitive miser principle may work as well here as it appears to work with newscasts. People who are inoculated may not remember exactly what attacks on their candidate they have been encouraged to resist, but they may remember that they should feel protective toward the candidate. That alone could lead to resistance of the opponent's views.

PRIMING

Like agenda-setting, priming occurs when television news calls attention to some matters while ignoring others. Priming, however, is concerned with the extent to which television news influences the standards by which governments, presidents, policies, and candidates for public office are judged.

From a priming perspective, what makes a candidate favorable depends on what voters are primed to consider when judging him or her. For example, if the public views communication skills as important, a presidential candidate like Ronald Reagan would do well. The candidate who can make his or her strongest issue or character trait important to the public has a good chance of being elected.

Poll results serve to prime issues and create standards. The reporting of who is ahead in an election can convince the supporters of the losing candidate that the race is over before it truly is. News polls can influence who wins an election by placing emphasis on issues that favor one candidate over another (Paletz, 1980). President Nixon recognized this. He thought that polls, with their emphasis on negative information, serve to encourage feelings of disenchantment with public officials (Safire, 1980). They essentially prime people to think about negative aspects of the current government and the people running it.

ETHICS OF POLITICAL PERSUASION

It is obvious from the preceding sections of this chapter that there is much more to enhancing candidates' credibility than just having them tell voters what they think. As a result, more and more political candidates are hiring consultants to help them create positive images. Image consultants, public relations experts, and advertising experts are all part of the mix.

There are those who wonder whether all this manufacturing of images prevents voters from knowing what they are really getting when they support a candidate. Others argue that there should be some regulation of "mudslinging ads" so that political campaigns do not become uncivilized. One suggestion passed around Congress was that candidates for federal office should appear personally in all their commercials. Proponents of this proposal argued that candidates would be deterred from running mudslinging ads if they had to appear in them and declare that such ads were their own rather than the work of media consultants.

There is also the issue of buying television time. Candidates with large sums of money can afford to buy expensive ad time. Some critics argue that political discourse could be improved by granting free time to political parties. In 1990 a Senate task force on campaign reform approved a proposal that would require each television station and cable network to give four hours to the Republican and Democratic parties (R. Rothenberg, 1990).

Some political experts argue that bringing political discourse back to a higher plane will not come from free ad time. Sabato, a government professor at the University of Virginia, argues, "Lack of education, lack of demands by the public that a certain level of discourse be reached are the problem. That will not change with free time. That is corrected with more and better civic education, starting from kindergarten." If Sabato is correct, it may be a long time before persuasive strategies used by political candidates allow the voter to determine if "what you see is what you get."

CONCLUSION

Political persuasion is an art. Knowing how voters make sense of political information, what they attend to, and what they retain are all key elements. As this chapter indicates, it is not enough to have good, ethical ideas. Candidates must get those ideas on the news agendas and find ways to inoculate the voters against potential attacks from opponents. They must determine what actions and characteristics build credibility with the people they hope to persuade and must watch carefully to see what issues those people are being primed to consider when selecting and supporting a candidate. The candidate who says, "I'll just be me and they'll vote in my favor" has a lot to learn about the influence of mass media on political outcomes.

Concluding Remarks

As this book suggests, the study of persuasion intersects with many other fields. Whether you are a businessperson, parent, student, teacher, medical practitioner, politician, or astronaut, persuasion is a part of your daily life. Many researchers have devoted extensive time to the study of persuasion. In many cases they reached some degree of consensus regarding how persuasion is accomplished. For example, consistency theories were popular for some time and still have credibility today. More recent theories focus on how people receive and interpret information (ELM Model), strategies most likely to influence people provoked to reason (ACE Model), steps likely to bring success in persuasion endeavors (Communication/Persuasion Model), and strategies likely to be used by persuaders when attempting to gain compliance or by persuadees when attempting to resist persuasive messages.

Current theories treat persuasion as an activity rather than an end product. The labels *persuader* and *persuadee* are used to indicate who is consciously attempting to change whom, but in reality, persuasion is most often a reciprocal process. Each participant's actions influence the choices of the others involved. Even as a persuader is speaking, the persuadee's body language may influence the persuader to alter his or her argument. A persuadee who folds his arms, shakes his head from side to side, or sighs unenthusiastically may influence the persuader to alter her approach or to change her request. In interpersonal persuasion, persuaders also play the role of persuadees. Sometimes their dual roles are played simultaneously. As they attempt to influence, they are influenced by the responses of the people whose attitudes or behaviors they seek to change. Thus persuasion is something done *with* rather than *to* people. Even in mass media persuasion, the persuadee influences the persuader's choices. Both anticipated and actual audience reactions influence how print and electronic media sources present information.

This view of persuasion as an activity done with rather than to people emphasizes the importance of knowing the schemata and rules that guide people's decisions. This is where I started this book, and it is a useful place to end it. Persuasion requires curiosity. It demands a willingness to explore the mind-sets of others. People incapable of approaching persuasion with a Sherlock Holmes mentality usually find themselves resorting to manipulation or coercion. Sometimes they achieve success, but it is typically short-lived. Acquiescence may be achieved with manipulation and coercion, but private acceptance is unlikely. Unless people believe they have *chosen* to adopt a new attitude or behavior and feel rewarded, they are likely to revert to old ways. It does not take genius to understand this rule, but it appears to take a certain genius to remember to apply it when dealing with employees, spouses, children, acquaintances, and friends. The most persuasive people listen, empathize, negotiate, motivate, and reward skillfully. These people select strategies with the needs and desires of the persuadee in mind. They know that just as the perfect gift is not something the giver would like for himself but something the recipient would prize, so too the most effective persuasion strategies are the ones responsive to the interests of the persuadee.

So when all is said and done, the primary key to effective persuasion is a strong curiosity about the cognitive and emotional makeup of others. This may mean understanding such things as how they make decisions, what they consider rewarding, rules they use to determine behaviors, schemata they apply when interpreting experience, styles they may have learned as a result of culture or gender, their likely response to conflict, and their proficiency in negotiation. Such knowledge provides the persuader with a bridge between his own views and those of the persuadee. It provides the information he needs to select arguments, stories, or images likely to encourage another person to at least appreciate his views. Given the different schemata and rules people bring to any encounter, such appreciation is an important first step in the persuasion process.

References

Abelson, R. P., & Rosenberg, M. J. (1958). Symbolic psycho-logic: A model of attitudinal cognition. *Behavioral Science, 3,* 1-13.

Adorno, T. E., Frenkel-Brunswick, D. L., & Sanford, R. (1950). *The authoritarian personality.* New York: Harper & Row.

Aldrich, H. E. (1979). *Organizations and environments.* Englewood Cliffs, NJ: Prentice-Hall.

Allport, G. W. (1954). *The nature of prejudice.* Reading, MA: Addison-Wesley.

Alpert, M. I., & Anderson, W. T. (1973). Optimal heterophily and communication effectiveness: Some empirical findings. *Journal of Communication, 23,* 328-343.

Anderson, K., & Clevenger, T. (1972). A summary of experimental research in ethos. In T. D. Beiseker & D. W. Parson (Eds.), *The process of social influence* (pp. 223-247). Englewood Cliffs, NJ: Prentice-Hall.

Anderson, N. H. (1971). Integration theory and attitude change. *Psychological Bulletin, 78,* 171-206.

Argyris, C. (1962). *Interpersonal competence and organizational effectiveness.* Homewood, IL: Irwin.

Argyris, C. (1964). *Integrating the individual and the organization.* New York: John Wiley.

Aronson, E. (1968). Dissonance theory: Progress and problems. In R. P. Abelson et al. (Eds.), *Theories of cognitive consistency: A sourcebook.* Skokie, IL: Rand McNally.

Atkin, C. (1975a, October). Parent-child communication in supermarket breakfast cereal selection. In *Effects of television advertising on children* (Report 7). East Lansing: Michigan State University.

Atkin, C. (1975b, December). Survey of children and mothers' responses to television commercials. In *Effects of television advertising on children* (Report 8). East Lansing: Michigan State University.

Atkinson, J. W. (1957). Motivational determinants of risk-taking behavior. *Psychological Review, 64,* 359-372.

Baird, J. E., Jr., & Bradley, P. H. (1979). Study of management and communication: A comparative study of men and women. *Communication Monographs, 46,* 101-111.

Ball-Rokeach, S. J., Rokeach, M., & Grube, J. (1984). *The Great American Values Test: Influencing behavior and belief through television.* New York: Free Press.

Bandura, A. (1977). *Social learning theory.* Englewood Cliffs, NJ: Prentice-Hall.

Bannister, D. (1966). Psychology as an exercise in paradox. *Bulletin of the British Psychological Society, 19,* 21-26.

Bannister, D., & Fransella, F. (1977). *Inquiring man.* New York: Penguin.

211

Barrett, J. H. (1977). *Individual goals and organizational objectives.* Ann Arbor, MI: Institute for Social Research.

Bauchner, J. E. (1978). *Accuracy in detecting deception as a function of level of relationship and communication history.* Unpublished doctoral dissertation, Michigan State University.

Bauchner, J. E., Brandt, D. R., & Miller, G. R. (1977). The truth/deception attribution: Effects of varying levels of information availability. In B. Rubin (Ed.), *Communication yearbook 1.* New Brunswick, NJ: Transaction.

Bauer, R. A., & Greyser, A. A. (1968). *Advertising in America: The consumer view.* Cambridge, MA: Harvard Business School.

Baumeister, R. F., & Darley, J. M. (1982). Reducing the biasing effect of perpetrator attractiveness in jury simulation. *Personality and Social Psychology Bulletin, 8,* 286-292.

Bem, D. J. (1965). An experimental analysis of self-persuasion. *Journal of Experimental Social Psychology, 1,* 199-218.

Bem, D. J. (1968). Attitudes as self-descriptions: Another look at the attitude-behavior link. In A. G. Greenwald et al. (Eds.), *Psychological foundations of attitudes* (pp. 197-215). New York: Academic Press.

Bem, D. J. (1972). Self-perception theory. In L. Berkowitz (Ed.), *Advances in experimental social psychology* (pp. 1-62). New York: Academic Press.

Bem, D. J., & McConnell, H. K. (1970). Testing the self-perception explanation of dissonance phenomena: On the salience of premanipulation attitudes. *Journal of Personality, 14,* 23-41.

Benfare, R. C., Okene, J. K., & McIntyre, K. M. (1982). Control of cigarette smoking from a psychological perspective. *Annual Review of Public Health, 3,* 101-128.

Bennis, W. (1989). *Why leaders can't lead.* San Francisco: Jossey-Bass.

Bennis, W., & Nanus, B. (1985). *Leaders: The strategies for taking charge.* New York: Harper & Row.

Ben-Yoav, O., & Pruitt, D. G. (1984). Resistance to yielding and the expectation of cooperative future interactions in negotiation. *Journal of Experimental Social Psychology, 20,* 323-353.

Berkowitz, L., & Cottingham, D. (1960). The interest value and relevance of fear-arousing communications. *Journal of Abnormal and Social Psychology, 60,* 37-43.

Berlyne, D. E. (1960). *Conflict, arousal, and curiosity.* New York: McGraw-Hill.

Berlyne, D. E. (1963). Motivational problems raised by exploratory and epistemic behavior. In S. Kotch (Ed.), *Psychology: A study of a science* (Vol. 5). New York: McGraw-Hill.

Bies, R. J., Shapiro, D. L., & Cummings, L. L. (1988). Causal accounts and managing organizational conflict: Is it enough to say it's not my fault? *Communication Research, 15,* 381-399.

Blau, P. (1964). *Exchange and power in social life.* New York: John Wiley.

Boorstin, E. J. (1961). *The image: A guide to pseudo-events in America.* New York: Harper & Row.

Bostrom, R. N., Baschart, J. R., & Rossiter, C. M., Jr. (1973). The effects of three types of profane language in persuasive communication. *Journal of Communication, 23,* 461-475.

Bowers, J. W. (1964). Some correlates of language intensity. *Quarterly Journal of Speech, 50,* 415-420.

Bowers, J. W., & Osborn, M. M. (1966). Attitudinal effects of selected types of concluding metaphors in persuasive speeches. *Speech Monographs, 33*, 147-155.

Bradac, J. J., Bowers, J. W., & Courtright, J. (1979). Three language variables in communication research: Intensity, immediacy, and diversity. *Human Communication Research, 5*, 257-269.

Bradac, J. J., & Mulac, A. (1984). A molecular view of powerful and powerless speech styles: Attributional consequences of specific language features and communicator intentions. *Communication Monographs, 51*, 307-319.

Brehm, J. W., & Cohen, A. R. (1962). *Explorations in cognitive dissonance.* New York: John Wiley.

Brierly, D. W. (1966). Children's use of personality constructs. *Bulletin of the British Psychological Society, 19.*

Brigham, J. C., & Bothwell, R. K. (1983). The ability of prospective jurors to estimate the accuracy of eyewitness identifications. *Law and Human Behavior, 7*, 19-30.

Brock, T. C. (1963). Effects of prior dishonesty on post-decision dissonance. *Journal of Abnormal and Social Psychology, 66*, 325-331.

Brooks, R. D. (1970). The generality of early reversal of attitudes toward communication sources. *Speech Monographs, 37*, 152-155.

Brooks, R. D., & Scheidel, T. M. (1968). Speech as a process: A case study. *Speech Monographs, 35*, 1-7.

Brooks, W. D. (1971). *Speech communication.* Dubuque, IA: Wm. C. Brown.

Brown, J. R. (1976). Children's uses of television. In J. R. Brown (Ed.), *Children and television.* Beverly Hills, CA: Sage.

Brown, P., & Levinson, S. (1978). Universals in language usage: Politeness phenomena. In E. Goody (Ed.), *Questions and politeness* (pp. 56-323). Cambridge: Cambridge University Press.

Buck, R. (1975). *Human motivation and emotion.* New York: John Wiley.

Buck, R. (1984). *The communication of emotion.* New York: Guilford.

Burgoon, M. (1970). The effects of response set and race on message interpretation. *Speech Monographs, 37*, 264-268.

Burgoon, M., Cohen, A., Miller, M. D., & Montgomery, C. (1978). An empirical test of a model of resistance to persuasion. *Human Communication Research, 5*, 27-39.

Burgoon, M., Jones, S. B., & Stewart, D. (1974). Toward a message-centered theory of persuasion: Three empirical investigations of language intensity. *Human Communication Research, 1*, 240-256.

Burgoon, M., & Miller, G. R. (1971). Prior attitude and language intensity as predictors of message style and attitude change following counterattitudinal advocacy. *Journal of Personality and Social Psychology, 20*, 246-253.

Burns, T., & Stalker, G. M. (1961). *The management of innovation.* London: Tavistock.

Byrne, D. (1969). Attitude and attraction. In L. Berkowitz (Ed.), *Advances in experimental social psychology* (Vol. 4, pp. 30-89). New York: Academic Press.

Cacioppo, J. T., Petty, R. E., & Morris, K. J. (1983). Effects of need for cognition on message evaluation, recall, and persuasion. *Journal of Personality and Social Psychology, 45*, 805-818.

Campbell, J. D. (1986). Similarity and uniqueness: The effects of attribute type, relevance and individual differences in self-esteem and depression. *Journal of Personality and Social Psychology, 50*, 281-294.

Capon, N., & Kuhn, D. (1978). *The development of consumer information processing strategies.* Unpublished manuscript, Harvard University.

Carbone, T. (1975). Stylistic variables as related to source credibility: A content analysis approach. *Speech Monographs, 42,* 99-106.

Cartwright, D. (1971). Some principles of mass persuasion: Selected findings of research on the sale of U.S. war bonds. In W. Schramm & D. F. Roberts (Eds.), *The process and effects of mass communication.* Chicago: University of Chicago Press.

Cartwright, D., & Harary, F. (1956). Structural balance: A generalization of Heider's theory. *Psychological Review, 63,* 277-293.

Chapanis, N., & Chapanis, A. (1964). Cognitive dissonance: Five years later. *Psychological Bulletin, 61,* 1-22.

Chein, I. (1967). Behavior theory and the behavior of attitudes: Some critical comments. In M. Fishbein (Ed.), *Attitude theory and measurement* (pp. 51-57). New York: John Wiley.

Child, J. (1974, October). Managerial and organizational factors associated with company performance: Part I. *Journal of Management Studies,* pp. 175-189.

Christie, R. (1968). Some consequences of taking Machiavelli seriously. In E. F. Borgatta & W. W. Lambert (Eds.), *Handbook of personality theory and research.* Skokie, IL: Rand McNally.

Cialdini, R. B. (1985). *Influence: Science and practice.* Chicago: Scott Foresman.

Cialdini, R. B. (1987a). Compliance principles of compliance professionals: Psychologists of necessity. In M. P. Zanna, J. M. Olson, & C. P. Herman (Eds.), *Social influence: The Ontario Symposium* (Vol. 5, pp. 165-184). Hillsdale, NJ: Lawrence Erlbaum.

Cialdini, R. B. (1987b). Interpersonal influence: Being ethical and effective. In S. Oskamp & S. Spacapan (Eds.), *Interpersonal processes: The Claremont Symposium on Applied Social Psychology.* Newbury Park, CA: Sage.

Clark, R. A. (1984). *Persuasive messages.* New York: Harper & Row.

Clark, R. A., & Delia, J. G. (1977). Cognitive complexity, social perspective-taking, and functional persuasive skills in second to ninth grade children. *Human Communication Research, 3,* 128-134.

Cody, M. J., & McLaughlin, M. L. (1985). Models for the sequential construction of accounting episodes: Situational and interactional constraints on message selection and evaluation. In R. L. Street, Jr., & J. Capella (Eds.), *Sequence and pattern in communication behavior* (pp. 50-69). London: Edward Arnold.

Comstock, G., & Cobbey, R. (1979). Television and the children of ethnic minorities. *Journal of Communication, 29,* 104-115.

Conover, P. J. (1984). The influence of group identification on political perception and evaluation. *Journal of Politics, 46,* 760-785.

Conover, P. J., & Feldman, S. (1986). The role of inference in the perception of political candidates. In R. R. Lau & D. O. Sears (Eds.), *Political cognition* (pp. 127-158). Hillsdale, NJ: Lawrence Erlbaum.

Conway, M., & Ross, M. (1984). Getting what you want by revising what you had. *Journal of Personality and Social Psychology, 47,* 738-748.

Cook, P. D., & Flay, B. R. (1978). The persistence of experimentally induced attitude change: An evaluative review. In L. Berkowitz (Ed.), *Advances in experimental social psychology* (Vol. 11, pp. 1-57). New York: Academic Press.

Cooper, J., & Scalise, C. (1974). Dissonance produced by deviations from life styles: The interaction typology and conformity. *Journal of Personality and Social Psychology, 29*, 566-671.

Cooper, J., & Worchel, S. (1970). Role of undesired consequences in arousing cognitive dissonance. *Journal of Personality and Social Psychology, 16*, 199-206.

Cooper, J., Zanna, M., & Goethals, G. (1974). Mistreatment of an esteemed other as a consequence affecting dissonance reduction. *Journal of Personality and Social Psychology, 20*, 224-233.

Corner, J. (1979). Mass in communication research. *Journal of Communication, 29*, 26-32.

Courtright, J. A., Fairhurst, G. A., & Rogers, L. E. (1989, August). *Interact patterns in organic and mechanistic systems.* Paper presented at the annual meeting of the Academy of Management, Anaheim, CA.

Cox, D. F. (1962). The audience as communicators. In J. T. Wheatley (Ed.), *Measuring advertising effectiveness* (pp. 201-213). Homewood, IL: Irwin.

Crockett, W. H. (1965). Cognitive complexity and impression formation. In B. A. Maher (Ed.), *Progress in experimental research.* New York: Academic Press.

Cronen, V., & Pearce, W. B. (1978). *The logic of the coordinated management of meaning: An open systems model of interpersonal communication.* Paper presented at the annual meeting of the International Communication Association, Philadelphia.

Cronkhite, G. (1976). Effects of rater-concept-scale interactions and use of different procedures upon evaluative factor structures. *Human Communication Research, 2*, 316-329.

Culley, J. D., Lazer, W., & Atkin, C. K. (1976). The experts look at children's television. *Journal of Broadcasting, 20*, 3-21.

Cummings, R. (1979). Double play and replay: Living out there in television land. In G. Gumpert & R. Cathcart (Eds.), *InterMedia.* New York: Oxford University Press.

Danowski, J. A. (1975). *An information theory of communication function: A focus on information aging.* Unpublished doctoral dissertation, Michigan State University.

Darwin, C. (1965). *The expression of emotion in man and animals.* Chicago: University of Chicago Press.

Davidson, J., & Kiesler, S. (1964). Cognitive behavior before and after decisions. In L. A. Festinger (Ed.), *Conflict, decision, and dissonance* (pp. 10-19). Stanford, CA: Stanford University Press.

Deaux, K., & Emswiller, T. (1974). Explanations of successful performance on sex-linked tasks: What is skill for the male is luck for the female. *Journal of Personality and Social Psychology, 29*, 80-85.

Deaux, K., & Farris, E. (1977). Attributing causes for one's own performance: The effects of sex, norms, and outcome. *Journal of Research in Personality, 11*, 59-72.

De Charmes, R. (1968). *Personal causation.* New York: Academic Press.

DeFleur, F. R., & Ball-Rokeach, S. J. (1982). *Theories of mass communication* (4th ed.). New York: Longman.

Delia, J. G., & Clark, R. A. (1977). Cognitive complexity, social perception, and the development of listener-adapted communication in six-, eight-, ten-, and twelve-year-old boys. *Communication Monographs, 44*, 326-345.

Delia, J. G., Clark, R. A., & Switzer, D. E. (1974). Cognitive complexity and impression formation in informal social interaction. *Speech Monographs, 41*, 209-308.

Dervin, B. (1989). Audience as listener and learner, teacher and confidante: The sense-making approach. In R. Rice & C. K. Atkin (Eds.), *Public communication campaigns* (pp. 67-86). Newbury Park, CA: Sage.

de Sousa. (1980). Self-deceptive emotion. In A. Rorty (Ed.), *Explaining emotions*. Berkeley: University of California Press.

Deutsch, M., & Krauss, R. M. (1965). *Theories in social psychology*. New York: Basic Books.

Deutsch, M., Krauss, R. M., & Rosenau, N. (1962). Dissonance or defensiveness? *Journal of Personality, 30*, 16-28.

Dimitrovsky, L. (1964). The ability to identify the emotional meanings of vocal expressions at successive age levels. In J. R. Davitz (Ed.), *The communication of emotional meaning*. New York: McGraw-Hill.

Doob, L. W. (1947). The behavior of attitudes. *Psychological Review, 54*, 135-156.

Dubin, R. (1956). Industrial workers' worlds: A study of the "central life interests" of industrial workers. *Social Problems, 3*, 131-142.

Dubois, B. L., & Crouch, I. (1975). The question of tag questions in women's speech: They don't really use more of them, do they? *Language and Society, 4*, 289-294.

Dwyer, F. R., Schurr, P., & Oh, S. (1987). Developing buyer-seller relationships. *Journal of Marketing, 51*, 11-27.

Dwyer, F. R., & Walker, O. (1981). Bargaining in an asymmetrical power structure. *Journal of Marketing, 45*, 104-115.

Eagly, A. H., & Himmelfarb, S. (1978). Attitudes and opinions. *Annual Review of Psychology, 29*, 517-554.

Eagly, A. H., Wood, W., & Fishbaugh, L. (1980). *Sex differences in conformity: Surveillance by the group as a determinant of male nonconformity*. Amherst: University of Massachusetts.

Ekman, P., & Friesen, W. V. (1974a). Detecting deception from the body or face. *Journal of Personality and Social Psychology, 29*, 288-298.

Ekman, P., & Friesen, W. V. (1974b). *Unmasking the face*. Englewood Cliffs, NJ: Prentice-Hall.

Elms, A. C. (1967). Role playing, incentive, and dissonance. *Psychological Bulletin, 68*, 132-148.

Enis, B., & Reardon, K. K. (1989). *Internal marketing*. Unpublished manuscript, University of Southern California.

Etaugh, L., & Brown, B. (1975). Perceiving the causes of success and failure of male and female performers. *Developmental Psychology, 11*, 103.

Falcione, R. L., McCroskey, J. C., & Daly, J. A. (1977). Job satisfaction as a function of employees' communication apprehension, self-esteem, and perceptions of their immediate supervisors. In B. Rubin (Ed.), *Communication yearbook 1* (pp. 363-366). New Brunswick, NJ: Transaction.

Farace, R. V., Taylor, J. A., & Stewart, J. P. (1978). Criteria for evaluation of organizational communication effectiveness: Review and synthesis. In B. Rubin (Ed.), *Communication yearbook 2* (pp. 271-292). New Brunswick, NJ: Transaction.

Feldman, A., Wolf, A., & Warmouth, D. (1977). Parental concern about child-directed commercials. *Journal of Communication, 27*, 125-137.

Festinger, L. A. (1954). A theory of social comparison processes. *Human Relations, 7*, 117-140.

Festinger, L. A. (1957). *A theory of cognitive dissonance*. Evanston, IL: Row, Peterson.

Festinger, L. A., & Maccoby, N. (1964). On resistance to persuasive communication. *Journal of Abnormal and Social Psychology, 68*, 359-366.

Festinger, L. A., & Walster, E. (1964). Post-decision regret and decision reversal. In L. A. Festinger (Ed.), *Conflict, decision, and dissonance* (pp. 100-112). Stanford, CA: Stanford University Press.

Fishbein, M. (1963). An investigation of the relationships between beliefs about an object and an attitude toward that object. *Human Relations, 16*, 233-240.

Fishbein, M., & Ajzen, I. (1975). *Belief, attitude, intention and behavior: An introduction to theory and research.* Reading, MA: Addison-Wesley.

Fiske, S. T., & Taylor, S. E. (1984). *Social cognition.* New York: Random House.

Fitzpatrick, M. A. (1977). A typological approach to communication in relationships. In B. Rubin (Ed.), *Communication yearbook 1* (pp. 263-275). New Brunswick, NJ: Transaction.

Fitzpatrick, M. A. (1984). A typological approach to marital interaction: Recent theory and research. In L. Berkowitz (Ed.), *Advances in experimental social psychology* (Vol. 18, pp. 1-47). Orlando, FL: Academic Press.

Fitzpatrick, M. A. (1988). *Between husbands and wives: Communication in marriage.* Newbury Park, CA: Sage.

Fitzpatrick, M. A., & Badzinski, D. (1985). All in the family: Communication in kin relationships. In M. L. Knapp & G. R. Miller (Eds.), *Handbook of interpersonal communication* (pp. 687-736). Beverly Hills, CA: Sage.

Fitzpatrick, M. A., & Indvik, J. (1982). The instrumental and expressive domains of marital communication. *Human Communication Research, 8*, 195-213.

Fitzpatrick, M. A., & Winke, J. (1979). You always hurt the one you love: Strategies and tactics in interpersonal conflict. *Communication Quarterly, 27*, 3-11.

Flay, B. R. (1985). *Psychosocial approaches to smoking prevention: A review of findings.* Unpublished manuscript, University of Southern California.

Frazier, G. L., & Summers, J. O. (1986). Perceptions of interfirm power and its use within a franchise channel of distribution. *Journal of Marketing, 23*, 169-176.

Frentz, T. S. (1976). *A generative approach to episodic structure.* Paper presented at the annual meeting of the Western Speech Association, San Francisco.

Friedman, H. (1979). The concept of skill in nonverbal communication: Implications for understanding social interaction. In R. Rosenthal (Ed.), *Skill in nonverbal communication: Individual differences.* Cambridge, MA: Oelgeschlager, Gunn & Hain.

Friedman, L., Lichtenstein, E., & Biglan, A. (1985). Smoking onset among teens: An empirical analysis of initial situations. *Addictive Behaviors, 10*, 1-13.

Frost, J. H., & Wilmot, W. W. (1978). *Interpersonal conflict.* Dubuque, IA: Wm. C. Brown.

Gantz, W., Gartenberg, H., & Rainbow, C. (1980). Approaching invisibility: The portrayal of the elderly in magazine advertisements. *Journal of Communication, 30*, 56-60.

Gerbner, G. (1978). The dynamics of cultural resistance. In G. Tuchman et al. (Eds.), *Hearth and home: Images of women in the mass media* (pp. 46-50). New York: Oxford University Press.

Gilchrist, L. D., & Schinke, S. P. (1984). Self-control skills for smoking prevention. In P. F. Engstrom, P. N. Anderson, & L. E. Mortenson (Eds.), *Advances in cancer control, 1983* (pp. 125-130). New York: Allen R. Liss.

Gillig, P. M., & Greenwald, A. G. (1974). Is it time to lay the sleeper effect to rest? *Journal of Personality and Social Psychology, 29*, 132-139.

Ginsberg, A., & Grant, J. H. (1985). Research on strategic change: Theoretical and methodological issues. *Academy of Management Proceedings*, pp. 11-15.

Goethals, G. R., & Cooper, J. (1972). The role of intention and postbehavioral consequences in the arousal of cognitive dissonance. *Journal of Personality and Social Psychology, 23*, 293-301.

Goffman, E. (1967). *Interaction ritual*. Garden City, NY: Doubleday.

Goldberg, P. (1968). Are women prejudiced against women? *Transaction, 5*, 28-31.

Gollin, E. S. (1958). Organizational characteristics of social judgment: A developmental investigation. *Journal of Personality, 26*, 139-154.

Golub, S., & Canty, E. M. (1982). Sex-role expectations and the assumption of leadership by college women. *Journal of Social Psychology, 116*, 83-90.

Graber, D. A. (1980). *Mass media and American politics*. Washington, DC: Congressional Quarterly Press.

Graham, J. L., & Sano, Y. (1984). *Smart bargaining: Doing business with the Japanese*. Cambridge, MA: Ballinger.

Gray, B., & Ariss, S. S. (1985). Politics and strategic change across organizational life cycles. *Academy of Management Review, 10*, 707-723.

Greenberg, B. S., & Miller, G. R. (1966). The effects of low-credible sources on message acceptance. *Speech Monographs, 33*, 127-136.

Greenberg, M., & Gorn, G. (1978). Some unintended consequences of TV advertising to children. *Journal of Consumer Research, 5*, 22-29.

Greiner, L. E., & Bhambri, A. (1988, September 29-October 1). *New CEO intervention and dynamics of deliberate strategic change*. Paper presented at the Strategic Leaders and Leadership Colloquium, New York.

Gross, N., Mason, W., & McEachern, A. (1958). *Explorations in role analysis*. New York: John Wiley.

Guterman, S. (1970). *The Machiavellians*. Lincoln: University of Nebraska Press.

Haaland, G. A., & Venkatesan, M. (1968). Resistance to persuasive communications: An examination of the distraction hypothesis. *Journal of Personality and Social Psychology, 9*, 167-170.

Hall, J. A. (1978). Gender effects in decoding nonverbal cues. *Psychological Bulletin, 85*, 845-857.

Hamner, W., & Tosi, H. (1974). Relationship of role conflict and role ambiguity to job involvement measures. *Journal of Applied Psychology, 59*, 497-499.

Hannan, M. T., & Freeman, J. R. (1977). The population ecology of organizations. *American Journal of Sociology, 82*, 929-964.

Hart, R. P. (1987). *The sound of leadership: Presidential communication in the modern age*. Chicago: University of Chicago Press.

Hastie, R. (1981). Schematic principles in human memory. In E. T. Higgins, C. P. Herman, & M. P. Zanna (Eds.), *Social cognition: The Ontario Symposium* (pp. 39-88). Hillsdale NJ: Lawrence Erlbaum.

Heider, F. (1946). Attitudes and cognitive organization. *Journal of Psychology, 21*, 107-112.

Heider, F. (1958). *The psychology of interpersonal relations*. New York: John Wiley.

Herman, J. B. (1977). Cognitive processing of persuasive communications. *Organizational Behavior and Human Performance, 19*, 126-147.

Herzberg, F. (1966). *Work and the nature of man*. Cleveland: World.

Hocking, J., Bauchner, J., Kaminski, E., & Miller, G. (1979). Detecting deceptive communication from verbal, visual and paralinguistic cues. *Human Communication Research, 6,* 33-46.

Hops, H., Weissman, W., Biglan, A., Thompson, R., Faller, C., & Severson, H. H. (1986). A taped situation test of cigarette refusal skill among adolescents. *Behavioral Assessment, 8,* 145-154.

Hosman, L. S. (1989). The evaluative consequences of hedges, hesitations and intensifiers: Powerful and powerless speech styles. *Human Communication Research, 15,* 383-406.

Hosman, L. S., & Wright, J. W., II. (1987). The effects of hedges and hesitations on impression formation in a simulated courtroom context. *Western Journal of Speech Communication, 51,* 173-188.

Hovland, C., Janis, I., & Kelley, H. (1953). *Communication and persuasion.* New Haven, CT: Yale University Press.

Hovland, C., & Mandel, W. (1952). An experimental comparison of conclusion-drawing by the communicator and by the audience. *Journal of Abnormal and Social Psychology, 47,* 581-588.

Hovland, C., & Weiss, W. (1951). The influence of source credibility on communication effectiveness. *Public Opinion Quarterly, 15,* 635-650.

Howie-Day, A. M. (1977). *Metapersuasion: The development of reasoning about persuasive strategies.* Unpublished doctoral dissertation, University of Minnesota.

Hoyt, M., Henley, M., & Collins, B. (1972). Studies in forced compliance: The confluence of choice and consequences on attitude change. *Journal of Personality and Social Psychology, 23,* 205-210.

Huber, G., O'Connell, M., & Cummings, L. (1975). Perceived environmental uncertainty: Effects of information and structure. *Academy of Management Journal, 18,* 725-740.

Huseman, R. C., Logue, C. M., & Freshly, D. L. (1977). *Readings in interpersonal and organizational communication.* Boston: Holbrook.

Insko, C. A. (1967). *Theories of attitude change.* Englewood Cliffs, NJ: Prentice-Hall.

Iyengar, S., & Kinder, D. R. (1987). *News that matters.* Chicago: University of Chicago Press.

Jackson, J. (1966). A conceptual and measurement model for norms and roles. *Pacific Sociological Review,* pp. 35-47.

Janis, L., & Feshback, S. (1953). Effects of fear-arousing communications. *Journal of Abnormal and Social Psychology, 48,* 78-92.

Janis, L., & Field, P. (1956). A behavioral assessment of persuasibility: Consistency of individual differences. *Sociometry, 19,* 241-259.

Jecker, J. D. (1964). The cognitive effects of conflict and dissonance. In L. A. Festinger (Ed.), *Conflict, decision, and dissonance* (pp. 21-30). Stanford, CA: Stanford University Press.

Jones, E., & Davis, K. (1965). From acts to dispositions: The attribution process in person perception. In L. Berkowitz (Ed.), *Advances in experimental psychology* (pp. 220-266). New York: Academic Press.

Jones, E., & Nisbett, R. (1971). *The actor and the observer: Divergent perceptions of the causes of behavior.* New York: General Learning Press.

Kahn, R. L., Wolfe, D. M., Quinn, P., Snoek, J. D., & Rosenthal, R. A. (1964). *Organizational stress.* New York: John Wiley.

Kaplan, M., & Miller, L. E. (1978). Reducing the effects of juror bias. *Journal of Personality and Social Psychology, 36,* 1443-1455.

Kaplan, M., & Schersching, C. (1980). Reducing juror bias: An experimental approach. In P. D. Lipsitt & B. D. Sales (Eds.), *New approaches in psycholegal research* (pp. 149-170). New York: Van Nostrand Reinhold.

Katz, D. (1960). The functional approach to the study of attitudes. *Public Opinion Quarterly, 24,* 163-204.

Kelly, G. (1955). *The psychology of personal constructs.* New York: W. W. Norton.

Kelman, H. C. (1961). Processes of open change. *Public Opinion Quarterly, 25,* 57-78.

Kelman, H. C., & Hovland, C. (1953). Reinstatement of the communicator in delayed measurement of opinion change. *Journal of Abnormal and Social Psychology, 48,* 327-335.

Kiesler, S., & Mathog, R. (1968). Distraction hypothesis in attitude change: Effects of effectiveness. *Psychological Reports, 23,* 1123-1133.

Kinder, D. R. (1986). Presidential character revisited. In R. R. Lau & D. O. Sears (Eds.), *Political cognition* (pp. 233-256). Hillsdale, NJ: Lawrence Erlbaum.

Kirsch, I., Tennen, H., Wickless, C., Saccone, A., & Cody, S. (1985). The role of expectancy in fear reduction. *Behavior Therapy, 14,* 520-533.

Knapp, M., & Comadena, M. (1979). Telling it like it isn't: A review of theory and research on deceptive communications. *Human Communication Research, 5,* 270-285.

Knapp, M., Stahl, C., & Reardon, K. K. (1980). *Memorable messages.* Unpublished manuscript.

Kohlberg, L. A. (1966). A cognitive developmental analysis of children's sex-role concepts and attitudes. In E. Maccoby (Ed.), *The development of sex differences.* Stanford, CA: Stanford University Press.

Kohlberg, L. A. (1969). The cognitive developmental approach to socialization. In D. Goslin (Ed.), *Handbook of socialization theory and research.* Skokie, IL: Rand McNally.

Korzenny, F., & Neuendorf, K. (1980). Television viewing and self-concept of the elderly. *Journal of Communication, 30,* 71-80.

Kramer, C. (1974). Women's speech: Separate but unequal? *Quarterly Journal of Speech, 60,* 14-24.

Krugman, H. (1965). The impact of television advertising: Learning without involvement. *Public Opinion Quarterly, 29,* 349-356.

Kuhn, T. (1975). *The structure of scientific revolutions.* Chicago: University of Chicago Press.

Lakoff, R. T. (1975). *Language and a woman's place.* New York: Harper & Row.

Lane, R. E. (1986). What are people trying to do with their schemata? The question of purpose. In R. R. Lau & D. O. Sears (Eds.), *Political cognition* (pp. 303-318). Hillsdale, NJ: Lawrence Erlbaum.

LaPiere, R. G. (1954). *A theory of social control.* New York: McGraw-Hill.

Larson, C., & Sanders, R. (1975). Faith, mystery, and data: An analysis of "scientific" studies of persuasion. *Quarterly Journal of Speech, 61,* 178-194.

Lau, R. R. (1986). Political schemata, candidate evaluations, and voting behavior. In R. R. Lau & D. O. Sears (Eds.), *Political cognition* (pp. 95-126). Hillsdale, NJ: Lawrence Erlbaum.

Lau, R. R., & Sears, D. O. (1986). An introduction to political cognition. In R. R. Lau & D. O. Sears (Eds.), *Political cognition* (pp. 3-10). Hillsdale, NJ: Lawrence Erlbaum.

Lehmann, S. (1970). Personality and compliance: A study of anxiety and self-esteem in opinion and behavior change. *Journal of Personality and Social Psychology, 15,* 76-86.

Leventhal, H. (1970). Findings and theory in the study of fear communications. In L. Berkowitz (Ed.), *Advances in experimental social psychology.* New York: Academic Press.

Leventhal, H., & Niles, P. (1964). Field experiment on fear arousal with data on the validity of questionnaire measures. *Journal of Personality, 32.*

Leventhal, H., Singer, R., & Jones, S. (1965). Effects of fear and specificity of recommendations upon attitudes and behavior. *Journal of Personality and Social Psychology, 2,* 20-29.

Leventhal, H., & Watts, J. C. (1966). Sources of resistance to fear-arousing communications on smoking and lung cancer. *Journal of Personality, 34,* 155-175.

Little, B. R. (1972). Psychological man as scientist, humanist, and specialist. *Journal of Experimental Research in Personality, 6,* 95-118.

Livesley, W. J., & Bromley, D. B. (1973). *Person perception in childhood and adolescence.* New York: John Wiley.

Locke, E. A. (1968). Toward a theory of task motivation and incentives. *Organizational Behavior and Human Performance, 3,* 157-189.

Loevinger, L. (1979). The ambiguous mirror: The reflective-projective theory of broadcasting and mass communication. In G. Gumpert & R. Cathcart (Eds.), *InterMedia* (pp. 243-260). New York: Oxford University Press.

London, H. (1973). *Psychology of the persuader.* Morristown, NJ: General Learning Press.

Lumsden, D. (1977). An experimental study of source-message interaction in a personality impression task. *Communication Monographs, 44,* 121-129.

Macneil, I. R. (1978). Contracts: Adjustment of long-term economic relations under classical, neoclassical, and relational contract law. *Northwestern University Law Review, 72,* 854-902.

Macneil, I. R. (1980). *The new social contract: An inquiry into modern contractual relations.* New Haven, CT: Yale University Press.

Manz, C. C., & Angle, H. (1986). Can group self-management mean a loss of personal control? Triangulating a paradox. *Group and Organization Studies, 11,* 309-334.

Manz, C. C., & Sims, H. P. (1987). Leading workers to lead themselves: The external leadership of self-managing work teams. *Administrative Science Quarterly, 32,* 106-128.

Marks, G. (1984). Thinking one's abilities are unique and one's opinions are common. *Personality and Social Psychology Bulletin, 10,* 203-208.

Marwell, G., & Schmitt, D. (1967). Dimensions of compliance-gaining behavior: An empirical analysis. *Sociometry, 30,* 350-364.

McCall, M. W., Lombardo, M. M., & Morrison, A. M. (1988). *The lessons of experience: How successful executives develop on the job.* Lexington, MA: Lexington.

McCroskey, J. C. (1979). *A critique of the top five papers in interpersonal and small group communication.* Paper presented at the annual meeting of the Speech Communication Association, San Antonio, TX.

McCroskey, J. C., & Burgoon, M. (1974). Establishing predictors of latitude of acceptance-rejection and attitude intensity: A comparison of assumptions of social judgment authoritarian personality theories. *Speech Monographs, 41,* 421-426.

McCroskey, J. C., & Mehrley, R. S. (1969). The effects of disorganization and nonfluency on attitude change and source credibility. *Speech Monographs, 36,* 13-21.

McDougall, W. (1980). *An introduction to social psychology.* London: Methuen.

McEwen, W. J. (1969). *Counterattitudinal encoding effects on message style and performance.* Unpublished doctoral dissertation, Michigan State University.

McEwen, W. J., Watt, J. H., & Shea, C. G. (1977). *Content and style attributes as predictors of TV commercial recall.* Paper presented at the annual meeting of the International Communication Association, Berlin.

McGarry, J., & Hendrick, C. (1974). Communication credibility and persuasion. *Memory and Cognition, 2,* 82-86.

McGuire, W. J. (1961). The effectiveness of supportive and refutational defenses in immunizing and restoring beliefs against persuasion. *Sociometry, 24,* 184-197.

McGuire, W. J. (1964). Inducing resistance to persuasion: Some contemporary approaches. In L. Berkowitz (Ed.), *Advances in experimental social psychology* (Vol. 1). New York: Academic Press.

McGuire, W. J. (1969). The nature of attitudes and attitudinal change. In G. Lindzey & E. Aronson (Eds.), *Handbook of social psychology* (2nd ed., Vol. 3, pp. 136-314). Reading, MA: Addison-Wesley.

McGuire, W. J. (1973). Persuasion, resistance, and attitude change. In I. Pool et al. (Eds.), *Handbook of communication* (pp. 216-252). Skokie, IL: Rand McNally.

McGuire, W. J. (1985). Attitudes and attitude change. In G. Lindzey & E. Aronson (Eds.), *Handbook of social psychology* (3rd ed.). New York: Random House.

McGuire, W. J. (1989). Theoretical foundations of campaigns. In R. E. Rice & C. K. Atkin (Eds.), *Public communication campaigns* (2nd ed., pp. 43-65). Newbury Park, CA: Sage.

McKay, H. B. (1988). Humanize your selling strategy. *Harvard Business Review, 2,* 36-47.

McKelvey, W. H. (1969). Expectational noncomplementarity and style of interaction between professional and organization. *Administrative Science Quarterly.*

McLaughlin, M. L., Cody, M. J., & O'Hair, H. D. (1983). The management of failure events: Some contextual determinants of accounting behavior. *Human Communication Research, 9,* 208-224.

McLaughlin, M. L., Cody, M. J., & Robey, C. S. (1980). Situational influences on the selection of strategies to resist compliance-gaining attempts. *Human Communication Research, 7,* 14-36.

McLaughlin, M. L., Cody, M. J., & Rosenstein, N. E. (1983). Account sequences in conversations between strangers. *Communication Monographs, 50,* 102-125.

McQuail, D. (1979). Alternative models of television influence. In R. Brown (Ed.), *Children and television* (pp. 343-359). Beverly Hills, CA: Sage.

McQuillen, J. S., & Higginbotham, D. C. (1986). Children's reasoning about compliance-resisting behavior. In M. L. McLaughlin (Ed.), *Communication yearbook 9* (pp. 673-690). Beverly Hills, CA: Sage.

McQuillen, J. S., Higginbotham, D. C., & Cummings, M. C. (1984). Compliance-resisting behaviors: The affects of age, agent, and types of request. In M. L. McLaughlin (Ed.), *Communication yearbook 8* (pp. 747-762). Beverly Hills, CA: Sage.

Merton, R. K. (1957). *Social structure and social theory.* New York: Free Press.

Miles, R. H. (1977). Role-set configuration as a predictor of role conflict and ambiguity in complex organizations. *Sociometry, 40,* 150-163.

Miller, G. R. (1980). On being persuaded: Some basic distinctions. In G. R. Miller & M. Roloff (Eds.), *Persuasion: New directions in theory and research.* Beverly Hills, CA: Sage.

Miller, G. R., Boster, F., Roloff, M. E., & Seibold, D. (1977). Compliance-gaining message strategies: A typology and some findings concerning effects of situational differences. *Communication Monographs, 44,* 37-51.

Miller, G. R., & Burgoon, M. (1973). *New techniques of persuasion.* New York: Harper & Row.

Miller, G. R., & Hewgill, M. A. (1964). The effects of variations in nonfluency on audience ratings of source credibility. *Quarterly Journal of Speech, 50,* 36-44.

Miller, G. R., & Steinberg, M. (1975). *Between people: A new analysis of interpersonal communication.* Chicago: Science Research Associates.

Miller, M., & Burgoon, M. (1979). The relationship between violations of expectations and the induction of resistance to persuasion. *Human Communication Research, 5,* 301-313.

Miller, N., Maruyama, G., Beaber, R. J., & Valone, K. (1976). Speed of speech and persuasion. *Journal of Personality and Social Psychology, 34,* 615-624.

Millman, S. (1968). Anxiety, comprehension, and susceptibility to speech influence. *Journal of Personality and Social Psychology, 9,* 251-256.

Mintzberg, H., & Waters, J. A. (1985). Of strategies, deliberate and emergent. *Strategic Management Journal, 6,* 257-272.

Mischel, H. (1974). Sex bias in the evaluation of professional achievements. *Journal of Educational Psychology, 2,* 157-160.

Moltz, H., & Thistlethwaite, D. (1955). Attitude modification and anxiety reduction. *Journal of Abnormal and Social Psychology, 50.*

Morgan, G. (1986). *Images of organization.* Beverly Hills, CA: Sage.

Mulac, A. (1976). The effects of obscene language upon three dimensions of listener attitude. *Communication Monographs, 43,* 300-307.

Mulac, A., Incontro, C., & James, M. (1985). Comparison of the gender-linked language effect and sex-role stereotypes. *Journal of Personality and Social Psychology, 49,* 1098-1109.

Mulac, A., & Lundell, T. L. (1980). Differences in perceptions created by syntactic-semantic productions of male and female speakers. *Communication Monographs, 47,* 111-118.

Mulac, A., & Lundell, T. L. (1982). An empirical test of the gender-linked language effect in a public speaking setting. *Language and Speech, 25,* 243-256.

Mulac, A., & Lundell, T. L. (1986). Linguistic contributors to the gender-linked language effect. *Journal of Language and Social Psychology, 5,* 81-102.

Mulac, A., Wiemann, J. M., Widenmann, S. J., & Gibson, T. W. (1988). Male/female language differences and effects in same-sex and mixed-sex dyads: The gender-linked language effect. *Communication Monographs, 55,* 315-335.

Nel, E., Helmreich, R. K., & Aronson, E. (1969). Opinion change in the advocate as a function of the persuasibility of his audience: A clarification of the meaning of dissonance. *Journal of Personality and Social Psychology, 12,* 117-124.

Newcomb, H. (Ed.). (1979a). *Television: The critical view* (2nd ed.). New York: Oxford University Press.

Newcomb, H. (1979b). Toward a television aesthetic. In H. Newcomb (Ed.), *Television: The critical view* (2nd ed.). New York: Oxford University Press.

Newcomb, T. M. (1953). An approach to the study of communicative acts. *Psychological Review, 60,* 393-404.

Newman, I. (1984). Capturing the energy of peer pressure: Insights from a longitudinal study of adolescent cigarette smoking. *Journal of School Health, 54,* 146-148.

Nietzke, A. (1977). The American obsession with fun. In L. Sellers & W. Rivers (Eds.), *Mass media issues* (pp. 337-345). Englewood Cliffs, NJ: Prentice-Hall.

Novak, M. (1977). Television shapes the soul. In L. Sellers & W. Rivers (Eds.), *Mass media issues* (pp. 41-56). Englewood Cliffs, NJ: Prentice-Hall.

Nunally, J., & Bobren, H. (1959). Variables concerning the willingness to receive communications on mental health. *Journal of Personality, 27,* 38-46.

O'Keefe, B. J., & Shepherd, G. J. (1987). The pursuit of multiple objectives in face-to-face persuasive interactions: Effects of construct differentiation on message organization. *Communication Monographs, 54,* 396-419.

Osgood, C., & Tannenbaum, P. (1955). The principle of congruity in the prediction of attitude change. *Psychological Review, 62,* 42-55.

Osterhouse, R. A., & Brock, T. C. (1970). Distraction increases yielding to propaganda by inhibiting counterarguing. *Journal of Personality and Social Psychology, 15,* 344-358.

O'Toole, J. (1987). *Vanguard management.* New York: Berkley.

Paletz, D. L. (1980). Polls in the media: Content, credibility, and consequences. *Public Opinion Quarterly, 44.*

Patterson, T. E. (1980). *The mass media election.* New York: Praeger.

Pearce, W. B. (1976). The coordinated management of meaning: A rules-based theory of interpersonal communication. In G. R. Miller (Ed.), *Explorations in interpersonal communication* (pp. 17-36). Beverly Hills, CA: Sage.

Petty, R. E., & Cacioppo, J. T. (1981). *Attitudes and persuasion: Classic and contemporary approaches.* Dubuque, IA: Wm. C. Brown.

Petty, R. E., & Cacioppo, J. T. (1984). The effects of involvement on responses to argument quantity and quality: Central and peripheral routes to persuasion. *Journal of Personality and Social Psychology, 46,* 69-81.

Petty, R. E., Cacioppo, J. T., Kasmer, J. A., & Haugtvedt, C. P. (1987). A reply to Stiff and Boster. *Communication Monographs, 54,* 257-263.

Petty, R. E., Kasmer, J. A., Haugtvedt, C. P., & Cacioppo, J. T. (1987). Source and message factors in persuasion: A reply to Stiff's critique of the elaboration likelihood model. *Communication Monographs, 54,* 233-249.

Petty, R. E., Wells, G., & Brock, T. (1976). Distraction can enhance or reduce yielding to propaganda: Thought disruption versus effort justification. *Journal of Personality and Social Psychology, 34,* 874-884.

Pfau, M., Kenski, H. C., Nitz, M., & Sorenson, J. (1990). Efficacy of inoculation strategies in promoting resistance to political attack messages: Application to direct mail. *Communication Monographs, 57,* 25-43.

Piaget, J. (1962). *Comments on Vygotsky's critical remarks.* Cambridge: MIT Press.

Plummer. (1988, August 11). How basic values are changing. *Adweek.*

Pruitt, D. G. (1983). Integrative agreements: Nature and antecedents. In M. H. Bazerman & R. J. Lewicki (Eds.), *Negotiation in organizations* (pp. 35-50). Beverly Hills, CA: Sage.

Pruitt, D. G. (1986). Achieving integrative agreements in negotiations. In R. K. White (Ed.), *Psychology and the prevention of nuclear war* (pp. 463-478). New York: New York University Press.

Putnam, L. L. (1985). Bargaining as task and process: Multiple functions of interaction sequences. In R. L. Street, Jr., & J. N. Capella (Eds.), *Communication behavior* (pp. 225-242). London: Edward Arnold.

Putnam, L. L. (1989). Reframing integrative and distributive bargaining: A process perspective. In R. J. Lewicki, B. H. Sheppard, & M. H. Bazerman (Eds.), *Research on negotiation in organizations* (Vol. 2). Greenwich, CT: JAI.

Putnam, L. L., & Wilson, S. R. (1989). Argumentation and bargaining strategies as discriminators of integrative outcomes. In M. A. Rahim (Ed.), *Managing conflict: An interdisciplinary approach* (pp. 121-141). New York: Praeger.

Ray, M. (1973). Marketing communication and the hierarchy of effects. In P. Clarke (Ed.), *New models for communication research*. Beverly Hills, CA: Sage.

Reardon, K. K. (1979). *Conversational deviance: A structural model*. Falls Church, VA: Speech Communication Association.

Reardon, K. K. (1981). *Persuasion: Theory and context*. Beverly Hills, CA: Sage.

Reardon, K. K. (1982). Conversational deviance: A structural model. *Human Communication Research, 9*, 59-74.

Reardon, K. K. (1986). *Gift-giving around the world*. Palo Alto, CA: Passepartout.

Reardon, K. K. (1987). *Interpersonal communication: Where minds meet*. Belmont, CA: Wadsworth.

Reardon, K. K., & Enis, B. (1990). Establishing a companywide customer orientation through persuasive internal marketing. *Management Communication Quarterly, 3*, 376-387.

Reardon, K. K., Greiner, L. E., & Leskin, B. D. (1989). *Values implementation plan*. Unpublished manuscript, University of Southern California.

Reardon, K. K., Noblet, C., Carilli, T., Shorr, M., & Beitman, M. (1980). *A theoretical model of rules invalidation: A study of new faculty*. Paper presented at the annual meeting of the International Communication Association, Acapulco.

Reardon, K. K., Sussman, S., & Flay, B. R. (1989). Are we marketing the right message? Can kids "just say, 'no' " to smoking? *Communication Monographs, 56*, 307-324.

Reardon-Boynton, K. (1978). *Conversational deviance: A developmental perspective*. Unpublished doctoral dissertation, University of Massachusetts.

Reardon-Boynton, K., & Fairhurst, G. (1978). *Elaboration on the concept rule: A case study with the military*. Paper presented at the annual meeting of the International Communication Association, Philadelphia.

Reinard, J. C. (1988). The empirical study of the persuasive effects of evidence: The status after fifty years of research. *Human Communication Research, 15*, 3-59.

Reynolds, P. D. (1975). *A primer in theory construction*. Indianapolis: Bobbs-Merrill.

Richmond, V. P., & McCroskey, J. C. (1975). Whose opinion do you trust? *Journal of Communication, 25*, 42-50.

Robertson, T. S. (1979). Parental mediation of television advertising effects. *Journal of Communication, 29*, 12-25.

Robertson, T. S., & Rossiter, J. R. (1977). Children's responsiveness to commercials. *Journal of Communication, 27*, 101-106.

Robicheaux, R., & El-Ansary, A. (1975). A general model for understanding channel member behavior. *Journal of Retailing, 52,* 13-30, 90-94.

Robinson, M. J. (1981). The media in 1980: Was the message the message? In A. Ranney (Ed.), *The American elections of 1980* (pp. 171-211). Washington, DC: American Enterprise Institute.

Rogers, E., & Shoemaker, F. (1971). *Communication of innovations: A cross-cultural approach.* New York: Free Press.

Rohrbach, L. A., Flay, B. R., & Reardon, K. K. (1989, November). *An analysis of disc jockeys' drug-related remarks during live radio broadcasts.* Paper presented at the annual meeting of the American Association of Public Health, Chicago.

Rokeach, M. (1960). *The open and closed mind.* New York: Basic Books.

Rokeach, M. (1980). The role of values in public opinion research. *Public Opinion Quarterly, 44,* 514-529.

Rokeach, M., & Ball-Rokeach, S. J. (1988, May 22). *Stability and change in American value priorities, 1968-1981.* Paper presented at the meeting of the American Association for Public Opinion Research, Toronto.

Rokeach, M., & Rothman, G. (1965). The principle of congruence and the congruity principle as models of cognitive interaction. *Psychological Review, 72,* 129-156.

Rosenthal, P. (1972). The concept of the paramessage in persuasive communication. *Quarterly Journal of Speech.*

Rosenthal, R., & DePaulo, B. (1979). Sex differences in accommodation of nonverbal communication. In R. Rosenthal (Ed.), *Skill in nonverbal communication: Individual differences.* Cambridge, MA: Oelgeschlager, Gunn & Hain.

Rosten, L. (1977). The intellectual and the mass media: Some rigorously random remarks. In L. Sellers & W. Rivers (Eds.), *Mass media issues.* Englewood Cliffs, NJ: Prentice-Hall.

Rothenberg, R. B. (1970). Children's social sensitivity and the relationship to interpersonal comfort and intellectual level. *Developmental Psychology, 2,* 335-350.

Rothenberg, R. (1990, July 15). Politics on TV: Too fast, too loose. *New York Times,* pp. 1, 4.

Rotter, J. B. (1954). *Social learning and clinical psychology.* Englewood Cliffs, NJ: Prentice-Hall.

Rubin, J. Z., & Brown, B. R. (1975). *The social psychology of bargaining and negotiation.* New York: Academic Press.

Safire, W. (1980, Winter). The press is the enemy: Nixon and the media. *Public Opinion Quarterly, 44.*

Schachter, S. (1959). *The psychology of affiliation: Experimental studies of the source of gregariousness.* Stanford, CA: Stanford University Press.

Schachter, S. (1964). The interaction of cognitive and physiological determinants of emotional states. In L. Berkowitz (Ed.), *Advances in experimental social psychology* (Vol. 1). New York: Academic Press.

Schachter, S. (1967). Cognitive effects on bodily functioning: Studies of obesity and eating. In D. C. Glass (Ed.), *Neurophysiology and emotion.* New York: Rockefeller University Press.

Schenck-Hamlin, W. J., Wiseman, R. L., & Georgacarakas, G. N. (1980). *A typology of compliance-gaining strategies and the logic of their underlying relationships.* Paper presented at the annual meeting of the International Communication Association, Acapulco.

Schinke, S. P., & Gilchrist, L. D. (1983). Primary prevention of tobacco smoking. *Journal of School Health, 53,* 416-419.

Schinke, S. P., & Gilchrist, L. D. (1984). Preventing cigarette smoking with youth. *Journal of Primary Prevention, 5,* 48-56.

Schramm, W., & Roberts, D. F. (Eds.). (1972). *The process and effects of mass communication.* Urbana: University of Illinois Press.

Schuler, R. (1975). Role perceptions, satisfaction and performance: A partial reconciliation. *Journal of Applied Psychology, 60,* 683-687.

Sears, D. O., & Freedman, J. L. (1967). Selective exposure to information: A critical review. *Public Opinion Quarterly, 31,* 194-213.

Shatz, M. (1977). The relationship between cognitive processes and the development of communication skills. In H. E. Howe (Ed.), *The Nebraska Symposium on Motivation.* Lincoln: University of Nebraska Press.

Sheikh, A. A., & Moleski, L. M. (1977). Conflict in the family over commercials. *Journal of Communication, 27,* 152-157.

Shroder, H., Driver, M., & Streufert, S. (1967). *Human information processing.* New York: Holt, Rinehart & Winston.

Shulman, G. (1973). *An experimental study of the effects of receiver sex, communicator sex, and warning on the ability of receivers to detect deception.* Unpublished master's thesis, Purdue University.

Sigelman, L., & Knight, K. (1983). Why does presidential popularity decline? A test of the expectation/illusion theory. *Public Opinion Quarterly, 47,* 310-324.

Singer, R. (1965). *The effects of fear-arousing communication on attitude change and behavior.* Unpublished doctoral dissertation, University of Cincinnati.

Smith, M. (1982). *Persuasion and human action.* Belmont, CA: Wadsworth.

Smith, T. J. (1976). *Communication and multiple generative mechanisms: A theoretical extension.* Unpublished manuscript, Michigan State University.

Snow, C. C., & Hambrick, D. C. (1980). Measuring organizational strategies: Some theoretical and methodological problems. *Academy of Management Review, 5,* 527-538.

Staats, A. (1967). An outline of an integrated learning theory of attitude formation and function. In M. Fishbein (Ed.), *Readings in attitude theory and measurement.* New York: John Wiley.

Staats, A. (1968). *Learning, language, and cognition.* New York: Holt, Rinehart & Winston.

Stern, L. (Ed.). (1969). *Distribution channels: Behavioral dimensions.* Boston: Houghton Mifflin.

Stern, L., & Heskett, J. L. (1969). Conflict management in interorganization relations: A conceptual framework. In L. Stern (Ed.), *Distribution channels: Behavioral dimensions.* Boston: Houghton Mifflin.

Stewart, J. B. (1964). *Repetitive advertising in newspapers: A study of two new products.* Cambridge, MA: Harvard Business School.

Stiff, J. B. (1986). Cognitive processing of persuasive message cues: A meta-analytic review of the effects of supporting information on attitudes. *Communication Monographs, 53,* 75-89.

Stiff, J. B., & Boster, F. J. (1987). Cognitive processing: Additional thoughts and a reply to Petty, Kasmer, Haugtvedt, and Cacioppo. *Communication Monographs, 54,* 250-256.

Stimson, J. A. (1976). Public support for American presidents: A cyclical model. *Public Opinion Quarterly, 40*, 1-21.

Street, R. L., & Giles, H. (1982). Speech accommodation theory: A social cognitive approach to language and speech behavior. In M. Roloff & C. Berger (Eds.), *Social cognition and communication* (pp. 193-226). Beverly Hills, CA: Sage.

Sussman, S., Brannon, B. R., Flay, B. R., Gleason, L., Senor, S., Sobel, D. F., Hansen, W. B., & Johnson, C. A. (1986). The television school and family smoking prevention/cessation project II: Formative evaluation of television segments by teenagers and parents—implications for parental involvement in drug education. *Health Education Research: Theory and Practice, 1*, 185-194.

Sutton, S. (1982). Fear-arousing communications: A critical examination of theory and research. In J. R. Eiser (Ed.), *Social psychology and behavioral medicine*. New York: John Wiley.

Sypher, H. E. (1980). Illusory correlation in communication research. *Human Communication Research, 7*, 83-87.

Sypher, H. E., & O'Keefe, D. (1980). *The comparative validity of several complexity measures as predictors of communication-relevant abilities*. Paper presented at the annual meeting of the International Communication Association, Acapulco.

Tannenbaum, D., & Norris, E. (1966). Effects of combining congruity principle strategies for the reduction of persuasion. *Journal of Personality and Social Psychology, 3*, 233-238.

Taylor, S. (1981). The interface of cognitive and social psychology. In J. H. Harvey (Ed.), *Cognition, social behavior, and the environment* (pp. 189-211). Hillsdale, NJ: Lawrence Erlbaum.

Taylor, S., & Brown, J. (1988). Illusion and well-being: A social psychological perspective on mental health. *Psychological Bulletin, 103*, 193-210.

Thibaut, J. W., & Kelly, H. H. (1978). *Interpersonal relations: A theory of interdependence*. New York: John Wiley.

Thompson, E. L. (1978). Smoking education programs, 1969-1976. *American Journal of Public Health, 68*, 250-257.

Thompson, J. D. (1967). *Bureaucracy and innovation*. University: University of Alabama Press.

Tobler, N. (1986). Meta-analysis of 143 adolescent drug prevention programs: Quantitative outcome results of program participants compared to a control or comparison group. *Journal of Drug Issues, 16*, 537-567.

Tolman, E. C. (1932). *Purposive behavior in animals and men*. Englewood Cliffs, NJ: Prentice-Hall.

Tosi, H. (1971). Organizational stress as a moderator of the relationship between influence and role response. *Academy of Management Journal, 14*, 7-20.

Toulmin, S. E. (1958). *The uses of argument*. Cambridge: Cambridge University Press.

Triandis, H. C. (1971). *Attitude and attitude change*. New York: John Wiley.

Tuchman, G. (1978). The symbolic annihilation of women by the mass media. In G. Tuchman et al. (Eds.), *Hearth and home: Images of women in the mass media* (pp. 3-38). New York: Oxford University Press.

Ugwuegbu, D. C. E. (1979). Racial and evidential factors in juror attribution of legal responsibility. *Journal of Experimental Social Psychology, 15*, 133-146.

Vandenberg, S., & Watt, J. (1977-1978). *Changes in audience perceptions of sex and violence on television*. Unpublished manuscript, University of Connecticut.

Vohs, J. L., & Garrett, R. L. (1968). Resistance to persuasion: An integrative framework. *Public Opinion Quarterly, 32*, 445-452.

Wackman, D. B., & Ward, S. (1976). The development of consumer information processing skills: Contributions of cognitive development theory. In B. B. Anderson (Ed.), *Advances in consumer research.* Cincinnati: Association for Consumer Research.

Walster, E. (1964). The temporal sequence of post-decisional processes. In L. A. Festinger (Ed.), *Conflict, decision, and dissonance* (pp. 112-127). Stanford, CA: Stanford University Press.

Wartella, E., & Ettema, J. S. (1974). A cognitive developmental study of children's attention to television commercials. *Communication Research, 1*, 46-69.

Wartella, E., Wackman, D. B., Ward, S., Shamir, J., & Alexander, A. (1979). The young child as consumer. In E. Wartella et al., *Children communicating: Media and development of thought, speech, understanding.* Beverly Hills, CA: Sage.

Watson, G., & Johnson, D. (1972). *Social psychology: Issues and insights.* Philadelphia: J. B. Lippincott.

Watt, J. H., & Krull, R. (1976). An examination of three models of television viewing and aggression. *Human Communication Research, 3.*

Weber, M. (1947). *Theory of social and economic organization.* New York: Oxford University Press.

Weick, K. E. (1969). *The social psychology of organizing.* Reading, MA: Addison-Wesley.

Weick, K. E. (1987). Theorizing about organizational communication. In F. Jablin, L. L. Putnam, K. H. Roberts, & L. W. Porter (Eds.), *Handbook of organizational communication* (pp. 97-122). Newbury Park, CA: Sage.

Weimann, J. M. (1977). Explication and test of a model of communication competence. *Human Communication Research, 3*, 195-213.

Weiss, R. F., Rawson, H. E., & Pasamanick, B. (1963). Argument strength, delay of argument, and anxiety in "conditioning" and "selective learning" of attitudes. In S. Himmelfarb & A. H. Eagly (Eds.), *Readings in attitude change.* New York: John Wiley.

Werner, H. (1957). *Comparative psychology of mental development.* New York: International University Press.

Wheeless, L. R. (1974). The effects of attitude, credibility, and homophily on selective exposure to information. *Speech Monographs, 41*, 329-338.

Wicker, A. W. (1969). Attitudes vs. actions: The relationship of verbal and overt behavioral responses to attitude objects. *Journal of Social Issues, 25*, 41-78.

Wilkinson, I., & Kipnis, D. (1978). Interfirm use of power. *Journal of Applied Psychology, 63*, 315-320.

Witteman, H., & Fitzpatrick, M. A. (1986). Compliance-gaining in marital interaction: Power bases, power processes, and outcomes. *Communication Monographs, 53*, 130-143.

Wolf, M. A., & Hexamer, A. (1980). *Children and television commercials: A look at the child's frame of reference.* Paper presented at the annual meeting of the International Communication Association, Acapulco.

Woods, M. A. (1975, January). What does it take for a woman to make it in management? *Personnel Journal,* pp. 38-41.

Zahn, C. J. (1989). The bases for differing evaluations of male and female speech: Evidence from ratings of transcribed conversation. *Communication Monographs, 56*, 59-74.

Zajonc, R. B. (1960). The process of cognitive tuning in communication. *Journal of Abnormal and Social Psychology, 61,* 159-164.

Zajonc, R. B. (1968). Cognitive theories in social psychology. In G. Lindzey & E. Aronson (Eds.), *The handbook of social psychology* (Vol. 1, pp. 320-411). Reading, MA: Addison-Wesley.

Zimbardo, P. G., & Ebbesen, E. B. (1970). *Influencing attitudes and changing behavior.* Reading, MA: Addison-Wesley.

Zimbardo, P. G., Ebbesen, E. B., & Maslach, C. (1977). *Influencing attitudes and changing behavior.* Reading, MA: Addison-Wesley.

Index

About the Author

Kathleen Kelley Reardon, Associate Professor of Management and Organization in the Business School at the University of Southern California and core faculty member in the Executive MBA Program, teaches and conducts research in persuasion, negotiation, and interpersonal communication. She is the author of *Persuasion: Theory and Context* (Sage), *Where Minds Meet* (Wadsworth), and a book for business travelers, *Gift-Giving Around the World* (Passepartout). She has been a speaker and consultant for numerous organizations, including the Conference Board, Xerox, ITT, Cigna, and AT&T. Her current research and lectures focus on methods of persuasion to manage and motivate employees, negotiation within the United States and across cultures, the role of gift-giving in international business negotiations, persuasion methods for changing health-related behaviors, and using the business environment to change such behaviors. She also serves on the Preventive Medicine Faculty at USC and has been principal investigator or coinvestigator on several national health grants. She has been a member of the editorial boards of *Communication Monographs, Communication Yearbook,* and *Communication Quarterly,* and she is currently a Member-at-Large of the International Communication Association Board of Directors.

Dr. Reardon is a Phi Beta Kappa graduate of the University of Connecticut, B.A., and received her M.A. and Ph.D. summa cum laude and with distinction from the University of Massachusetts.